GW00859416

Westward Fever

by

James Taylor

Published by New Generation Publishing in 2020

Copyright © James Taylor 2020

First Edition

ISBN

Paperback	978-1-80031-961-5
Hardback	978-1-80031-960-8
Ebook	978-1-80031-959-2

www.newgeneration-publishing.com

New Generation Publishing

About the Book

A wise old lady once said…

'You should be able to take your retirement now, then work right up until you're eighty. Maybe then we'll all appreciate how precious this life really is. Go see the world now, when you're young, fit, and able. Maybe then we can all give something back!'

Back in the winter of 2010, I quit my well-paid corporate job in the midst of the worst ever recession to go rail-tracking across America. Everyone thought I was crazy. *'You're doing what? In a middle of a recession? Have you lost your flipping mind lad?'*

Luckily for me, my beautiful girlfriend, Angela, shared my dreams and quickly followed suit to accompany me on my journey.

The following spring, and inspired by our great British ancestors, we set off to cross the Great American continent by railroad – from north to south, from east to west. In search of hope and inspiration we followed a dream, along the old railroad routes of the vast American West. What started as an adventure to fulfil a goal, ended up in discovering a lost American soul.

Inspired by Bill Bryson's *The Lost Continent*, the occasional 'once in a lifetime' trip to Disney, and watching countless spaghetti westerns with my father – the story of *Westward Fever* describes our exploits as we whisk our way across the continent in search of the great American Dream. However, unlike Bryson's discoveries beforehand, where he only found a land of lost folk, what we found was a land full of hope, inspiration and opportunity.

Westward Fever is a sharp, nostalgic and comical look into the American way of life, drawing much of its inspiration from the westward migration of the late 19th century – although the real star of the show is undoubtedly the awesome, all inspiring American landscape in which the story is framed.

Aimed at readers of all ages, *Westward Fever* provides hope and inspiration for every hard-working lost soul who dares to live the dream.

The American Dream

Wake up and smell the coffee

Who says life ends at thirty? I recently turned thirty-five and ever since then my life has been one major roller coaster after another. Let me be straight with you, this roller coaster hadn't been planned, provisioned, or partially desired. I wasn't trying to find myself, run away from anyone, or feed some desperate need by a wannabe teenager in the hope of clinging onto a lost youth. It wasn't a midlife crisis, a result of some messed up relationship, and it certainly wasn't one final play before quietly moving aside and melting back into the soulless suburbs. It was so much more. This was one of those roller coaster rides where I always knew I'd end up on. For the first time in my life I wasn't entirely sure where I was gonna go or who I was going to meet along the way. But I knew the time was coming and knew it was soon, then one cold wintery morning as I lay next to my sleeping girlfriend, I knew it was time to wake up, smell the coffee and completely turn our lives upside down.

As my girlfriend shuffled against my back I realised our lives would never be the same, well not for the foreseeable future anyway. You see today was going to be a different day, a mad, extraordinary day where I would finally awake from my long hibernation and take control of my life once and for all. Turning to Angie I gave her one last lingering cuddle. I wanted to make this moment last, just a little longer. We were safe here in our little haven between the sheets, no one could get us here. I kissed her cheek one final time, and then quietly slipped away into the night. What I was about to do was going to change our lives forever.

The Drive

The drive to work was a surreal experience. The M4 near Bristol was unusually calm that morning. Yes, it was early, must have been around six, but why was everyone driving so painfully slowly? And why was I overtaking everyone with ease today? I wasn't driving that fast. Seventy, perhaps, but was still way faster than everyone else on the road. Normally I'd expect to see some light resistance, like the good old gently tapping on the accelerator trick. Why do they always do that? Suddenly speed up when you're trying to overtake them? Can't they just accept you're the faster driver and let you pass on by? If you're gonna drive like a granny, fine, but don't speed up and make my life difficult just because you can't be arsed to move out of that comforting middle lane, you lazy little sod. But today was different, everyone was letting me pass. What the hell did they know that I didn't? Then the phone rang.

'Mawning, James. Where are you?' Clayton said in his deep Bristolian accent. 'Tune your radio into the local station then give me a call back... alwright!'

'Anything a matter?' I replied.

'Just turn it on then call me back... alwright!'

This was slightly worrying. I could tell by the tone of his voice that something wasn't quite right. What the hell could he possibly want at this time in the morning? Looking in my mirror I began to panic, for an early morning call from Clayton could only mean one thing... *Trouble!*

To put you in the picture, Clayton was rapidly approaching retirement and had been working for the company for longer than anyone could ever care to remember. He is what we all call a dinosaur, one of those sorry old chaps who has been slowly and surely been demoted and now has absolutely nothing positive to say about anyone. There's one like him in every company so I'm told. Although I can't blame the old fellow, for this old boy had seen it all on his slippery descent down the corporate ladder. Sadly for Clayton, he'd had to put up with all sorts of useless idiots progress above him and slowly bugger things up for this once great corporation – and now he had to report to me – this suave, have a go, fast track cowboy, thirty years his junior, strutting around in a crumpled Hugo Boss suit. Poor old sod, it's no wonder why he's a tad bitter – so if there's bad news to be had then you can bet your bottom dollar that a phone call from Clayton is never too far away. I swear the only thing that gets this prehistoric beast out of bed each morning is to deliver me the daily bad news. This must be bad I thought to myself, it's 6 o'clock in the bleeding morning!

I turned on the radio to be greeted by what can only be described as a bunch of disgruntled farmers all claiming to be victimised drivers. *'No one told us about this, my luvvy.'* One said. *'It's a bleeding conspiracy luvvy, they're all in it, my luvver!'* Another suggested. *'Why didn't they tell us why?'*

And so it went on for the next ten minutes – country bumpkins randomly ranting over the radio. I shouldn't have been surprised with their impassioned reactions – they were all West Country folk after all, Britain's very own equivalent to the American Hillbilly. A wild, savage, homegrown breed of folk who get their kicks by dancing like drunken fools around Combine Harvesters: *Now I've got a Combine Harvester!* Celebrate Guy Fawkes by carrying burning barrels of fire through crowded streets, and insist on rolling a month's worth of cheese over the top of the hill before hurling themselves after it in the most hopeless of pursuits. It's amazing any of them live to see the age of thirty. Then the penny dropped. *So that's why they're all crying in their milk!* Word had spread that the local council had just installed a whole load of speed cameras between the Bath and Bristol stretch of the motorway – the very same stretch of road that I had been booting it down all morning. Typical, you get out of bed at the crack of dawn for another hard day's graft and all they can do is find another way of stitching you up. If it's not the local council trying to steal your money, then it's the Government raising your taxes to fund their reckless waste. If it's not the Government on the take then it's that useless idiot of a boss telling you. *'Thanks for last year you did a great job, turned your accounts right around – but regrettably the board feel there are some "development areas" you need to work on, so unfortunately I cannot put you forward for that promotion that you absolutely, wholeheartedly, bloody deserve!'*

What a joker. I had literally propped that little clown up for the past two years and privately he knew it, but in public it would be him claiming all the glories while secretly informing the directors that I wasn't really cut out for it after all. Don't you just hate the rat race? What a waste of time, I thought to myself as I exited the motorway westbound and rejoined it eastbound. All the stress and migraines, was it really worth the pain? *Sorry old buddy, you're just going to have to deal with today's meeting on your own* I said to myself looking down at Clayton's number. For I had some very important business of my own that I needed to attend to.

The Office

I was first to arrive in the office that morning. The clock above the reception said 7.45 but you'd never guess it with it being so dark outside. How depressing, I thought as I fumbled for the light switch, lighting up my office prison for yet another mundane day of checking emails, fudging forecasts and attending pointless supply chain meetings. No doubt there'd be a few angry voicemails I'd have to deal with as well – our logistics team wasn't exactly the most reliable bunch of cowboys I'd ever worked with.

I logged onto my computer and waited for it to load. Soon this bland space of office would steadily come to life with the quiet murmurings of my fellow colleagues. Most of which I would have absolutely no time for whatsoever, our only bonding being a ridiculously low pay packet and a common desire to be anywhere but here. Credit to everyone though, as we'd all hide behind our steely poker faces pretending to be all busy and important, stopping only to laugh at our boss's pathetic banter every once in a while. And that was it. That was my miserable life for five days a week. Not to mention all the stress and migraines – the direct result of being constantly squeezed by a slacker of a boss all too willing to delegate every last one of his principal duties to me. That guy was so useless he could barely work out how to switch on his calculator, let alone work out a simple profit on return calculation without asking me to double check his numbers first. The weekends couldn't come any quicker, only when they did finally arrive I was way too bloody knackered to do anything remotely productive. This was not what I wanted; this was not what I signed up for when I first jumped onto the corporate ladder as an eager graduate all those years ago. If I'd known then what I know now then maybe I would have taken life a little less seriously and appreciated what I had a bit more.

I opened Outlook to find twenty-three unread emails, most of which were from my lazy arse boss: *Can you ACTION this please... Can you ACTION that please... End of the day for this... End of the day for that!* Oh, how I wished I was somewhere else. Oh, how I missed those long carefree days of my childhood. A magical time of fun and adventure, a time of innocence and excitement, not knowing what one day would bring to the next. Quite simply it was the best time of my life but a time so long ago I could barely remember it now. I wanted to experience that feeling again, to experience those sensations, and to recapture that part of my life where the days were long and the sun always shone. I wanted one last summer holiday, and at the back of my mind I knew where that would be.

I first visited North America when I was a twelve-year-old boy. Well I'm not sure Florida actually technically counts. Let's face it, since the introduction of Disney World in the early seventies, it has effectively evolved into one giant of a theme park. Hardly the real America, I agree, but better than nothing, I guess. Prior to this 'once in a lifetime trip' my only exposure to American culture had been somewhat limited to my Monday night fix of *The Wonder Years*, my Wednesday night dose of *Dallas* and perhaps my favourite of all, *Degrassi Junior High, technically Canadian*

in a Sunday morning. It is at this point I must add that
a late developer in life, only acquiring my graceful
good looks at a much later age. You see for the majority of
my teenager years I was often compared to one of the actors
in *The Wonder Years* – although sadly for me it wasn't the
cute little one that all the girls seemed to fancy. Much to my
mates' pleasure I was apparently the spitting image of the
slightly chubby and considerable uglier older brother. I
could never see it myself, but in hindsight it was probably
my 80s-style greasy mullet and ever expanding rash of acne
that drew the unfavourable comparisons. Either way I was
now scarred for life and my fragile confidence now
completely shattered. *Growing up in the playground was
never easy, my friend.*

Although my first visit to America gave me real hope.
From out of nowhere I had suddenly found this far away
haven, a place I felt comfortable in, and for the first time in
my life a place I belonged. It was all so very exciting I
remember thinking as the sun burnt down on my dainty pink
shoulders. There was just so much to do and so many
intriguing places to see. Everything was just so incredibly
big. The streets were wide, the burgers were fat, and as for
the cars, well they were simply enormous. However, what I
loved most about the place was its sense of history. A
strange concept when you consider American history only
really gets interesting from the 18th century onwards. But to
me it actually meant something. It was fun, it was exciting,
and it was adventurous. It had the cowboys chasing the
Indians, the outlaws shooting the sheriffs, and the good old
men of the north whipping the bad old boys from the south.
It was home to the greatest gold rush the world has ever
seen, yet at the same time witnessed the largest ever human
land migration the world has ever known. In a land of few
inherent privileges, America represented real hope. I've
always had such fond memories of that first Floridan
holiday. I remember how thrilling it was laying on my
Quality Inn bed watching ESPN on cable TV. When I got
thirsty I would gather up my quarters and venture down the

hallway to the shiny new vending machine at the bottom of the stairs. Feeling adventurous I would press for Mountain Dew and listen intently as the can rumbled its way down the tray. Next to it was the free ice machine and what a privilege that was filling up my silver bucket with chunks of ice so big I could easily crunch on them back in my room. Sometimes in life it's the small things that give us the most delight.

It was these cherished memories that now occupied my mind, nearly a quarter of a century later. As I sat at my desktop staring into an abyss of mind-boggling numbers, I wondered at what point did I decide to pull over and let life pass me by? How many more years would I continue to watch from the sidelines? Was this it, was this my destiny? To be nothing more than a miserable underappreciated account manager? No, actually it was far worse than that – for I had become a run of the mill account manager who sold bread for a living! Of all the most exciting things in life that I could do, I had somehow managed to end up selling the dullest and most lackluster product in the history of mankind. And yes, I can assure you, that I have heard just about every bread pun there ever was. Social functions were partially challenging especially for any poor sod who accidentally asked what I did for a living. On hearing my reply my inquisitor would often be left starry eyed, dumbfounded and void of any sensible response, they would usually reply *'Oh... well... err... now that's interesting? Bet you must make lots of DOUGH for a living hey? Ha ha ha ha ha! Oh well gosh is that the time? I'd best be off. I assume you must be up early?'* Now in full retreat and at a safe distance my inquisitor would then deliver the killer blow. *'So what time do you begin baking then?'*

In hindsight I'd often wondered how the hell I'd actually managed to hold onto a girlfriend knowing the amount of ribbing they'd undoubtedly receive the moment my secret vocation had been revealed. *'Yes dear, but have you ever considered a career change?'*

It was approximately a quarter to four on a bleak wintery afternoon when I finally plucked up the courage to approach my boss's office. This was it; there was no turning back now, I thought to myself as I banged on his office door. I had some very important news I needed to deliver.

The Big Picture

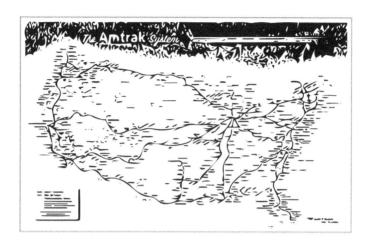

Quitting my job was the easy part. Telling everyone about this mad hotchpotch of a plan was proving to be slightly more difficult.

'You did what?' Angie screamed. 'You quit your job? Well you can just go right back and beg for it back, Mr. Mid-Life Crises. And if you think I can just drop everything to go gallivanting around America with you, then you are sadly mistaken, my friend!'

'Sorry babe, can't do that,' I replied rather sheepishly.

'Oh yes you can so you'd better start grovelling for your old job back, my friend.'

'Yes, well that could be a little tricky, my darling.'

'What? What do you mean that could be bloody tricky?'

'I kind of had a heart-to-heart with my boss.'

'Good, so even more reason to go back to him and ask for your old job back. I'm sure he will understand.'

'Well it wasn't exactly that kind of heart-to-heart, babe.'

'So, what kind of heart to heart was it then, James?' Angie demanded to know.

15

'The kind where I told him he was a useless twat and he grassed me to HR. The deed's been done now, darling, there's no turning back now!'

There was a pause and for the briefest of moments a smile unravelled across her face. Deep down she knew I was miserable and that my boss had been the primary cause. I used to go to work happy and with a spring in my step, then gradually over time the powers that be would find a way to slowly squeeze every last drop of enthusiasm out of me. I wasn't the only one who felt this way, we all did, the entire office, but each too afraid to do anything remotely constructive about it.

'I promise, babe, it's not a midlife crisis, just a realisation I don't want to do this shit anymore. For the first time in my life, I've finally woken up. I can't be that man they want me to be. All that social networking nonsense and raising your profile malarkey. That corporate arse slapping just ain't for me. Why can't they just recognise me for who I am; a bloody good businessman. I'm sorry babe, I can't play that game anymore.'

By now Angie had softened, stroking her hands across my back. 'We'll get through this, James, I promise, but you gotta have a plan. We can't just go and quit our jobs without some kind of plan. What would everybody think?'

She was right, she always was. Deep down she understood, shared my pain even, but I needed to justify our reasons for going. If I was going to cash in our life savings and roll the dice then I needed a bloody good reason for doing it. It was fair to say I needed a plan, and besides, every great journey needs a little direction, I guess.

I spent the next few months studying maps of America trying to figure it all out. One in particular was so big I had to Blu Tac it across my bedroom wall in order to fully appreciate it's size. I stepped back to assess the task in hand. Stretching over 3,000 miles from east to west and 1,000 miles from north to south, it was quite possibly the most diverse country I had ever studied – with landscapes so vast and terrain so varied you could be skiing down the mountains one minute then sweltering on the valley floor the next. There was so much to see with such limited resource. I checked my online savings account which I had been steadily building up. There was a little over 12k in there, not bad. Add to this a couple more from Angie, and then we had enough cash for a couple of flights and a generous allowance of $200 a day, if we plumped for the 90-day visa waiver option. Angie's dad had also kindly donated a handful of Marriott discount forms from his local office which would come in very handy. Well he had worked there his entire life so only fair then they give us a little something in return. That should cover us; we were only going to do this the once so there was no need to rough it.

To be honest I'd had my fair share of dodgy hostels the last time I travelled around Australia in the late nineties. Although what an amazing trip that turned out to be – fresh out of Uni, completely carefree, and with a sense of freedom like never before. One day you're climbing the Sydney Harbour Bridge the next you're jumping aboard the Greyhound bus and heading for the tropics. There is no better feeling then catching a bus not really knowing what adventures lies ahead. It was without a doubt a journey of a lifetime. I was young, full of zest with my whole life ahead of me. It was fun, it was exciting and an experience I'll never forget no matter how distant the memory may be. My life wasn't all bad now. I had done OK since - steady job, nice family, and good friends. There was also Angie, my beautiful girlfriend and soulmate of five years. With stunning looks inherited from the hills of Madeira, I was most definitely punching way above my station with that one. And who else would pack it all in to go follow her man? Yet still I yearned for more adventure.

I returned home from the Australian trip promising to do it all again and now here I was over ten years later attempting to fulfil that promise. My eyes diverted to the huge map on the wall. There were so many options and so many places to see. Ninety days was clearly not going to be enough time to see it all. I needed to be more strategic, more specific, no point going back on yourself I had learnt many years before. The plan was beginning to take shape. We would target each region, checking out the highlights before moving onto the next. Starting in the far north, we could hit the major cities then work our way down. No doubt after that we would fancy a change so heading into the Deep South looked the most likely option. After that a decision would have to be made. We could venture westwards into the Southwest or head diagonally into the Midwest. Either way we would cross the Great Plains at some point and eventually end up in the Wild West. Nice, I was liking it, keep it simple and all should be fine. There was only one more thing to sort out – travel arrangements. With a landscape so vast and varied we would have to use a combination of planes, trains and automobiles to get ourselves around. But let's get there first and work out the rest later – no need to worry about that now, as long as we had regular access to Wi-Fi we'd be OK.

The plan was set and Angie went for it, walking out on her job the following week. All our friends thought we were mad. *'You what? You're doing what? In a middle of a recession? Are you flipping mad?'* It's fair to say it probably wasn't the most sensible thing we had ever done, but sometimes in life you simply have to go to the edge to see what lies beyond. A few weeks later we packed our bags and headed for the airport. Our American adventure was about to begin.

Leaving on a Jet Plane

'Good afternoon folks, this is errrrr your captain speaking. I hope you all had an enjoyable flight with us today. We will shortly be starting our descent into Boston Logan. Local temperatures are currently errrrr 56 degrees and conditions are looking a errrr tad cloudy. This may hamper our descent somewhat, but all things being well we should be touching down at approximately errrrr 16.00 hrs. I trust you all had a errrrrrr very good flight with us and look forward to seeing you flying with Air Canada again very soon.'

'Yeah right,' I whispered into Angie's ear. 'If he thinks we're ever using this two bob bit of an airline again he's got errrrr another think coming, my friend.'

Angela glumly looked at me, nodding her head in agreement. Our once in a lifetime travelling adventure hadn't exactly got off to the most promising of starts. It all started the day before when my iPhone 3 had informed us that our flight had been cancelled. I wasn't surprised, to be fair I was kind of half expecting it, what with the volcanic ash cloud that was now sweeping its merry way over half of Europe. Now I'm not one to usually moan but there's just something about airport delays that can bring out the very worst in a man. I must reiterate one cannot lay the blame solely on the ash cloud itself, it was what it was, a random, natural event that few could have predicted and even fewer prepare for. Dare I even suggest it was slightly gripping watching the world's most sophisticated airlines crumble into pieces the moment that fluffy cloud of ash suddenly wafted into their airspace. Even the slickest of operators nervously began to ask themselves questions. '*How dangerous is this mysterious cloud of dust? Could it really interfere with a plane's engine? Could it possibly even bring one down? And holy shit this has never happened before, we're all gonna fucking die!* It was fair to say it was pure pandemonium. The skies had never been more precarious and as a result hundreds of flights were cancelled in the immediate overreaction. Still, there is nothing like a good old crisis to seriously test one's mettle and in times of adversity it's reassuring to know that the cream will always naturally rise to the top. Regrettably our plucky little airline was up to no such challenge, as getting any sensible information out of them was proving to be frustratingly difficult. Customer services were being as helpful as you'd expect *refusing to answer any calls before the 9 o'clock tea run,* and when we did finally get through we were transferred to some far away call centre in the middle of French Quebec – which made about as much sense as listening to a French cassette tape in one of those solitary, old school language laboratories. Correct me if I'm wrong, but aren't you supposed to mingle with other people to learn a friggin' language?

Anyway, with time running out we jumped into the car and headed to the airport to find out more. We needn't have bothered. For some reason the management had decided to gag all staff, only allowing them to hand out a hurriedly put together piece of paper instructing all passengers in felt tip pen to *please immediately phone customer services*! *You've got to be joking!* These guys were clearly professionals. After much finger pointing we finally secured a seat on the next available plane.

And that my friend was the good news. The bad news being this would entail a seven-hour flight to Nova Scotia, then a pointless stopover for four hours before catching our connecting flight to Boston. It all looked so reasonable when Angie Googled up cheap flights a couple of weeks before.

'What do you reckon James? It is £50 cheaper this way?'

'I dunno babe, think I'd rather fly direct' I remember replying.

'Well we're in no rush to get there, and we are on a budget you know.' she shrugged.

Left with little choice I reluctantly agreed, but did we ever stop to think that any pennies saved on the booking would almost certainly be frittered away at the airport bar in a desperate attempt to pass away the mindless hours of boredom? champagne bars ain't exactly cheap, you know.

'Champagne? You've got to be kidding me, darling?'

'Yes, champagne it must be... and you're paying my handsome friend!'

No, of course we didn't, nobody thinks of that, do they? Anyway, after several rounds of expensive bubbles our Air Canada Jazz plane eventually arrived revealing itself to be nothing more than the runt of the litter. Never had the term 'flying in a tin can' been more appropriate, as despite it's funky name it clearly was the biggest heap of junk I'd ever seen. And here we were now coming into land and the captain telling me *'All things being well we should land at 16.00 hours!'* All things being well? What the hell's that supposed mean? Isn't the captain supposed to relax his passengers by reassuring them that everything's gonna be alright? It's hardly the most convincing statement you want to hear as you nosedive into the clouds?

I needn't have worried, the captain got us down in one piece and almost simultaneously I could feel ten years of stresses ebbing away. As the plane taxied into position I peered outside my window, wondering what fun adventures lay ahead. A tinge of excitement ran through me. This was going to be the start of something great, a rare, once in a lifetime opportunity to follow in the footsteps of our great British ancestors. I had seen the pictures, read many stories and now here I was finally about to experience that great westward fever for myself. They had a lifetime, we only had ninety days and the clock was now ticking.

The East

Boston

After the trials and tribulations of the preceding days we had finally arrived on American soil. And so where better place to start our adventure, than in the historic city of Boston, located in the far northern reaches of the country. It was fair to say it was love at first sight which was no mean feat considering the treacherous conditions we encountered upon our arrival – as like our forefathers before, we too had crossed the ocean in the vain hope of finding just a smidgen of friggin' sunshine only to discover it to be colder, windier and far wetter than we could possibly have imagined. Typical and one could only imagine as to what our Pilgrim ancestors must have made of it all?

'Fucking raining again, Captain? You promised the crew it would be sunny this time, sir?'

'Hmmmm? Well observed, ship boy. I knew we should have invested in a decent set of compasses. Those barrels of rum will be no use to us here. Right from this day forward I hereby declare that these cold and dreary lands shall forever go by the name of New England, to remind us of home. Now

where the hell are those Caribbean islands supposed to be then, boy?'

Departing the airport we flagged down a taxi for the short ride into town. As a goodbye treat my father had kindly booked us into the Omni hotel, one of Boston's oldest and grandest establishments, although it was here where the planning would end. From this point forward we were well and truly on our own.

We were up early the next morning eager to explore our new surroundings and it didn't take too long to find our bearings. On first impressions it was remarkable how similar it was to England. Navigating around the city was a piece of cake and with everything being so close it was proving virtually impossible to get lost. Granted, the weather was hugely disappointing, but despite the gloom there was a radiance of old school charm I hadn't experienced in a long, long time. The place was literally dripping in history – in every shop, on every window, in every corner, on every street. Historic pride was everywhere. Never before had I seen such passionate, nationalistic fever on quite such a scale. Old men in costumes roamed the streets ringing out their bells in notification of the next available Freedom tour. In Boston you simply cannot go anywhere without at some point crossing the path of this much talked about trail – Boston's very own *Wizard of Oz*-style red bricked road taking you through the heart of the city on an evolutionary journey through revolutionary America. Not wanting to miss out we tagged onto the back of one of the many Ranger led tours and much to Angie's delight it was completely free of charge. 'Didn't I do well saving us all that money?' She gleed in excitement.

The next few hours were really quite splendid as our enthusiastic Ranger, *who by the way was a spit of the late Steve Irwin,* led his merry bunch of mature students through the city's cobbled streets. And it didn't take long for Stevie to get us fully up to speed. First settled by the British in 1630, Boston is considered to be the birthplace of modern America, the cradle of the revolution he quickly informed us. For it was in these very waters where the first hints of rebellion played out, when a group of activists commandeered an English vessel throwing its contents, a boat load of tea, into the harbour in protest against the extortionate taxes which the British had recently imposed. *'No taxation without representation*' being the buzzwords of the day. This show of defiance would become known as the Boston Tea party and what many believe to be the catalyst for the American Revolution. It is these events that have undoubtedly shaped Boston into what it is today – a strong, affluent, powerhouse of a city, proud of its heritage, yet not backwards in reminding you of this once great feat. It's fair to say Boston is not the most modest city you will ever come across, but then I guess that's half its charm and charming it most certainly was. We passed through sixteen historic landmarks that afternoon – churches, meeting houses, graveyards – each one revealing its own significant tale into the past. It was fascinating stuff if you could stomach the pomp, and even Angie managed to stay interested for a while. We finished the tour in the North end of town. Stevie thanked us for listening then hovered somewhat uncomfortably before the tips generously began to flow in.

'Go on Angie, give him twenty bucks. He was brilliant, don't you think?'

'Yes James, he was excellent, very passionate but twenty bucks? Come on? We're unemployed, remember? How about we give him ten and I'll buy you a drink later?'

Never one to turn away a free drink I agreed and we were soon heading to the Bull & Finch pub *aka the Cheers Bar* and set of the 1980s smash hit comedy, where movie legends Woody Harrelson, Kirstie Alley and Ted Danson would eventually make their name. The walk across town to the bar's location on Beacon Hill was as pleasant as could be. The long rows of Victorian buildings were particularly enchanting, reminding me of a cold winter's day back home in London. We passed the common, one of the oldest and most beautiful of city parks, while to our right the quaint lantern filled cobbled streets of the plush Beacon Hill district got me believing that one day too I could live in such a place.

It was late afternoon when we entered the *Cheers* bar. My recollections of the series are understandably very sketchy due to the embarrassing admission it was shown on a school night so I was never really allowed to stay up and watch it. Bedtimes came early in the Taylor household. Even on those long and glorious summer evenings when every other kid was allowed to play out late – I would usually be the one watching enviously from afar, safely locked away behind my dreary prison windows.

'But Mum, it's still light outside?' I would challenge scratching my head.

'Yes, well your father and I want our evening together. Now get to bed,' my mother would reply running her finger along her prized video collection searching for something to watch. Undeniably I had strict parents, the kind of parents that would insist on dropping you right outside the school gates directly in front of your jeering mates. Our morning conversations would usually pan out in a familiar way.

'Thanks Mum, that's great. You can drop me round the corner if you like?'

'It's ok darling, it's no problem.'

'No really Mum, I don't mind. I could do with the walk. Look, just here will be fine.'

'Don't be silly darling, we're nearly there.'

'No Mum, honestly it's fine, you really don't have to!' I would reply in haste, spotting a rival gang member fast approaching.

Then with impeccable timing she would wait for the leader, usually the biggest and nastiest of the bunch, to pass my window before declaring. *'Mummy still loves you, baby. Now give your mummy a kiss!'* Sheepishly I would exit the door only to hear my mother screaming behind me. *'Now you boys stick together... ok!'* Oh, the humiliation! It would take months to recover from the taunts that would inevitably follow the moment she was out of sight.

Anyway, upon entering the Cheers bar, my memories of the show came immediately flooding back. *Large square mahogany bar, scattering of bar stools, dimpled pint glasses, freakishly scary moose head nailed onto the Wall?* Although I must say I don't ever remember Woody Harrelson and his buddies getting stitched up for a whopping sixteen bucks a round? It's no wonder why they were all so bloody miserable, but what the heck, 16 dollars for a couple of dimpled pints was a small price to pay to be sitting at the very same bar where such legends once graced. 'Worth every last cent, my darling.' I commented slurping down my pricey beer. Only problem being it wasn't the same bar at all, the barman would later inform us. The Bull and Finch pub only provided the inspiration for the series. The bar scenes themselves were actually filmed over 3,000 miles away in some run-of-the-mill Californian studio. I was shocked, dumbfounded that I could be so duped into handing over sixteen big ones on the promise that I was actually drinking inside the genuine article not some fake replica bar. Suddenly my beer didn't taste quite as good after all. *Well thanks, thanks for nothing, don't suppose you offer refunds do you? Cheers!*

It soon became clear that Boston is a city that trades heavily on its heritage. The amount of claims, dubious or not, to be the first American this or the first American that is really rather striking. If it's not the first Irish pub then it's the first city park, or the first public library, or the first man made shop? *Okay I'm stretching it now*! And so the list goes on, so long in fact the city has even drawn up an official list to remind everyone. But as contentious as these claims may be, few can deny that one of Boston's most important contributions to American society was the creation of the country's first institute of higher education, the one and only Harvard University. Over the years seven US presidents have graduated from Harvard and a staggering seventy-five Nobel prize winners have been affiliated to the institution. Founded in 1636, in the pleasant riverside suburb of Cambridge, the university is as old as the city itself, but thanks to the yearly influx of students it will forever be blessed with an eternal youth and optimism.

Keen to relive our own student days we boarded the metro with the hope of rekindling some of our own dwindling memories. A short while later we ascended the escalator and were immediately collared by a wave of freshman girls kindly offering their services for a free tour of the Yard. And man, these girls were good, as not only were they all exceptionally beautiful, but being from Harvard they were all naturally of the highest intelligence. A dangerous combination if ever I'd seen one and like a pack of hungry lionesses they hunted for their prey before homing in on the weak. Not surprisingly then they clocked onto me the moment I walked out onto the street and one in particular, a stunningly beautiful Myleene Klass lookalike, wasted little time in singling me out as her next prized victim.

'Hey sir, would you like a tour around my cam... puss?' She provocatively suggested with a cheeky twinkle in her eye.

'I'm fine, thank you,' I replied

'It's completely free,' she said mischievously arching her back to reveal a tight little torso.

'Come on, you know you want to!' she giggled.

You're damn right I do... wooooooo... steady on, boy! Her forwardness had clearly caught me off guard. For a moment I stood there dazed and confused, struck by her audacity, yet curiously excited she had chosen me first. I pondered my next move. 'Hmmm free, you say? So what's in it for you then?'

'Errr nothing really we just want to show you around our lovely home. Share with you our wonderful place. But you can give me a nice tip at the end of the tour if you like!'

'Ahhhh, so it's not really free then, is it?' I said with a raise of the eyebrow and tilt of the head.

'Errrr well you don't have to give us a tip, sir.'

'So, tell me,' I paused. 'What kind of tip would you expect then?'

By now the young Harvard freshman was getting seriously tongue tied, clearly not used to such a skilled interrogation.

'Errr well, we can discuss that after the tour?'

'Hmmm I tell you what, let me think about that "f, tour" and I'll get back to you later.'

My beautiful young friend had clearly met her match and sensing defeat her once mesmerising smile had now turned into a shocking grimace. 'Never mind darling. It's not every day you'll come up against a pro!' I said patting her on the back to consolidate her crushing defeat.

We continued onwards to the main entrance, above which I noticed a sign over the bricked passageway proclaiming 'Enter here to gain wisdom'. Wow, what a great sign and a perfect photo opportunity if ever I'd seen one. I retrieved my iPhone and snapped a couple of students walking through, but for some reason it was so much more fun snapping away at Angela's silhouette as she passed through. 'Stop right there, babe, just a couple more, last one, perfect!' *This will definitely find its way on Facebook later,* I chuckled to myself.

We ambled around the famous yard before finally entering the library where we were immediately approached by security.

'Sir, I'm going to have to request you delete those immediately!'

'Really? It's only a couple of photos? They're not doing any harm are they?' I shrugged.

'Sorry sir, I'm going to have to insist you remove them. It's more than my job's worth!' he replied shaking his head.

A smile broadened across my face. It had been a while since I'd heard that one.

'Bloody jobsworth,' Angie muttered not so quietly.

I nodded in agreement suddenly remembering why everybody hates a jobsworth. They love giving it out, throwing their weight around and enforcing their petty little rules, but the moment someone plucks up the courage and calls them a jobber they suddenly get all very angry and upset.

'Excuse me madam, what did you just say? What did you just call me?' the security man replied clearly irritated.

'Nothing, we're just leaving,' Angie replied sensing it was time to exit the building.

Clearly not welcome without an official guide we decided to grab a coffee in the local coffee bar overlooking the yard. Sitting at the table and watching the students going about their daily lives was a humbling experience. For all we knew it might have been this very spot where a young Mark Zuckerberg once sat ogling girls before coming up with an idea that would change the world. Maybe, maybe not? But one thing's for sure, he would most certainly have sat here at some point slurping away on a latte drawing inspiration from the world beyond. I sat in silence. It had been nearly thirteen years since I had graduated, a lifetime ago, but at that moment I felt closer to being a student now than ever before *living on a budget, with an unknown future.* Only now I was a little older, a little wiser, and with a lifetime of experiences behind me. I watched the students scurrying around with their lattes and laptops wishing I too could go back and do it all again – only this time I would do it better *like actually bothering to attend my lectures.* I sat and pondered. Do they really appreciate what a gift of opportunity they have here? To be given the freedom and opportunity to explore life without any external responsibility whatsoever – is truly a wonderful gift to be given. I sincerely hope they realise this, as these really are the best days of their lives.

We spent the next few days immersing ourselves deep within American culture. For the majority of the time, this entailed devouring dunking donuts on the streets, downing pints of Bud Light in multi-screen sports bars, and trawling around numerous grocery stores marvelling at the huge variety of products at ridiculously low prices. However, as fun as it all was, my favourite pastime was undoubtedly our daily visits to the American food hall located inside Quincy Market. Set in historic surroundings, this place really is the future of food. Offering a cultural variety of on the go delicacies, from New England Clam Chowder to Japanese Teriyaki, the thriving food hall in the heart of town quickly won over our bellies. Now obviously the abundance of sampling ladies handing out free food may have helped somewhat – so not wanting to look a gift horse *or free sample* in the mouth, we immediately set to work sweeping the stalls and tucking into as many freebies as we could possibly lay our hands on. 'Ohhhh can I try some please? Ohh thank you very much,' I said snatching another chicken skewer from the now not so friendly Japanese lady. Although after several rounds of munching I soon realised it was time for a strategic retreat the moment I inadvertently started tucking into a poor old lady's bag of chips. 'Thanks very much, very kind of you, my friend,' I said delving into the lady's warm bag of fries. The old girl was not amused and could only stare back in amazement when I rummaged back for seconds.

Yes, it's fair to say I fell in love with Boston during our short stay. Undoubtedly I could have stayed longer but unfortunately time was not on our side. The next morning we packed our rucksacks and headed for the airport – but what we were about to encounter was going to be a far more challenging experience then just catching a simple flight.

On the Road

I was very much looking forward to the next couple of weeks in the Verdant north east. Prior to arriving, I had spent several weeks familiarising myself with New England's six rolling states –Massachusetts, Maine, Rhode Island, Connecticut, New Hampshire and Vermont – and with the help of my trusty Lonely Planet it was the only section of the trip I had bothered to plan for. There was a reason for this. Back in the summer of 2003 I was going through a really tough time, you could say I was going through a bit of a mid-twenties crises – I was unemployed, looking for work and as a result residing at my grandad's house *God rest his soul*. I must have attended at least ten interviews that summer and as hard as I tried the right opportunity simply wouldn't present itself, much to the frustrations of my grandad who believed that laying outside on the grass reading Bill Bryson travel tales all day wasn't perhaps the best way to motivate myself into a new job.

'Grandad, you couldn't bring me out some more of that lovely homemade lemonade, could you?'

Perhaps he had a point. Although those long lazy days drinking lemonade on the lawn did at least offer some perspective that there was a wider world out there to be explored beyond the M4 corridor. One book in particular, *The Lost Continent*, had me absolutely captivated from the very start, whilst quickly becoming my main source of inspiration. The book itself depicts a young Bill trawling through small town America in search of the perfect American town. A simple concept, but delivered with such intuitiveness, I was immediately suckered into the dream as well. At the end of his journey Bill returns home not declaring whether he had found what he was looking for – however in subsequent books the winning town is somewhat revealed with frequent references to his newfound lifestyle in Hanover, a small college town on the New Hampshire border. So, if it's good enough for Bill Bryson then it's got to be worth a look, I thought to myself as I planned our New England adventure in and around the Appalachian Mountains. And with Angie taking care of the hotel it was left to me to sort out the car hire.

'This will be a piece of cake, honey,' I said with a hint of arrogance. 'Just leave the talking to me.' I smiled as we entered the downtown Boston car rental. Little did I know we were about to enter the fluid world of the slippery car salesman.

'Ahhh good morning sir, madam, and how can I help you today?' the smiling salesman said beckoning us over to his desk.

'Yes, hi there, we need a car for the week. I was wondering what you could do for us?' I smiled back.

'Ok. Going anywhere special, sir? A nice coastal drive? The mountains perhaps?' the smiling man replied writing down some notes.

'Mmmm, not sure yet? We're still in the planning process,' I said sensing it perhaps best to give away as little as possible.

'And what type of car are you looking for, sir? Oh, have we got some fabulous deals for you today,' the man said presenting me with a list of comprehensive options.

'The cheapest one would be nice, thanks,' I replied running my eyes over the list of cars.

'Ok, like that, is it? I see. So, sir would like the cheapest model then, hey?' he questioned subtly glancing up towards my girlfriend. 'And how many drivers will be driving, sir?'

'Just me please, probably best if you want the car returned safely in one piece!' I chuckled.

'Yes, very good, sir, now let me get you that price,' he said tapping away into his computer. 'Ok... nearly there... give me one moment... just a few more seconds. Right that's it, that will be $67 a day for a small compact plus the insurance.'

'Plus the insurance? Well how much extra is that then?' I replied nearly spilling over my cup of coffee I had just that moment purchased from the vending machine.

'Well sir, I do recommend you take out our most popular cover, sir – our category A Gold Star package, it's a most excellent package and for an additional $35 a day you can be rest assured that you will be completely covered. It's an absolute must if I don't say so myself!' he smirked leaning back in his chair clasping his hands behind his head.

'One hundred bucks a day! Wow, that's a bit bloody expensive, don't you think? No, I'm sorry, I'm not sure we can afford that. You got anything else?'

'Well you can't be too careful these days, can you, sir? You need to get those tyres insured especially if you're driving up into the mountains. Don't want to be popping one of those big boys up there, uh uh absolutely not! They can be pretty damn expensive to replace, you know,' he said shaking his head like he gave a damn.

'Yes, well thanks for your concern but I'm sure we'll be fine. How much for the basic cover please?'

'Well you can't blame a man for trying can you, sir? We are in a recession, you know.'

'Indeed we are, my friend, so even more reason to give you less of my money then!' I replied trying to usher the conversation along.

'Very well sir, but I must inform you that you will be held entirely responsible for any damages to the tyres. Not to mention it will be your responsibility to pay for the tow truck should the need arise. Are you sure you wish to proceed with the basic cover, sir?'

'Yes, positive,' I snapped back tiring of his persistence.

'Well how about something more comfortable then, sir? Stretch out those tired old legs. We have some excellent options available for you today, sir.'

'Yes, I'm sure you do, but if you can just give me your best price for the compact car that would be great, thanks.'

'I understand, sir... but I must inform you that we will have to include the cost of a full tank of petrol in the price, sir.'

'You what? And how much is that then?' I asked, immediately wishing I hadn't!

'That's approximately $75, sir.'

'Seventy-five bucks! Can't I just take the car and sort my own petrol out. It's gotta be cheaper than that, surely?'

'I'm sorry sir, a full tank of petrol comes as standard. It's stated in our terms and conditions. See?' He said presenting me with a written document which in reality could have said absolutely anything for all I knew; the writing was so bloody small!

'Thank you but no thank you, my friend,' I said turning my back in disgust. 'Come on girl, we're leaving. This joker clearly doesn't want a sale today, does he?'

Who would have thought hiring a car could be so stressful? It was an experience I didn't want to repeat again, but luckily enough we would soon learn that booking online was by far the cheaper option, allowing us to hire a car at a third of the price and ironically from the exactly same place. The next day we picked up our car from the now not so smiling salesman and were soon dashing around the streets frantically searching for the main highway out of town.

'Which way? Which way? Which way?' I said panicking at the vast array of options suddenly opening up before my very eyes.

'Left, no straight, no left... no right, right, right!' Angie shouted flinging both hands into the air trying desperately to figure out her left from her right – before screaming in my ear...

'Pull over! You're in the wrong bloody lane, you idiot!'

'Yeah alright girl, steady on. You're supposed to be the one navigating me, remember! Didn't they teach you anything at school, stupido!' I said darting across the lanes to a crescendo of irate irons.

The next few intersections proved just as scary, but gradually my fragile confidence began to grow.

'This ain't so hard is it, darling? Quite frankly I don't know what all the fuss was about?' I said with one hand on the wheel just to prove my point.

'Yeah yeah you weren't saying that five minutes ago. Oh look babe, signs for Highway 1. Let's get the hell out of here, my darling.'

And so within a blink of an eye we were exiting the city and heading towards the rolling countryside of New England – the next leg of our trip – and what a fabulous little place that would turn out to be.

New England

The drive up through the rural forests of New Hampshire to Hanover was as stunning as could be. According to the local radio station, the weather had been unseasonably hot that week and with temperatures well into the eighties, the bright blanket of deep blue sky that painted the horizon formed the perfect backdrop to the surrounding green hills.

'This is what we came to find, darling,' I said smiling to Angie while rolling down my window.

For the next few days we had booked ourselves into a local Residence Inn. *'A home away from home'* the website had claimed and upon our arrival it was easy to see why. Nestled high above the road overlooking dense woodland, the sweeping views of the valley were nothing short of sensational. In truth, we couldn't have wished for a more perfect setting to choose as our first real base. And if we were worried about our creature comforts beforehand, we needn't had done. The Residence Inn offered us functionality beyond our wildest dreams. Equipped with our very own kitchenette, en suite bathroom, living room, free Wi-Fi and perhaps best of all, a full English breakfast completely free of charge it really was every modern-day ~~backpacker's~~ cash-packer's dream.

'Oh my God!' Angie shrieked with delight as we walked down the main corridor. 'I can't believe it? They've even got their own washing machines here. Baby, we can do all our washing. Look, they've even got tumble driers,' she said fumbling the dial back and forth. Sometimes it's the small things in life that bring us the most joy, and knowing our washing would now not be a problem was particularly good news.

That evening as we tucked into our complementary Hot Dogs, one of the hotel's staff approached our table to say hello. We were captivated almost immediately.

'Hi, I'm Tyler from reception,' the handsome man began. 'Everything OK for you folks? Can I get you guys another beer? It's on the house.'

'Oh yes please,' Angie replied fluttering her eyes, big smile beaming across her face.

'Ah well go on then, it would be rude not to,' I replied necking the last few remaining dregs from my can of Bud Light.

'Wow, you guys from England? That's totally awesome! How long you folks staying with us for?'

'Well we're not quite sure yet.' Angie smiled with a subtle tilt of the head. 'Just recently quit our jobs so we thought we'd come and explore your wonderful country for a while.'

'Oh my god, that's so amazing! You guys are so brave what with the recession 'n' all. I really hope you have a fantastic time with us.'

'Ahh thank you, Tyler. You have such a fabulous place up here. It's so green everywhere, never seen anything like this before,' she said gesturing towards the window.

'Stunning, isn't it. Heaven on earth we all reckon. You folks gonna love your stay here, there's so much to do in these parts,' he said pulling a cartoony styled map from his back pocket.

'Wow cool map,' I said looking at the cutesy images depicting the local landmarks.

'Sure is, my friend. Only in New England do you get maps this pretty,' he said unfolding the map before giving us a quick rundown of the local attractions. 'You gotta go to the White Mountains. There's loads to do there and it's only an hour or so away. Oh, you can't miss the Greens Mountains either and if you think it's green here? Well boy you ain't seen nothing yet, my friend. But don't forget Hanover and Woodstock,' he said pointing to the cute little drawing of a white clapboard church. 'Quintessential New England they all reckon, whatever the hell that's supposed to mean?'

'No idea either, mate?' I shrugged. 'But thanks for the advice, really appreciate it, always good to get the lowdown.'

'No worries, my English friends, and if there's anything you need then please don't hesitate to ask,' he said skipping off to aid another table.

'What a lovely young man. Don't get that sort of service in *olde* England do we, dear?' Angie giggled.

'We certainly don't, my darling. The only time I get any sort of small talk is at the end of the evening when they're friggin' well trying to turf me out. Miserable sods!' I said chuckling at the irony.

Nevertheless, it was comforting to be welcomed with such open arms. Being English and all we're not usually used to such lavish introductions '*You fooking English bastards'* being the more usual greeting – so to be actually respected for once was indeed very reassuring, even if it did take a little while to get used to.

We were up early the next morning for our much-anticipated jaunt into Hanover – and it didn't take too long to figure out why CNN magazine once voted it one of America's most desirable places to live. With its towering clock tower, immaculate green and delightful downtown buzz – it was as if time had stood still as you're immediately taken back to bygone era. This was undoubtedly the small-town America that Bill Bryson had been looking for and that I was now searching for myself. We parked the car and headed to the main coffee shop in the centre of town. It was Saturday morning yet the place was a hive of students, no doubt all busily preparing for their upcoming exams at the prestigious Dartmouth College on the other side of the green. Then in the corner of my eye I spotted a strange looking bearded man, *no not Bill Bryson,* approaching Angie from behind. *'Look away girl, don't acknowledge him, just ignore him... No... don't smile back at him... Nooooo!'*

'Excuse me, young peoples, could you tell me the way to the college bookstore please?' the peculiar looking man asked.

'Sorry sir, we don't know where that is,' Angela politely replied.

'Ohhhh helloooooooooo there Miss Engerlaaand, a pleasure to meet your acquaintance. Harry's the name, perhaps you know my aunt Elsie? She lives over there... in Englaaaaand you know. Maybe you've even had a nice cup of tea with her?' he said grinning from ear to ear like a demented clown. Angie's face dropped like a lead balloon.

'Jamie, he's an absolute fruitcake. Help me!' she whispered.

'Ohh I just love Englaaaand you know,' Angie's new friend continued. 'I love the Queen, I love Prince William, I love Prince Harry, and as for Diana well I loved her very much. Not sure about Camilla. But I'm sure I could eventually grow to love her too,' he said nodding his head.

'Yeah nice one, Angie, who's your new mate?' I muttered. 'I know you were keen to make friends but this really does take the...'

'I love Margaret Thatcher, I love John Major, I love Tony Blair...'

And so he carried on, talking a complete load of nonsense, leaving us little choice but to politely smile as we shuffled ever so slowly towards the safety of the coffee shop, which rather like a mirage teased us far away into the distance.

'I really love students too,' he continued. 'This place is full of them. I often come and sit in the park and watch them go by. Do you like students too?' he said looking at Angie.

'Errr I guess so?' she began.

'Ahhh maybe you are a student? An English student perhaps? Oh, I love students I really do. I'll do anything to them... Whoops did I really say that? Silly me how did I let that one slip out of the cat's bag?' he said smacking his hand as if to tell himself off before asking us. 'So why don't you come back to my place for a nice cup of tea?'

That was it, I'd heard enough! The thought of ending my days tied up half naked, underneath that fucker's basement wasn't exactly the most appealing offer on the table right now.

'No, we're fine, thanks,' I said nodding in the direction of the coffee shop window. 'Think we'll just stick to the coffee today, maybe next time. Although it was very nice to meet you... really... *now let's get the hell outta here!'* I muttered, grabbing Angie's hand and darting for the sanctuary of the coffee shop.

'Phew that was a close one, my darling. That'll teach you never to talk to strangers again, won't it?' I said with a hint of relief.

'Indeed so, my friend. This one is definitely on me,' she smiled, ordering a couple of Grande Lattes from the counter.

We chilled in the coffee bar for a while, and then meandered around the town's leafy streets, popping into the local bookstore where we were once again reminded of our distant student past. In the afternoon we ate lunch on the green underneath the University's famed clock tower and watched the world pass on by. It was a wonderful experience, doing nothing much in particular, but for once time was on our side. I looked around as a gentle breeze brushed passed my face. We really do live the majority of our lives in the fast lane, so sometimes it's nice to just sit back and take a moment to take it all in. It's fair to say we didn't have a care in the world that afternoon, and what a pleasant early summer's afternoon it was too.

The next few days continued in much the same vein as we weaved our way through the wooded heartlands of New England. Earlier that morning we had entered Vermont, crossing over the Quechee Gorge, Vermont's very own Grand

Canyon, although in truth if it wasn't for the brown signage on the rickety old bridge instructing us to 'Please drive carefully' I'd have barely noticed the open crevasse a hundred feet below. After that we explored the river town of Woodstock, before ascending into the Green Mountains towards the thriving village of Stowe, an affluent ski destination in winter but covered in white blossom in spring. Out of all the New England towns we'd visited perhaps Stowe was the most classical with its stunning white clapboard church instantly recognisable from a thousand picture postcards. Keen to see more we parked outside the Green Mountain Inn and wandered along the beautifully crafted Main Street. It really was the America I had seen in the movies. Grand properties set back on rolling lawns, all with these magnificent sweeping white verandas. Oh, how I wished I could sit on one of those wooden rockers watching the world pass me by. We ambled around, sampling on some of Vermont's finest culinary delights – from the freshly baked smell of sweet praline to the spicy tingle of pumpkin pie, and all completely delicious. After lunch we stopped off at Shaw's, Stowe's charming general store to check out its intriguing assortment of needful things.

It was late afternoon when we departed the village in the direction of the ski resort. The season may have long since gone, but we felt enough vibe to promise ourselves that one day we'd definitely be back to experience our first ever ski. It is fair to say I was falling in love with the place, perhaps even more so than Boston?

Driving home that day I looked out my window. With every shade of green from the darkest of forests to the lightest of lawns, it really was the greenest place I'd ever seen. At one point our surroundings were so breathtakingly beautiful we simply had to pull over on the grassy verge to take it all in. If indeed as Tyler had suggested that there was a heaven on earth then perhaps this was it.

The next day we hit the I-80 and headed to the region's other major mountain range, the White Mountains of New Hampshire. Located in the far north of the state, the expansive range completes the northern part of the Appalachian chain and is both the oldest and highest set of mountains on the eastern seaboard. Spanning over 3,000 miles from eastern Canada to the tip of Georgia, the ancient stretch of mountains was widely considered to be *the* natural barrier to the west, where only Indians and fur trappers dared go. Luckily for us times have changed and scaling the mountains was now not so precarious.

Earlier, over breakfast, I had come across a marketing flyer promoting the Mount Washington Auto Road. Ascending over 6,000 feet to the roof of New Hampshire '*The Road to the Sky*' is a fourteen-mile road journey into what is officially America's windiest place – the summit of Mount Washington. *Damn, these Americans really know how to sell!* Regrettably our trip to the top never actually materialised with us getting repeatedly side-tracked to explore the rocky gorges, numerous hiking trails and impressive cascades of waterfalls that would randomly pop up along the way. Although the highlight of the day was undoubtedly our visit to the Boulder Caves inside the Lost River Gorge – a narrow, steep-walled set of caverns hidden deep within the forested mountains. So with the thought of squeezing our butts into the tightest of crevices suddenly becoming all very appealing, we wasted little time in following a group of kids along a twisted boardwalk to the murky depths below. *I really must stop reading those marketing brochures*!

'Excuse me mister, you'll never get through that one, you're way too big!' one of the boys shouted, noticing me eyeing up a tight opening within the rocks.

Never one to shirk a challenge I responded with a nonchalant. 'No problem, little one, I'll see you on the other side!' I said crouching down on all fours confidently shuffling my head through the darkest of cracks. And then it happened, this unexplainable wave of claustrophobia that immediately set in the moment I squeezed my body in behind. Tight spaces have never really been my thing and when I couldn't twist my head back, a bolt of pure adrenalised panic swept through every nerve ending in my body *'Holy fuck... I'm... I'm... I'm... I'm fucking stuck!'* And so for a brief moment my fate was sealed. For not only was my life about to abruptly end in the most undignified of ways *with my big head lodged firmly between two boulders* – but my abiding memory being the unfortunate image of my hairy butt waving goodbye to the world as the fire teams tried desperately in vain to drag my sorry arse out. My heart raced as the news headlines flashed before me. 'What an ARSE... Man's head stuck in HOLE!'

Eventually after the tears had subsided I managed to regain my composure, twisting my head free and thus escaping my rocky doom, whilst also saving my family a whole lot of very difficult explaining. *'Yes, yes, we know his pants were falling down but they needed to take his belt off! Now leave us alone, you bastards!'*

That evening to celebrate my lucky escape Angie treated me to a full rack of BBQ ribs at the local smoking steakhouse, and they were absolutely delicious. The last few days had been fantastic; a real eye-opener into another simpler way of life, but sadly it was now time to move on. New England had been good to us but technically we were still going backwards on our westward adventure. Some serious questions now needed addressing. Did we continue with the car and drive for the majority of the trip or look at other more viable options? Trading in the car would certainly be difficult. As much as we loved the freedom it provided, it would probably be a nightmare getting around some of the bigger cities, whilst not to mention very costly. In truth I didn't really fancy the buses either as I'd heard way too many Greyhound horror stories. Therefore we were left with only one real option – the train, more specially the Amtrak. Not that this was bad, on the contrary, for it was actually rather good. You see like many a boy I'd always been fascinated with trains. I don't know what it is but there's just something about the railroad that stirs a man's emotions. Riding the Amtrak would be particularly captivating, like going back in time to a bygone era of hope and discovery. An incredible journey that would inevitably lead us down the very same pathway the early pioneers would've undoubtedly embarked upon over 150 years ago. Well it was supposed to be a westward adventure, wasn't it?

Over dinner I tapped away on my iPhone learning we could buy a forty-five-day rail pass for less than 800 hundred bucks. Not bad when you consider this entitled us to eighteen segments of travel – and with each segment counting as one journey, you could either jump off at the next station to use up a segment or ride the train all the way from Chicago to sunny San Francisco to use another. An absolute bargain if ever I'd seen one and although we'd probably never pull off such a stunt it was clear we could certainly cover a fair bit of distance in the upcoming weeks, maybe even get as far as the Rockies?

'Are you sure about this?' I said to Angie positioning the curser over the *complete reservation* icon.

'Go for it, cowboy,' she replied with the biggest smile. 'Let's go live the dream!'

The Train to NYC

The next day we returned the car and headed to Boston train station to begin the next leg of our journey. No more car, no more plans, just me, my girl, and a couple of rucksacks to accompany us on our first ever trip to New York City. A tinge of excitement ran through me as we cobbled our way across the station's marble floor. I looked around to assess our impressive surroundings. Built to reflect the time, South Station Boston is one of those grand old railway buildings that still very much dominates the immediate area, its imposing half domed facade standing proud after all these years. In its heyday, in the early 20th century, the station was one of the busiest transportation hubs in America, escorting over one million passengers a month. To many, the station was considered *the* gateway to the American west where thousands would pass through in search of a better life. Over the decades much has changed. What was once effectively a thriving frontier has now evolved into a modern, relaxed, airport style business lounge with an intriguing array of market stalls, trendy coffee shops and plush wine bars – their primary purpose to satisfy the hordes of hungry commuters on their way down to the Big Smoke.

We collected our shiny new passes from the Amtrak ticket office, grabbed a couple of lattes and waited somewhat excitedly for the train to arrive. It was approximately an hour later when we first heard it, faint at first but then progressively louder *Choo Choo... Choo Choo... Choo Choo.* The closer it got the louder it became *Choo Choo... Choo Choo... Choo Choooooo,* while all around a crescendo of steel bells rattled frantically to announce the impending arrival. Then it arrived, *'The Silver Bullet',* one of the most impressive looking double decker liners I had ever seen, coming to a halt just a few yards away.

A moment later a man in a smart uniform stepped off the train to address the line of waiting passengers. 'All aboard cabin number 6 for New York City!' he shouted, carefully checking each and every ticket.

We clambered aboard where a smiling lady greeted us at the top of the steps.

'Welcome aboard sir, madam,' she said looking at our tickets. '12A and 12B, right over there by the window to your left. Now you folks have yourself a wonderful day.' She smiled, pointing us towards these two huge window seats with enough capacity to occupy a small family.

'This certainly beats travelling in cattle class, doesn't it, darling,' I said reclining my seat a notch or two.

'Stretch out those tired old legs, hey baby,' Angie smiled.

While outside on the platform the station master made his final call. 'All aboard for New York City. All aboard!'

A moment later he blew his whistle and we were gently rolling through the leafy suburbs of Boston, then out into the big wide world. Feeling tired I lent my head against the window saying goodbye to Boston with sleepy eyes.

Then out of the blue I was awoken by a sharp tingling pain to the ribs? 'Arrrrrrgh what the...' I said feeling somewhat disorientated. 'Where are we, babe?'

'Wake up sleepyhead, we're nearly there. Look, look out the window. It's amazing, don't you think?' Angie said kissing the side of my cheek.

I rubbed my eyes to notice the entire carriage looking out in awe to the world beyond. A hushed silence bestowed the train. Manhattan is truly a spectacular sight – breathtaking, awe-inspiring, a modern day space age city, instantly recognisable yet unimaginably bigger from afar. No amount of words can do it justice. You simply have to see it for yourself.

New York City

It's fair to say I took an immediate dislike to New York. That's not to say it didn't grow on me over the coming days, on the contrary, but as we found our feet in the heart of Manhattan, I'd have given anything to have been elsewhere. We disembarked at Penn Street Station to a scene of pure and utter chaos. It may have only been a few hours south, but on first impressions it was a world away from the quiet sophistications of Boston. There were people bloody everywhere, far too many of them, all bulling and barging, desperately scurrying around so as not to miss their vital connection. It was confusing stuff alright. Trying to navigate one's way around in normal circumstances would have been a challenge, but trying to do it while lugging our entire possessions on the base of our backs only added to the frustrations.

'Which line do we need, babe? You did make a note, didn't you?' Angie shouted above the noise.

'Not sure, honey? Could be the blue line? That one seems to go north? Then again could be the orange one as well? But it could also very feasibly be the green one too? Oh, I don't bloody know? What street we on again, babe?' I said scanning the tube map.

'Yeah, nice planning, Jamie. Knew I could rely on you to prepare in advance!' she said shaking her head. 'Yet another fine entry into the Taylor's guide book of care free travelling, hey?'

Totally overwhelmed by the sheer pace of it all, we decided to head up the escalators into the hustle and bustle of Manhattan to flag down a cab. A simple exercise on paper, as frequently demonstrated in many a mafia movie where the hero leaps out into the road shouting *'TWAXI'* *literally* commanding the nearest cab to pull over. Only this was not the movies. Clearly not impressed with our high pitched and quite frankly lame Italian gangster impersonations, those yellow babies weren't stopping for us anytime soon. To add to our woes the rain clouds had opened up giving them even more reason to ride on by, and us a nice soggy welcome to New York.

Stranded, miserable and getting wetter by the minute we were left with little choice but to navigate our way to the hotel on foot. At least I was properly equipped for the occasion. Prior to the trip I had invested a large handful of cash into a brand spanking new all-encompassing North Face wheeler trolley back pack – which I must add was coming in particularly handy now, as I didn't really fancy lugging three months' worth of panty liners on the small of my back for the next twenty blocks or so. Granted I may have looked like a rather camp trolley dolly wheeling my bag behind me, and yes, I did get a few inquisitive looks from the locals as I minced my way up Chinatown, but at least it made the journey bearable. Unfortunately the same could not be said for Angela. How can I put it? She had chosen to be slightly more prudent in her choice of luggage and had elected to go for the good old-fashioned holdall style rucksack – big, heavy, no support whatsoever, one word – totally useless. I had to double take when she first tried it on as for a brief moment I thought I was looking at some weird, hybrid, fucked up human tortoise. Bless her, it was nearly twice the size of her petit little frame. Well I did try to warn her.

'You planning on taking a hike up to base camp then?' I remember saying.

'Base camp? What the hell you taking about James?' she replied all defensively

'Your bag. That's the sort of thing you wanna take up the mountains dear not cart around the streets of New York, my darling.'

'James, it will be fine. And it has so much storage. I can fit my whole wardrobe in here.' she replied, clearly chuffed with her decision.

'Fine go for the tortoise shell look if you want but don't expect me to lug that thing around when you find you can't cope, my friend!'

'Oh you do bang on, James. I'll be alright,' she hastily replied. *'Don't you worry about me... and I don't see why you always have to go for the most expensive thing in the shop anyway? It's not like you've got a job now, is it?'*

'Your funeral, babe, just promise you won't shout at me when that piece of crap fails its first real test!'

And I have to say Angie kept to her word. Not once did she shout at me during her sixty-minute crawl through the streets of New York. Actually she was so quiet she never really spoke to me or anyone else for that matter for the rest of the entire day. Yes, it is fair to assume she was absolutely livid, although with whom I'm not entirely sure? It's not like I didn't try to help her. I did offer to share the burden by suggesting we swap over every now and then, but being a stubborn little mule she was having none of it. Although in hindsight perhaps my frequent demonstrations of just how well my roller wheels were standing up to the riggers of the street only riled her even more. Digging in she simply refused to trade, whilst I might add, making me look a complete numpty in the process – casually wheeling my trolley around while watching my poor lady struggle on with hers. But would she listen?

The second morning didn't fare much better. Being memorial weekend, the city was packed full of tourists, and despite our best efforts to avoid the much publicised Statue of

Liberty queues – we found ourselves stuck at the back of the longest ever line at only 9.30 in the morning. Still, at least it gave us a plenty of time to laugh at the hoards of Japanese tourists who had formed an alternative queue to have their picture taken with some random bloke covered head to toe in a glittering of silvery spray paint. Did they really just give that guy twenty bucks? For that? To have their picture taken with some silly fool who incidentally looked bugger all like the real stature of liberty. I'm obviously in the wrong type of business my friend? I need to go to the shop and get me some sparkling spray paint. Anyway, Angie didn't seem to mind waiting around. Always a sucker for her cheap tack she now had an extra hour to negotiate with the local vendors and acquire herself numerous pieces of useless trinkets in the process. She was particularly pleased with her $2 fridge magnet purchase and free pen giveaway. 'Didn't I do well?' she smiled, tucking her new pen into the depths of her bag.

We eventually got to the front of the queue and were shocked to discover there were only a couple of little dinky boats ferrying the tourists across to Liberty Island. I shook my head in disbelief. You'd have thought they may have lay on a few more boats considering it was supposed to be one of the city's most popular attractions. Was I missing something here? In a country that practically invented the word 'convenience' you'd expect they'd have come up with a better way to ferry the eager herds across – like maybe a *Key West*-style highway providing direct access across the water, or at the very least a subway link to the statue herself. Can't be that hard, can it? Instead they prefer to let us queue for hours on end and at the mercy of these street traders. Maybe the street venders were running the whole operation after all? Like some dodgy mafia splinter group paying a cut to the big guy above. It would make sense I guess, and by subjecting everyone to their tacky stalls was indeed the most cost-effective way to relieve a sucker from his money. What's one man's trash is another man's treasure, hey? The Japanese were certainly going for it. However, it did get everyone around to speculate on how many people actually visited the statue and what revenues it could raise?

'I reckon that they must make over a million dollars a day,' Angela confidently confirmed.

'You reckon?' I responded pulling out my iPhone calculator. 'I'm not so sure, sweetheart? Divide that by our $12 ticket and you're looking at 80,000 people a day? That's over 29 million visitors a year. At that rate they would need the entire fleet of the Spanish Armada to ferry us across, not those two poxy little fishing boats, my dear. I don't know babe, way off the mark as usual!'

'Yeah alright, Mr. I've got a calculator. Frankly I don't give a monkey's. And if I'd wanted a mind numbingly boring analysis I would have phoned up Steven bloody Hawking wouldn't I!'

For those that care, Google would later declare that there was a limit to 15,000 visitors a day.

We proceeded to the front and it was of no surprise to learn that security had understandably tightened up since 9/11. Although going through the new airport style checks was proving particularly embarrassing, as somehow I managed to set off the portable hand detector on three separate occasions?

I can only assume I must have been born with some metal rod rammed firmly inside my privates, as no other sod seemed to so frequently set the alarm off? It wasn't exactly a very manly buzz either, more a pathetic whimper that kind of indicated there really wasn't much down there at all. Then finally on the 4th attempt an amused security officer instructed me to flex my muscles above my head and miraculously the beeper didn't go off! All very strange?

I wish I could say the hassle was worth it. In truth it was one of the most overrated attractions I had ever visited. The queuing certainly didn't help, but our morning got a whole lot worse when the smug little git next to us gleefully informed us that we needed to have booked our tickets over three weeks in advance if we actually harboured any realistic ambition of climbing the statue. '*No point queuing up on the day, no one ever queues up on the day!'* Well thanks for that matey and I don't ever recall reading that one in the 'NYC *don't forget to bloody book before you go section?'* So left with little alternative, our trip to the statue encompassed no more than a quick circuit around its perimeter, a couple of photographs for the mandatory Facebook brag, and a quick visit to the official gift shop *Angie's idea* to purchase yet more overpriced junk that would no doubt serve to remind us of what a terrible morning we had just experienced.

However one of the most important things to remember about New York is that you should never ever write it off – as we were starkly reminded when we passed through the World Trade Centre on our return to central Manhattan. A lone man stood under a bridge preaching to those who would listen, telling tales, showing a handful of photographs of those terrible events. It still sends a shiver to recall that one of the most notorious acts of terrorism occurred at this very place over a decade ago. All the fear, all that suffering, a moment in time that will never be forgotten. They say there are some times in life where you never forget where you were. Me? I was away with work in a hotel bar when news of the first plane struck. The rest of the evening we just sat there motionless, sipping on our pints watching the second plane crash into the South Tower. Then the first tower came crashing down to earth, shortly followed by the second. Speechless. A day in my life I will never forget.

The next day we caught the subway to 5th Avenue. Earlier that morning Angie had made it perfectly clear that a visit to Manhattan was never going to be complete without a quick look inside the world-famous Tiffany's. Which begs the question, why is it that practically every girl I have ever known wants to be like Audrey Hepburn in *Breakfast at Tiffany's*? Correct me if I'm wrong, but wasn't she a slutty little call girl with a taste for the high life who'd do anything for a fat diamond ring? And this is supposed to be their role model? It's no wonder why standards have declined. Quite frankly I could never understand what all the fuss was about. But now we were here, I simply had to investigate this age old feminine obsession – and so what better place to start, than posing outside the store as the very own Holly Golightly *that's Audrey to me and you chaps* peering through the window with a take away latte in one hand and butter croissant in the other – leaving Angie the simple task of capturing the moment on camera to no doubt bribe me with for the rest of my sorry arse life. Unfortunately, due to the fact that several other million people had probably done exactly the same thing, Tiffany's had long since blocked out the window, denying me any chance of peering through. *Thanks guys, waste my bloody time why don't you?* Anyway so there I was staring vacantly into this bricked up wall, generally just being a bit of a nuisance, bumping into people and dripping hot melting butter all over their shoes as they tried to enter the store. *'Oh, I'm ever so sorry!'*

Anyway, after a couple of minutes of fumbling around we decided it probably best to get the hell out the way and actually enter the store ourselves. What immediately struck me was how miserable everybody was. The blokes I could understand, they were just about to get walloped for a whacking great bill. If ever there was a harmony of fear between our fellow brothers then it was here down the marble isles of Tiffany's. Scanning around I could see a poor sod wincing as a smooth-talking sales advisor casually cranked up the gears, effortlessly working his fiancée up the price bands.

'Yes madam, half a carat would be adequate for the day, but if you really want to stand out from the crowd then you really should be looking at the full carat range, madam. Over here we have some of our finest South African pieces.'

I could see the whites in his eyes light up as the penny dropped that it was going to be a very expensive afternoon after all. Dazed, staggered and utterly confused he looked at me for any kind of support, but all I could offer was a consolatory shake of the head. *I feel for you, brother, I'm sharing your pain.* However, what surprised me most was just how bloody miserable all the women were. What with their *'I want this and I want that'* diva attitudes, it was like a toxic combination *Mean Girls* meeting *Lord of the Rings*... *'The ring... I must have the ring!'* Suddenly I was surrounded by a bunch of spoilt brats! If your children behaved in such a way you'd send them to bed without any tea. Don't they realise how much this shit costs? You'd think they'd show a little more appreciation considering they were about to fritter away their partner's entire life savings on what is effectively a dull piece of stone dug up from the ground. Yes, ok it may be very shiny but come on girls, is it really worth three times his monthly salary? Sadly there's very little room for humility in this kind of place as all sense of perspective has clearly been left outside. It was at this point I noticed Angela slowly being lured towards one of the counters. *Not today my little friend.* I had seen enough. It was time for a strategic withdrawal. 'Come on girl, I'll buy you lunch, my treat!'

For the next few days we followed the tourist trail with the customary crossing of the Brooklyn Bridge, quick jaunt up the Rockefeller building and the daily pilgrimage to Times Square – whilst in between making a point to sample as many of the weird and wonderful on the go delicacies we could possibly find. If ever there was a place where street food ruled then it was here, out on the streets and inside the numerous multi-cultural delicatessens of New York.

The highlight of Manhattan though was undoubtedly our visit to Central Park. I wasn't expecting much but was pleasantly surprised to find the most enchanting urban oasis I had ever encountered. Measuring an impressive 843 acres and coming in nearly two and a half times the size of London's Hyde Park, Central Park is simply enormous. Fully completed in 1878, the landscaped grounds are a complete contrast to the urban hustle and bustle outside. Offering a wealth of activities from ice skating, running tracks, open air concerts, baseball pitches, restaurants and boating lakes – the sanctuary of the park is a far cry from what lies beyond. Although what really makes it so special is the maze of enclosed pathways that entwine you towards the park's heart. Shielded by a dense forested canopy, you are guided to the centre almost oblivious to the world outside. Walking around the park was an experience I will never forget. There was a serenity in the air that you could almost touch, a calmness, a sense of belonging, an unrivalled tranquility emitting out from every winding pathway – at times it was hard to believe you are walking through the heart of one of the most populated places the planet. We sat down for a while and once again found ourselves watching the world go by – the eager joggers, the happy picnickers, the active family playing baseball in the nets, the cyclists, the old romantics, the three guys playing Frisbee on the lawn – and so for a moment, be it ever so brief, I too felt what it was like to be a proper New Yorker. *Maybe one day we could live here too? I wonder if Friends is on tonight?*

It was late afternoon when we started to head back. 'Hang on babe, there's just one more thing we need to do,' I said gesturing towards the large floral monument on the west side of the park. It was precisely thirty years ago when the great John Lennon was shot outside the park at the entrance of the Dakota hotel, his beloved apartment overlooking the park. A random, senseless act of violence by a man who only hours before was photographed receiving a signed autograph at the very same spot where'd he later return to gun him down. A haunting photograph if ever I'd seen one. As John scribbles his name, at first glance his murderer appears to be looking down in his sunglasses. Only he is not, is he, for his piercing eyes are looking directly into the face of his next victim – plotting, scheming, and working out his next move, with the Devil's smile sprawled all across his face. Such a tragic waste of life. As we stood at the entrance to the park, paying our condolences at the John Lennon Memorial, you couldn't help but think what other great feats he may have accomplished if his life hadn't been so cruelly cut short on that dark December night all those years ago. Long may his memory live on.

And so, our time in New York was coming to an end. Initially I may have held a few reservations but the more I began to discover, the more I began to understand. They say to be bored of London is to be bored of life. I felt the same with New York, only so much more.

Atlantic City

I first saw the film *Philadelphia* in the mid-nineties. Tom Hanks had won an Oscar for playing a sick man dying of AIDS, while his mate Bruce Springsteen, can be heard proudly singing along to the Streets of Philadelphia somewhere in the background. A touching movie, but there was never any doubt that the film successfully achieved its main ambition in portraying the place as a complete dump and thus placing an eternal curse on the city ever since. It's fair to assume that I had absolutely no desire to spend too much time in Philly. The closest we came was a one-hour stopover at the train station while waiting for our connecting train from New York to Atlantic City. I didn't really have that much desire to explore Atlantic City either. This was Angie's call, I'm afraid. Prior to the trip she had repeatedly requested we pay Atlantic City a visit, but not for the famous gambling, beaches or hotels as one would normally expect, but for the mere fact she had recently seen a movie where her heroine, Jennifer Aniston, was filmed cycling along the boardwalk on one of those old fashioned rickshaws. *'How romantic'* Angie had commented and now she too was insistent on visiting the exact same spot. And that was it, the sole reason why were now waiting at the station to catch a train to 'AC', as she kept calling it, was to walk down a friggin' wooden plank!

'Really? It's a long way to go, darling. You sure about this?' I said trying to talk her out of it. 'It's supposed to be a right dump there, you know?'

'Yes, I'm very sure and don't try to talk me out of it, Taylor. We always do what you want to do. You never let me do what I want to do.'

'I'm not stopping you? Just can't see the point really? All this effort just to walk down some shabby boardwalk on a beach?'

'There is no point as you like to put it. I just want to do it. Is that OK? And if it's not OK with you, then tough, as this time we're gonna do it my way for a change. I'm not going to let you talk me out of this one. You got that, buster!'

'Yes, loud and clear, darling!' I said realising I was a beaten man. There was absolutely no negotiation on this one, no way, so against my better judgement we were going to AC whether I was up for it or not. Truth was I didn't really mind that much. It was Angie's holiday too and she had given up a lot to come away with me. No point just living out my own adventure. It was only fair that she got to live out her own dreams, even if they were a bit light and fluffy at times.

A short while later, our connecting train rolled into Philly and we were soon boarding the local New Jersey train for the hour-long commute to the coast. My fear that it was going to be a long couple of days were immediately raised the moment we stepped aboard the tatty old train, unlike the Amtrak before, the only silver bullets on this train were the ones the passengers were probably carrying. It really was a throwback to the late seventies and the bad old days of British Rail. A dull lifeless greying plastic covered the interior, litter spewed across the floor, and murky grease smeared the windows blocking out any chance of a decent view. The train was in complete decay and in desperate need of a makeover. It was depressing stuff alright and perhaps explained why everyone onboard all looked so bloody miserable. The majority of which probably wouldn't have known much better. All were most definitely poor, low income day trippers commuting from Philly and about to waste what little money they did have in the bright lights of the big casinos. There were certainly no checkered shirts and pressed chinos aboard this carriage, that's for sure. Looking back it was also the first time on the trip I felt a little insecure. Should we have been so quick to have ditched the car? Here we were two innocent backpackers nervously guarding what little possessions we had, while all around inquisitive eyes darted in our direction no doubt planning our imminent demise.

Thankfully we survived the hour-long journey, but things didn't improve much more in AC. Our hotel, although fairly close to the casinos on the waterfront was set a couple of blocks back, thus requiring a spine-tingling ten-minute walk through some of the most derelict streets I had ever encountered. The boardwalk was a huge disappointment too, for scattered between each Super Casino lay a plethora of rundown shops, bordered up massage parlors, and a mountain of rubbish simply tossed all over the street. By the looks of things it had been a while since the place had been cleaned up. The beach didn't fare much better either. Angie had been insistent we head out to shore, having promised her friends she would dip her feet in both sides of the ocean. A moment she would be determined to capture on camera, even if it did mean navigating her way through the masses of debris leading up to the sea.

'Be careful babe, watch those bottles and don't step on any needles. You sure this is worth it?' I said shaking my head.

'I'll be fine, James. You worry about yourself. Just take the bloody shot, will you!' she hastily replied.

After that, we then preceded to follow boldly in the footsteps of Jennifer Aniston by walking down the very stretch of boardwalk where the former *Friends* star had once graced. Only problem being we had no idea that Atlantic City had another very special claim to fame – in that its boardwalk is officially the longest boardwalk in the whole of the friggin' western world, nearly six miles long to be precise. Now that's one hell of a walk to undertake especially when you're so blatantly walking in the wrong direction!

'We nearly there yet, babe?' I said looking around at the surrounding slums.

'Not too far now, Jamie,' she insisted.

'You sure they filmed it all the way out here. Those casinos are starting to look a long way back now, darling?' I replied glancing over my shoulder noting the distant casinos in the background. 'It's starting to get a little scary now, darling. Everyone is looking at us?'

'Yes Jamie, shush will you!'

We continued onwards for another few minutes but it was clear the moment had passed; the bright lights of the casinos were long gone, while all around us nothing but urban decay. A few minutes later Angie finally admitted defeat, but only after another round of squabbling had made her finally see sense. The long walk back was a silent one.

Some time later we arrived at our hotel and Angie immediately got to the task of booking the first available train out of *AC* and into Washington. 'Come on babe, we're here now we might as well have some fun tonight,' I said doing my best to console her. My offer of an olive branch seemed to lighten the mood and we were soon heading back for a night out in the casinos. Now I must confess, I've always been partial to a little flutter, and given the choice of spending a week out on a beach or a few days in Vegas, then the bright flashing lights win every time. However the clientele in the casinos here bore little resemblance to the high rollers you'd expect to see out in Nevada, and it didn't take long to figure out that Atlantic City was basically a poor man's Vegas. With a chilly atmosphere prevailing across the gaming floor, there were no cries of joy or hoots of laugher, just serious people seriously cursing their bad luck. Once again I was left with the 'poor day trippers from Philly feeling' although what shocked me most was the fact the tables weren't priced accordingly. With the cheapest chips costing a staggering twenty bucks a piece, it was virtually daylight robbery, even more so when you consider the majority of punters probably take home little more than a few hundred bucks a week. This wasn't fun this was desperate and it was no wonder why nobody was smiling.

We played a few hands of Blackjack but quickly found ourselves digging heavily into the next day's budget. Deciding it probably best to cut our losses, we agreed to head back to the hotel in preparation for our early morning train trip to the Capitol.

The walk to the station the following morning offered only more tedium. Once again Angie struggled with her rucksack, needing regular stops to catch her breath, while again she stubbornly refused my kind offers of help. 'If you were a real man, James, then you shouldn't even have to ask!' she would reply shaking her head.

We eventually arrived at the station only to find the train had been delayed for over an hour. Finding a bench I unloaded my rucksack and nervously checked out our gloomy surrounds. Never before had I encountered such a wave of desolate people all in one place. In truth I don't think I'd ever seen such a crazier bunch of odds and sods in my entire life then the lot I was looking at right here. It was as if we'd entered the local nuthouse not the local train station. Some were gibbering complete nonsense to themselves, while others randomly hummed; although the majority of folk just sat back staring silently into their sad abyss.

It's fair to say, even with my low expectations, Atlantic City was a huge disappointment. In a city that promises so much it delivered so very little – for all we encountered was poverty, hardship and desperation. In truth it was the other side of America I had often read about but didn't really want to see. It was also the first time I realised how vulnerable we really were. Maybe this trip wasn't going to be such a breeze after all? But we were the lucky ones, I guess. On the first signs of trouble we could simply pack up and leave. Sadly, for the majority of folk sitting around me, they rarely had such a choice.

Washington D.C.

It was late afternoon when our train rolled into the capitol's eastern suburbs, and much to our relief, Washington D.C. would prove to be a pleasant contrast to the squalidness of Atlantic City. The metro was immaculate, the streets were clean and on first impressions its people appeared extremely orderly, although perhaps a little too orderly I thought to myself as we made our way across town towards the hotel.

A short while later we checked in to a rather pleasant looking Courtyard hotel – only to discover the White House was located literally down the end of our street. *Result*! So, deciding this was simply too good an opportunity to miss out on, we ditched our bags and immediately hurried out to *go and call* for the President to see if he wanted to come and play. Not that he wanted to see us of course; he'd probably just get his mummy to answer the door making up some pitiful excuse why he couldn't hang out with the two coolest kids on the block!

'Sorry kids, Barrack won't be coming out today... he's grounded for telling too many lies!'

'Oh, Ok, Mrs Obama could you tell him that James and Angela called please.' Ahhhh those were the days hey!

A few minutes later we reached the fabled gates of the most powerful office in the western world. The White House is an impressive building from whatever angle you see it and don't believe that cock and bull you normally hear about it being much smaller then expected. From the front it's one imposing building and on first impressions very similar in statue to our own Buckingham Palace. The only slight blot being the hordes of anti-war veterans, pot smoking hippies and other time-wasting losers parading their pointless banners declaring the end is nigh and all that nonsense. Why people feel the need to always blame the government for their misfortunes is beyond me? Hadn't they anything else better to do, like get themselves a proper job? Perhaps then they wouldn't be so bleeding miserable.

Founded in 1790, Washington officially resides in the District of Columbia and is the only city in America not to be controlled by an individual State – therefore falling under the jurisdiction of the Federal Government. Now New York may house the might of the financial institutions, but with nearly 30% of Washington D.C.'s employees belonging to the government in some form – be it the Feds, the Senate, the Secret Service *or anyone else driving a blacked out car for that matter* it will forever be the designated home of the State. When designing the city, former President and design guru Thomas Jefferson aimed to recreate a 'Paris of the west' and with its low rise buildings, wide open streets and ample parkland, Washington can proudly boast more open spaces then virtually any other American city – while also providing the perfect cover for the occasional private or off the record conversation. *'Meet me round the back of the Lincoln Memorial in 10 minutes... alone... or the dog gets it!'*

You see that's the thing about this place, for all its status, prestige and history you can't but help think you've just rocked up into a bad episode of *The X-Files*. *'The watchers'* they're flipping everywhere, on every street, on every corner, watching your every turn. If it's not a blacked-out car tailing your behind, then it's a man in dark disguise observing your every fart. *'Rodger, Rodger, Rodger, we have the suspects in sight sir. Rodger copy that, over!'*

If I wasn't paranoid beforehand, I most certainly was now. All of a sudden you're guilty? You're not sure why and you're not sure what for? Then your mind starts playing tricks with you. You don't understand it but you're scared? You can't quite fathom it but somehow they're all over you? You sense it, you can feel it, and they're there, everywhere, across the street, behind the windows, hiding in the bushes for all you know. Just watching, waiting, waiting for you to slip up... *run, James... just bloody run...*

'You ok babe, you look a little lost?' Angie said snapping me out of this weird paranoid trance in which I had now entered.

'Err yeah fine babe, just checking out the local scenery,' I replied nervously, checking my back to see who was behind.

'Well, catch up, slow coach, we're nearly there,' she said walking around to catch a view of the south side of the building.

And what a view it was too. Instantly recognisable from the southern railings, the White House is even more impressive than it is from the north. Set aback on a lush carpet of manicured lawn you can just about make out the familiar curvature of the Oval Office in the far away distance. I stood in silence for a moment simply taking it all in. Here I was peering through the gates of Barrack Obama's very own back garden. It's not every day you get the chance to do that. *Wonder what's he's up to*? And then you notice them, the three snipers perched high above the rooftop watching you through their rifles. *'We have visual on the suspects again, sir!'* A cold shudder broke my trance, as I envisaged the three separate cross hairs now firmly planted in the centre of my very sweaty forehead.

'Ready to fire, sir?'
'Fire at will... fire at will!'

I jolted away. 'Right, that's it, think I've had enough of this today. Can we go home please, babe?'

The next day we visited the National Mall, a huge open parkland in the southern part of town in what effectively is the heartbeat of Capitol Hill – and it's here where everything ticks. In the centre of the park, the Washington Monument towers above the grassy verge – standing at exactly 555 feet, the marbled obelisk is officially the tallest structure inside the city. Flanked by the Jefferson Building to the south, Congress to the east and the Lincoln Memorial to the west, it's up to the White House in the north to complete the specific triangular formation in what many believe to be part of an elaborate design by the mysterious Illuminati. This powerful, enlightened, yet very secretive bunch of Masons are said to have embedded their vast wisdoms within the structural design of the city. It is believed magical symbols have been incorporated into the city's DNA that allegedly contains hidden scientific messages. What these mysterious symbols are supposed to mean has been the subject of conspiracy theorists for years. The iconic Masonic Square, Compass and its two inverted triangles are clearly visible from the sky. While other more controversial symbols such as the sabbatical goat, can with a trained eye, be identified in the street formations leading up to the White House. Fascinating stuff, but in truth I suspect even the great Robert Langdon and his plucky little French assistant would struggle to decode many of the claims.

The Mall is also proud home to the world-famous Smithsonian museums, the largest set of museums in the world. Comprising a staggering nineteen museums, numerous research facilities and even a fully housed zoo – the Smithsonian museums are said to own virtually every notable piece of scientific collectible worth preserving. One item in particular hitting the news that week was the Giant Squid that had recently washed up from the Gulf of Mexico. Measuring an impressive 20 feet in length, the gentle giant is said to be one of the most elusive sea creatures known to man. Once so slippery, it now lay bare in a shiny glass box. The giant squid was causing quite a stir in the Natural History's main atrium. Keen to see what all the fuss was about we joined the back of the queue, but when we eventually got to the front I was overcome with a sense of sadness not intrigue as I had so eagerly anticipated. Almost alien in appearance, its huge oval eyes stared lifelessly back through the bright glass box, while its once powerful tentacles now lay completely dormant. In truth, I was horrified to see this once great magical monster of the deep paraded in a box like some kind of freak show for the children to point and peer. A sad way indeed to end one's days.

After lunch we headed out for a quick perusal of the Hill. The Capitol Building was hugely impressive; its domed shaped exterior is an exact replica of its more famous cousin in the grounds of the Vatican. Later we walked across the grassy Mall, passing the Washington Monument on our way towards the Lincoln Memorial in the west of the city. The view from the top of the Memorial steps is one of the most recognisable in all of Washington. In the foreground, the long rectangular reflection pool glistens in the afternoon sun, while further aback, the Washington Monument, grassy verge and Capitol Building rather spectacularly frame the background. I was now standing on the very platform where every President of America was once sworn in. Shuffling to the front of the steps I puffed out my chest and like Martin Luther King before, declared to the world '*I have a dreaaaaaam!*' Ok, I may have gotten a few inquisitive looks from the locals but it was well worth the public declaration. Perhaps the most famous speech of all was the one delivered by a courageous young solider at an anti-Vietnam War rally. Oh the memories as the young Forrest Gump took the stage to deliver those famous words... '*In Vietnaaaam... and that's all I have to say about Vietnaaaaam. Jenny? Jennnnnny!*' A classic movie moment if ever there was one, and one that still brings tears to the eyes just even thinking of it. Forrest Gump, what a true American legend!

That evening we stayed in our hotel room to plan the next stage of our journey. We had now reached the first major crossroads of our trip where the next decision would inevitably mean forgoing something else. It was time for some difficult choices. From our current position there were three basic alternatives. The first was to hire a car for a couple of days then backtrack north into Virginia to visit Gettysburg, the site of one the most brutal battles in the American Civil War. The second was to venture inland and drive along the crest of the mountains in the beautiful Shenandoah National Park – while the third would see us returning to the railroad to continue our journey southwards. All three were desirable options, but the logistics involved would only allow us one choice. The Gettysburg option was initially the most tempting. I had never been to a battlefield before and to visit the site where the momentum of civil war effectively swung was certainly very appealing. There were other reasons why I wanted to go. My grandparents had visited the site many years before and brought back a whole host of Gettysburg memorabilia. Sunday lunches were never the same again the day they laid out those cheap plastic placemats, depicting those battlefield monuments all over the top of their dining room table. I can still recall now trying to shove my peas and carrots inside one of those tiny Cannon barrels. Oh, the joys of childhood. On a separate note, Gettysburg was also one of the first wars to be depicted in film. It was also the first time I ever saw a dead body. Those graphic, haunting images taken in the brutal aftermath would never be allowed to be circulated today, but one thing they did do was so vividly bring the ghastly horrors of battle to life, if you pardon the irony. We eventually ruled out Gettysburg for the simple reason that we wanted to move forwards not backwards. Sometimes when travelling even the shortest of backtracks can be seen as a trek too far. Two choices now remained and after much debate we finally came to a decision. We packed our bags and headed for Union Station. 'I hope the creole and hospitality is as good as they say?' I said to Angie as the train rolled out of the station. It was now time to begin part two of our great American adventure.

The Deep South

Savannah

It was a slow trek down to the Deep South. The unusually warm weather we were experiencing may well have been a hit with sun worshipers, ice cream manufactures and lollipop lovers, but for rail companies it was proving a complete disaster – the excessive heat on the rails were causing no end of delays and cancelations on the network. On a normal day, the coastal journey from Washington to Savannah could take anywhere up to ten hours, but on a bad run like today it was anybody's guess. We were only three hours into our ten hour marathon when the driver delivered the bad news over the tannoy.

'Sorry folks, but due to the heat on the rails, the trains speed will have to be restricted to fifty-six miles per hour for the rest of journey, or at least until the rails cool down. Apologies folks, so why not in meantime put your feet up and take in some of that beautiful scenery we have to offer!'

It was a nice try from the captain but understandably this didn't go down well with the passengers and was received by a loud chorus of moans, groans and a whole load of *'Oh for fucks sakes!'* The bad news would almost certainly mean a late-night arrival. To make matters worse the train driver was clearly in no particular hurry to make up lost time, frequently pulling aside to let others pass. At first it was the fast trains that were allowed to bully their way through, then the coal trains started to pass, then the freight trains, then finally just about any other piece of rusty old junk that happened to be in the area seemed to be allowed to pass. The rumbles onboard continued.

It soon became clear that Amtrak were no more than glorified tenants leasing out the use of the tracks. I would later find out that out of a network of 22,000 miles – Amtrak is said to own only a measly 3% – the other 97% belonging to the big freight companies, hence all the pussyfooting around. My patience was further tested by the big oaf sprawled across the seats in front who had been snoring like a hound the last couple of hours. Nothing a sharp poke to the kidneys wouldn't sort out. Tempting but probably suicidal considering he was twice my size and all dressed up in gangsta bling. Best to let sleeping dogs lie, I reckon. After a while the carriage settled and we did exactly as the captain had instructed.

'It's not so bad is it, Angie?' I said looking out the window.

'Ssshhhh. I'm relaxing,' she smiled back.

And so for the next few hours we sat in silence looking out to the world beyond. The Amtrak may have had its shortcomings, but one cannot deny there is something uniquely special about riding the long-distance railroad. The sound of the horns, the smell of diesel, the cool summer breeze drifting in through the wide open windows – quite frankly it was the closest I had come to any kind of exhilaration in a long, long time. I gazed out the window, took a deep breath and watched with childlike excitement as we crawled our way through the lush forested lands of Virginia. Every once in a while the driver would *Choo Choo* the horns as we chugged our way through yet another small town. It really was quite a wonderful experience and one I shall never tire of recalling – the sound of those magnificent horns will forever be the abiding memory I have of that summer.

Later that afternoon the conductor nonchalantly strolled through the carriages addressing each passenger in person as he politely invited them to join him for dinner.

'Excuse me, ma'am, dinner will be served in the dining cart at 7.00 this evening. Would you care to join us?'

'Ohh, that would be lovely,' Angie excitedly replied. The thought of having a posh dinner on the train clearly appealed to her romantic side.

'Excellent, ma'am, and will sir be making a reservation too?'

'Ahhh that would be fantastic as long as madam has no objections?'

'Very good, sir. You two folks have a great ride. We look forward to seeing you at the table.'

I smiled at the conductor and was touched by his manners. It had been a while since I had been addressed so politely on my travels. I was more accustomed to grumpy old cabin crew whose best days were clearly behind them, shoving a plastic tray under my nose while grimacing... *'Teaaaaa? Coffeeeee... anyfing else?'*

Yes, how about a smile, you miserable sod?

It was dark when we eventually rolled into Savannah's Union Station and as much as I had enjoyed our little adventure, I was a little concerned about arriving so late to such a small and unpopulated station. We collected our gear and tentatively stepped out into the night. A few weary passengers followed behind, but they were the lucky ones, each and every one of them had clearly made prior arrangements and were immediately dispersed into the line of waiting cars. One by one they drove off into the night, leaving just the two of us to negotiate a ride with what appeared Savannah's only available taxi. Somewhat precariously we headed towards the lone yellow cab, only to be intercepted by a scary looking biker man dressed head to toe in tattooed Hells Angel attire.

'You two wannnna ride?' he shouted in a slow southern drawl.

It was at this precise moment when my heart skipped a beat as a jolt of pure fear struck me like never before. *We're sooooo dead!* It didn't take a genius to work out that this scary looking man was also unfortunately going to be our only ride outta here. Suddenly our chances of getting to the hotel in one piece were starting to look very bleak indeed, and not for the first time on this adventure we were left with a dilemma. Did we take our chances on the streets and walk into town? Or jump into the car with biker boy and pray to God he wasn't as creepy as he looked? I checked my iPhone to note it was a four mile trek into town. *Oh shit!* I looked round to assess the situation. All around a blanket of thick black covered the horizon, while up ahead nothing bar a distant light flickering in the wind. And so there we were surrounded in total darkness with nothing but this scary, scraggly bearded man for company, who by the way was almost certainly going to kill us no matter whatever we did? After a long deliberation I was left with no other choice...

'Thanks very much sir but it's such a lovely evening so I'll think we'll walk into town.' I nodded, trying my utmost to sound genuine.

'You sure you wannna walk into town? It's one hell of a long walk, Mr? Take you folks best part of an hour to geeet thereeeeee,' he said not taking too kindly to the rejection he had just received.

'Excuse me, sir?' I said not quite getting the lingo.

'I saaaaaaaid it will take you folks best part of an hour to geeeet thereeeeee!'

'Errr ok, really? An hour. Well maybe we'll have a think about it then,' I replied, a nervous grin now stretching across my face.

'Oh great, now you've only just gone and flipping offended him. Good one, you idiot!' Angie muttered from behind.

I turned to her and could see she was worried. Her right foot was tapping on the floor so hard she was starting to make indents. I needed to sort this out and fast. A deserted station is never the best place to be after dark, but then hitching a lift with scary biker boy didn't exactly fill me with confidence either. And so with little other choice we reluctantly clambered aboard and for the first time this journey our fate was entirely sealed in another man's hands.

It was a tense ride to the hotel and one where I have never kissed so much arse in my entire life. *Be nice and polite and maybe he will spare us*! '*Oh, hello, sir! Thank you very much for picking us up at such a late hour, sir! What a lovely car you have, sir! Such a beautiful town you have here, sir! What a wonderful beard you have, sir! Oh and can I now suck your cock please, sir!*

I was on the major arse kiss and my cunning plan was working until I dropped the schoolboy clanger...

'I hear they shoot many great films here, sir?'

Not the brightest question I had ever asked considering our predicament.

'Yeaaaaap they shoooooot lottsa moooovies here in Saaaaavaaaaaanh. Now you come to mention it...' he said snapping a thin biscuit between his teeth 'They shoooooot allota folk in those moooovies tooooo!' he drawled.

'They do, do they? Can't say I've really heard of any?' I replied not liking where this was going. It's fair to say the next few minutes will go down as some of the most uncomfortable I can ever remember – sitting in stunned silence as biker boy enthusiastically reeled off some of Savannah's most murderous and violent movies.

'White Deaaaath was a good un, City of the Deaaad another, Snap waaaas goooood tooooo. Me, I personally liked The Slaaayer. That evil son of a bitch, he kicked some serious motherfucking arse in thaaaat one!' he chuckled snapping another biscuit between his teeth.

'Oh re… really?' I stuttered. 'Can't say I've seen that one!'

A somewhat shell-shocked Angie turned towards me and subtly whispered.

'Shut the hell up, James. If we die here tonight. I'll never ever forgive you. You got that, bigmouth?'

Taking the hint I zipped it up, although making a point to throw in a nervous chuckle whenever he finished a sentence.

Truth being I found his deep southern accent a little hard to understand. I'm just relieved I didn't laugh too loudly when he confessed that his beloved dog Grizzler had recently passed on.

'What, you think that's funny, do you?' Sometimes you just don't know whether to laugh or cry and that precise moment I was firmly between two camps.

It was close to midnight when biker boy eventually dropped us off outside our hotel on the outskirts of town. Relieved to be alive, I thanked him for his warm hospitality, waved goodbye and hoped we'd never see each other again.

The next day we were up bright and early for a quick stroll around the historic district, on the banks of the Savannah River. Many say that Savannah is one of America's most enchanting cities and it's easy to see why, with its warm sub-tropical climate providing the perfect arena to explore the shady squares that surrounded the cobbled streets. However, it's the abundance of Spanish moss that really steels the show – this weird, almost lazy like plant, that literally droops down from every tree.

'We're certainly in the Deep South now,' I said weaving under another growth of this mysterious leafy cloak.

The city's design is also unique. Set around twenty-two enticing squares, the town was originally intended to house the vast colonial armies in what was effectively the first planned American city. These landmark squares were designed to facilitate military exercises whilst housing its residents. Each symmetric square was loosely based around an old-fashioned prison camp system – its residents dwelling in parallel blocks to the north and south, while civic structures like churches and libraries located in twinned blocks to the east and west. A brilliantly simple design that still has architects salivating today.

Within a short period of time we had advanced towards Forsyth Park, one of the city's largest and most spectacular parks on the outer fringes of town. We admired the fountains for a while, before stopping off for a bite to eat on the grass and some much-needed rest and relaxation. After lunch we ambled back to town making a point to visit Chippewa Square, the very place they filmed the famous bench scene from the movie *Forrest Gump*. Located a few blocks back from Main Street, the old set wasn't too hard to find, although we were disappointed to learn that due to local do-gooders, the bench had recently been removed and relocated to a nearby museum. Apparently, residents weren't too happy with the influx of empty chocolate boxes suddenly appearing in their park. Such a shame, as ever since our visit to the Lincoln Memorial in Washington we had gotten quite excited about *Forrest Gump* and all it entailed.

Not to be disheartened we quickly cheered ourselves up, posing for the camera on the grass where the bench would have been.

'Hello, Mr Gummmmmmmp,' Angie smiled.

'Would you liiiiiiiike a chocolaaaaaate,' I enquired back offering out my hand.

'Oh yes please, Mr Gummmmmmmp.'

'Liiiife is liiiike a box of chocolates,' I began.

'You never know what you're gonnnnna geeeeet,' Angie giggled back.

And so it continued for the rest of the day – reciting as many one liners we could possibly think of. Every time we crossed the road Angie would shout out 'Run, Forrrrrrest, run!' And when I bought an expensive round of cocktails at the bar, I wasted little time in declaring. 'I may not be a smart man Anjaaaaay... but I'll make a goooood husbaaaand!'

It was late afternoon when we reached the riverfront. Clambering down a succession of steep iron steps we descended onto the cobbles of River Street, the main touristy area running parallel to the Savannah River. It was certainly well worth the effort, for oozing out of every rusticity old store was the wonderfully enticing smell of freshly baked sweet praline. This southern fusion of butter, nuts, cream and sugar was the sweetest, godliest scent I had ever had the privilege to encounter – and never one to let a freebie pass me by, I wasted little time in rummaging through the endless selection of free samples pilling up from every store.

After my fill of Pralines I dragged Angie into the nearby visitors' centre to learn more of this intriguing place, and was surprised to learn that little old Savannah was once the busiest port in America, annually exporting over 2 million bales of cotton. This growth largely coincided with the introduction of the cotton gin, a large mechanical roller that separated the 'white gold' from the buds. This genius invention revolutionised the cotton industry, effectively reducing the man hours required to produce a bale of cotton from a whopping great 600 hours to a more manageable twelve hours. As a result, the southern plantations flourished. A combination of endless sunshine, fertile lands and an abundance of slave labour, provided the perfect mix for the wealthy investors to exploit. Money soon poured into the city – the lavish stately homes that line the streets today, a testimony to the vast amounts of wealth that the city once enjoyed. Hardly surprising that folks in these parts weren't too keen to abolish slavery back in the day.

Although perhaps one of the best stories that surmises Savannah occurred in 1864, when General Sherman, one of the most ruthless and revered leaders of the civil war, marched his union army throughout the State of Georgia ordering his men to burn everything in their path. However upon arriving in Savannah he was so taken back by its sheer beauty he couldn't possibly destroy it, so spared it by offering it as a gift to President Lincoln. A most heartening story if ever I'd heard one, while once again proving beauty can sometimes overcome the beast.

We spent our remaining days in Savannah generally lazing around and plotting our path through the American Deep South. We had originally intended to ride the train all the way to New Orleans, but had since discovered that particular stretch of railroad had been recently damaged during hurricane Katrina and was still awaiting repair. Hiring a one-way car was looking expensive, therefore leaving us little choice but to either retrace our route back into Virginia for another connection, or brave the Greyhound bus and cut across country towards the city of Atlanta.

'It's only a few hours away and look, it's really cheap?' Angie said clicking on the *Agree* button for the last two remaining bus tickets to Atlanta. 'And besides, how bad can it be?' she said, her famous last words.

Atlanta

Riding the Greyhound bus in America is certainly a once in a lifetime experience – you try it once then swear that you'll never be so foolish to do it again. And I must say a stark contrast to my last experience *riding the hound,* when a friend and I ventured up the east coast of Australia in the late 1990s. There we were riding aboard this brand-new Greyhound bus, chilling among fellow like-minded travellers, and all without a care in the world. Although regrettably the Greyhound bus that we were about to embark on couldn't have been more different.

To tell the truth, I was a little apprehensive about our five-hour trip to Atlanta as I had recently read that the American Greyhound was not exactly backpacker friendly. Rather alarmingly I had established that in the land of the free there was a clear hierarchy in place when it comes to long distance travel. The car, not surprisingly, coming out on top. With an estimated 240 million registered licensees, a whopping 90% of the adult population clearly preferring the comforts of their cars to braving the perils of public transport. In second place comes air travel, nice if you can afford it, but way too expensive for most. In third but way behind is the train, great for city commuters but a clear sign of financial prowess *or lack of* when chosen over longer distances. Thus leaving the bus as the least popular method of travel where only the drifters, undesirables, and, dare I suggest, socially inept dare to venture. Now I must be clear, drop into any conversation that you've recently rode the American Greyhound and you'll inevitably be met with a swift *'You were brave'* shake of the head in return. In hindsight perhaps riding the Greyhound wasn't the most suitable form of transportation for two freshly faced backpackers to undertake whilst travelling through the rural Deep South, but the reality being our budget left us with little real alternative. *'And it would be a shame not to try the Greyhound at least once on our travels!'* I seem to remember Angie preaching as we packed our bags and headed for the bus station. However it didn't take long to realise we were making another big mistake, huge, as like Atlantic City before, the Greyhound bus terminal on the outskirts of Savannah will go down as one of the grimmest stations I have ever had the misfortune to step foot in.

Fearing the worst, I collected our passes from the only available ticket counter then grimly assessed our *lavish* surroundings. There wasn't much to see. The waiting area was so eerily quiet you could almost see the tumbleweed bobbling along the filthy floor. A once thriving cafeteria now lay dormant, while the station's only air conditioning unit had long since packed up, leaving swathes of ear twitching flies as our only companions inside the sweltering heat. The place was a rundown, third world, decaying shit-hole and certainly not the most promising start to our Greyhound experience.

Twenty minutes later our bus hissed into the station leaving a plume of black smoke streaming from behind. Sitting next to us, the only other family gathered up their things and scurried aboard. Following behind we made our way to the back of the bus. This was my call. Forever the cynic I'd always insisted on sitting at the back even if it meant forgoing empty rows upfront. Be it a classroom, the cinema or a business conference room – a rear side position always offered the best view to asses one's surroundings. *'Right, can everybody please move to the front please.' 'Oh sod off!'*

Conditions on the bus didn't fare much better, while our immediate surroundings only offering further evidence that it was going to be another very long trip. My battered seat had a huge tear across the middle, allowing a grubby piece of foam material to spill out. To make matters worse my inner thigh was resting perilously close to a large piece of melted chocolate *that had BETTER be chocolate!* Angie wasn't exactly happy either; her left index finger had just made acquaintance with a squishy piece of gum that had only recently been discarded under her seat. 'Urrrgggh Jamie, that's flipping disgusting!' she screeched in horror. A wry smile spread silently across my face. *This was your call, girl. Enjoy the trip, my friend!* Slowly but surely the bus came to life with a stream of young men filling up the vacant seats up front. A short while later the bus started its engines and we were soon on the main highway, heading towards Atlanta.

It was about fifteen minutes into the journey when I realised something wasn't quite right. It was approximately the same time when the shifty guy next to me stood up to retrieve an interesting package from the overhead compartment. Looking oddly peculiar he pulled out a brown paper bag before returning to his seat. Shuffling through the contents he grabbed a handful of old letters before attempting to read one to the guy next to him, who by sheer coincidence was also holding a brown paper bag stuffed full of letters. Inquisitively I looked round to notice another guy, the guy behind, holding a clutch of letters. *Hmmmm?* Then it stuck me. They all looked exactly the same. Every one of them dressed in identical clothing. The guy next to me? White shirt, sandy pants, grey plimsolls. The guy opposite? White shirt, sandy pants, grey plimsolls. The guy three seats from the front? White shirt, sandy pants and you've guessed it GREY FLIPPING PLIMSOLLS! *Oh dear.*

My eyes flickered around nervously as the alarming truth began to dawn. Twenty shifty young men all embarking together, all identically dressed, all clutching old photographs, while all attempting to decipher hand written letters they could barely even read! *Oh dear? They can't be, can they?* And that's when the panic set in. *Prisoners!* Stomach churning, heart racing I looked across to notice Angie happily tapping away on her laptop blissfully unaware of our current predicament.

'PUT THAT BLOODY THING AWAY!' I snarled.

'You what?' she replied, somewhat defiantly.

'Away... NOW!'

Never one to be told what to do she snapped down the lid as hard as she could. A loud thump vibrated throughout the bus. A few curious heads turned towards us.

'Nice one, girl. Just stand on your chair and wave that tacky thing around, why don't you!'

Angie stared back, still unaware that we were most probably sharing our seats with a bus load of murderers. What the hell they were doing on here was anyone's guess? It didn't look like there was anyone in charge either. 'What's your problem anyway, James?' she challenged back.

'Take a look around, babe. What do you see?'

'I see a big pussy who's scared of everything, so leave me alone please, James!'

The next few hours were perhaps the most uncomfortable I had ever experienced on any of my travels. Trapped and unable to move, time passed by with about as much pace as listening to your other half banging on about her exciting day at work. Every now and again we would pull off the highway for a quick smoke stop at some rundown backstreet station, gathering up even more strays along the way. Each town was depressingly the same – grotty, underprivileged and all with an element of menace. I looked out the window to notice a small congregation of juveniles lighting up their rollies. *Theres absolutely no bleeding way I'm going out there!* Then Angie nudged me.

'Budge up, buster, I'm hungry. I need to get some food!'

'You wh... wh... what, babe? Can't you just wait a bit longer, we're nearly there?' I practically pleaded.

'No, James, I can't wait a *bit* longer! You haven't let me leave my seat once yet! I'm hungry and gonna get myself some food. Is that OK, boss?'

'It's a bit dodgy out there, babe.'

'Oh come on James, nothing's going to happen to us. Now shift your arse or I'll go out on my own!'

Well I couldn't exactly let her do that now, could I? I'd probably never ever see her again? Reluctantly and against all sensible rationale I followed behind, as we slowly headed towards the lone vending machine on the far side of the station.

To say it was an uncomfortable experience was probably the understatement of the year. We couldn't have been more out of place if we'd tried. A hushed silenced prevailed as we entered the room, conversations momentarily coming to a halt as twenty sets of menacing eyes tracked our every move. We were at the vending machine when it happened, when the big scary guy in dreads approached us from behind.

'Excuse me boss, could you tell me liiiiikkkkeeeee what time da bus leaves, boss?' he said with a confident swagger of the shoulder.

'I'm sorry, I don't know. I think it leaves in a few minutes,' I politely replied sensing serious danger ahead.

Hunching his back, he glanced to his right, gave me the once over then whispered into my ear, 'The Lord's gonna kill you, white boy!'

What the...? 'You what?' I replied.

'For your sins. The Lord cannot forgive you!' he said shaking his head, eyes popping out with pure malice in his face. 'And now the Lord must finish what you started!' he continued, revealing a blade handle popping out from the corner of his pocket.

Shocked, confused and utterly terrified, no amount of words could come close to describing the fear that passed through me that moment. You see there's only one thing worse in life then being threatened by a nutter telling you he's gonna kill you, and that's being threatened by a *religious* nutter telling you he's gonna kill you. No point in negotiating with those bastards, probably only hurt you even more. Cornered and surrounded there was only one thing left to do... *Run, Forrrrrest, run!* 'Right, we're leaving,' I said, grabbing Angie's arm away from the machine. 'Now!' I demanded, but amazingly she had somehow missed all the shenanigans. She was too busy debating whether the American Milky Way was actually the British Mars Bar in disguise!

'But I haven't got my chocolate yet.'

'Forget the chocolate, we're leaving before this nutter BLOODY kills us! You got that!' I shouted literally dragging her out of the station never daring to look back.

I sat motionless for the rest of journey reflecting on the incident. The whole episode had completely shaken me up. I couldn't believe we had been so naive. The risks we take when we're on a budget, was it really worth it? Twice in a matter of days we had been put into a situation because we had chosen the wrong option. How on earth we got away without being either mugged or killed I will never know. The simple fact being in the American Deep South was a far more dangerous place than I could possibly have imagined. In a land of excessive wealth and opportunity it had been a real eye-opener to be taken through the parts where the dollar had barely yet to reach. Were we really travelling through America here? Felt more like the slums of Soweto to me, the chasm between rich and poor only sadly too evident. Somewhat unsurprisingly then it was an immense relief to finally roll into Atlanta, where we departed the American Greyhound for the first and most definitely very last time!

A trip to Atlanta wasn't exactly in our plans either, truth being I had barely given it a moment's thought until the last couple of days. The most I knew about the city was that it had recently been redeveloped to host the 1996 Olympics, had a major international airport, and was one of the few cities in the world to be lucky enough to have had a space shuttle named after it. Yeah, I'm not sure about that one either? But since we were here we agreed we may as well check it out.

The next morning we left our dependable Residence Inn and walked the two blocks south to the nearest subway station. I remember being in good spirits that morning, partly because it was a beautiful walk along a glorious tree lined avenue, *it's not called the City of Trees for nothing, you know,* but mainly for the sheer audacity of the hotel's team of delightful waitresses – who had wasted little time in exploiting the hotel's all you can eat free breakfast policy, by strategically placing themselves at the end of the sausage section to subtly shake their 'Thank you for dining' collection boxes at us. Nice touch ladies, now that's certainly one way to raise a few easy bucks, I smiled. And if by chance you managed to avoid their wonderfully enchanting toothy grins, then the two cheeky ladies blocking the exit door shaking their 'See you tomorrow xxx' collection buckets were simply impossible to ignore. Ten out of ten for initiative and they certainly didn't do that in Vermont!

Still chuckling to ourselves, we departed the Metro in the heart of downtown and headed through the business district to check out the Olympic site. Clean, tidy, modern and efficient, the business district had clearly been the recipient of much-needed investment over the years. The tall modern glass skyscrapers lay testament to the city's emergence as the new '*New York of the South*'. The Olympic Park itself though was exceptionally quiet and much like a previous pilgrimage I had once made to the site of the Munich Olympics, we barely passed a soul all morning – making me wonder was it all really worth the huge investment? Although it didn't take too long to figure out where all the tourists were hiding – for located just around the corner was the American headquarters of the almighty Coca-Cola corporation and its legendary World of Coke exhibition centre. Needless to say, it didn't take too much convincing to join the back of the queue for our guided tour of what is possibly the greatest consumer product ever produced. To many, Coke is *the* iconic American brand, its pioneering marketing and advertising campaigns defining a nations culture. To me though, Coca-Cola will always represent the good old days of my youth.

From my first day of school to my final exams, every day would have almost certainly began purchasing a cool can of Coke from the local ramshackle of a corner shop down the end of my street. Oh, the memories and touring the exhibition centre was certainly bringing them all back – especially inside the Coke theatre where we watched with fond nostalgia as the legendary adverts looped its way through the decades.

'Come on, Angie, we must have seen all of them now, my friend?' I said after some considerable time.

'I'm not leaving now, Jamie, no way sirree. I'm still waiting to see the '*Coca Cola is it*' one, baby. The one where Robin Beck sang *For the very first time*!' she said like an excited school child.

'Darling, don't you realise how sad this actually is? If it's so bleeding important then why don't you just bloody YouTube it?'

'No, I don't want to YouTube it, as you put it. I want to watch it here, right now, every last one of them. I still haven't seen the '*Can't beat the feeling'* one yet either. You know the one... The feeeeeeling you get from a Coca Colaaaaaaa...' She began to proudly sing, eyes closed and all.

'Yes, darling, I remember that one. No need to recite the whole friggin' song now, is it? You'll scare off all the children!'

A few songs later I dragged Angie out of the theatre promising her even more thrills in the museum finale, in the grand tour of the tasting room. Categorised by country, a collection of multinational pods await the eager tester, offering a free squirt of just about every variation of soft drink that particular country has ever made. From Chilean Coke to Mexican pop, we frantically scurried between the pods gulping down as much fizzy pop as our poor stomachs could take. Ironically then it came as no real surprise to see the biggest queues of the day were for the ladies' restrooms. For some reason they always do seem to have the biggest queues?

The exertions of the last few days were beginning to take their toll. After a sluggish start, our crossing of America was slowly but surely beginning to gather pace. This would only escalate over the coming weeks and with that in mind we spent the rest of our time in Atlanta planning the days ahead. Looking at the map we had covered much of the East Coast and were now moving rapidly inland towards the south. I traced my finger southwards along the imaginary train line to see where it would lead. A broad smile crept across my face as I pondered our next destination.

Ever since a boy I had dreamt of going to the Big Easy. A strange one really considering the alternatives, but then romantic notions never are that rational, are they? So why would a strapping young lad have a yearning for the Deep South? If I told you it was for the jazz, then I would be fibbing. If I stated southern hospitality, then it would be too cliché. Maybe if I said it was to try some of momma's good old-fashioned home cooking, then perhaps we would be getting closer. No, my reasons were far simpler. I wanted to ride aboard a steamboat along the great Mississippi just like my boyhood idols, Tom Sawyer and Huckleberry Finn did all those years ago.

New Orleans

Our journey into New Orleans was unforgettable and one that will stay in my mind for evermore. The preceding eleven-hour train ride through the cotton fields of Georgia and Alabama had been fairly uneventful, but my senses were immediately aroused the moment we entered the swamplands of the marshy Mississippi Delta region.

The topography of New Orleans had long since fascinated me. Situated on the mouth of the Mississippi River, the city was built upon an ancient high ground of soil and clay on what is effectively a huge bed of debris deposited from the river as it entered the sea. Hardly the most stable foundation to build a city upon, and to complicate matters further the surrounding areas are said to be gradually subsiding into the Gulf of Mexico. One can only imagine the astronomical levels of cash needed to get that one through planning?

'I'm sorry, Mr. Louis, your plan is utterly ludicrous. The city will be bombarded by hurricanes and sink within a hundred years. It's an absolute no from me I'm afraid... and what is this you present before me? One hundred French

francs, hey? And it's definitely not that funny Monopoly money you say? Well on that note then the State of Louisiana declares your city to be legally safe!

Word had it that King Louis and his merry men specifically chose the location as not only did it provide great access along the river to their southern territories, it was also believed to be situated far enough away from the coast to avoid the torrential hurricanes that were common in the area. *Yeah right*! The fact remains much of New Orleans is situated below sea level and in some cases up to 10 feet lower than the surrounding lakes and rivers. Now that's one gaping hole and if it wasn't for the construction of the numerous man-made concrete walls known as levees, the city would have no doubt been submerged under water years ago.

However, it took until the early sixties for officials to finally agree the levees needed improving and with the help of the Army Corps, the city undertook one of the most ambitious projects of the time. In hindsight it may have been wiser to have hired a private team of workman, as like most publicly run programs the project overran somewhat and by the time Hurricane Katrina washed ashore nearly forty years later, the city's defences were barely three quarters complete. As a result the rising water levels from the surrounding waterways were able to breach the levees, flooding an estimated 80% of the city and nearly wiping it out altogether. Quite shocking really and I doubt such a project would have taken so long to complete in the more affluent areas of the north?

It was approximately quarter to five when our train approached the city's outskirts – where outside we were given a grim reminder of the human cost and suffering in the wake of Hurricane Katrina. A hushed silence fell upon the carriage as we passed by hundreds of freshly painted white crosses, marking the spot where its victims were buried. The train preceded onwards taking us through some of the most decaying and depressing places I have ever seen. It had been five years since the disaster struck, yet much of the outskirts have barely been touched since that infamous day, simply left to rot and be forgotten. I sat uncomfortably and pondered how in a country so rich can there be so much blatant poverty. Approaching Union Station there were at least some signs that the city was finally rebuilding, most notable the erection of several red brick buildings, a common sight in England but a rarity out here in America. We departed the train, where I overheard two young college girls discussing what they had just seen.

'I never knew it was this bad?' one commented.

'A complete shit hole,' the other dismissed, shaking her head.

We collected our baggage and joined the back of the taxi queue, where a middle-aged man with an uncanny resemblance to James Brown was busily negotiating the taxi fares. Dressed in a white T-shirt, grubby jeans and nursing a can of Bud Light, he didn't look like he was officially employed as chief taxi negotiator, but the drivers didn't seem to mind him peddling the lines of weary passengers their way. We eventually got to the front of the queue and along with the two college girls were frogmarched to the back of the next available taxi.

'Hey, Jimbo, got another one for you!' he said opening one of the driver's rear doors.

'How much to the French Quarter?' one of the girls enquired.

'You folk both going there?'

'Yes, mate, absolutely,' I replied expecting it to be no more than a few dollars apiece.

'That will be thirty bucks a couple, then, boss.'

'How much? I can virtually see it from here!' I said pointing towards the bright lights beaming in the near distance.

'Well then you better start walking then, Mr!' he snapped back, taking a long slurp of his beer.

Reluctantly I agreed to his extortion. It was getting dark and I didn't really fancy lugging our rucksacks through the back streets of what is often labelled as Americas's most dangerous, Americas's most violent, and Americas most murderous city, with a murder rate of 59 people per 100,000. Now that may not sound much, but compared to New York's murder rate of 5.6 and London's murder rate of 1 per 100,000, then the true picture of America's Deep South begins to emerge.

'Fine, I'll pay you your 30 bucks then, Mr,' I said clambering aboard not really having much choice.

'Hey man, where's my tip?' he grunted back, holding out his hand.

Now in normal circumstances I would be loathe tipping anyone with the manners of a hyena, let alone pay for a service that I was more then capable of doing for myself. However, these were not normal circumstances and after what we had just witnessed I felt obliged to help the man even if he was a little rude. I reached into my pocket but could only spare a few bucks; I had barely enough to cover the taxi fare myself. A small smile broke across his face as he snatched the bills from my grasp.

'Thank you very much, now you folks have a nice day... and what da fuck is that?' He shrugged in disgust, looking down into his hand.

'Sorry man, that's all I got,' I replied

Unimpressed with his small but in my opinion more than adequate donation, he gave me a long hard stare before showing me some of that good old southern hospitality they all keep banging on about, by slamming my door, nearly smacking me in the face. Now that's smashing service, I thought as we pulled away into the night.

Our short drive to the hotel situated in the heart of the French Quarter was an altogether different experience, almost as if we were being taken back to another more dreamy time. As our taxi wound its way through the mazy streets, I could only watch on with a youthful wonder as the golden lanterns flickered their yellowy glow over the old colonial townhouses. Just an ordinary summers night to some, but to me it was so much more. You see after all those years of dreaming I had finally made it to the Big Easy. I opened my window, closed my eyes and all that could be heard was playful sounds of rhythm and blues.

The next day we ventured into the French Quarter to explore the historic district in more detail. Built by the French in the 1720s, then completely redesigned by the Spanish in the late 18th century, very little has changed in the intertwining years – the flowering wrought iron balconies we see today no doubt looking exactly the same as they did way back in the day. In the city's heart lies Bourbon Street, a mad, over excessive melting pot of a carnival street with its jazzy sounds, indulgent temptations and a whole mix of southern spirit thrown in too. We strolled around the infamous street, stopping frequently to take in some of the numerous bands playing along on their trumpets and trombones. The place was absolutely buzzing – the sounds, the smells, never before have I witnessed so much life in one little street. We walked a little more but were unable to resist the sweet smell of creole that lingered long into the air - the thought of tucking into some of momma's good old-fashioned cooking was simply too irresistible to refuse. Quite who this momma is supposed to be, I have absolutely no idea. But for some reason I've always had this weird and wonderful obsession with momma's cooking in the Deep South. One thing for sure though the Creole sauce they conjure up in these parts is very special indeed. How they make a simple blend of tomatoes, peppers, onions and spices taste so good is beyond me. Regrettably though the first restaurant we tried must have been the only one in town that would have given my mother's bland microwaveable cooking a decent run for its money. The swathes of empty chairs outside the restaurant perhaps a firm indication of what was to follow. Naively we choose to ignore the signs and were quickly fooled into believing the waiter's smooth-talking assurances that his Gumbo special was in fact *'definitely the finest tasting creole in the whole of New Orleans.'* On reflection my dish wasn't that bad, at least it looked edible. Unfortunately for Angela, as being something of a fish connoisseur *as she would often suggest* she daringly opted for the 'Crab a la Bowl' – and that's precisely what she got – a fully shelled crab staring back at her from the centre of her bowl. Her face was a picture of utter contempt as their eyes met for the first time. 'Oh, that's disgusting!' she shrieked, pushing away her bowl.

To make matters worse, the smooth-talking waiter had clearly taken a shine to her, insisting on giving her the lowdown on just about every jazz musician she'd never heard off or frankly ever cared about, while constantly asking how her food was going down. 'Hmmm, mine's delicious, thank you.' I replied. 'How's your crab, Angie? Given him a name yet? He looks a little sad!' I whispered in her ear.

A short while later I made our excuses...

'Yeah, she never could handle her afternoon drinking,' I said shaking my head to the smooth-talking waiter.

'But you didn't finish your lunch?' he said looking down at Angie's plate.

'A bloody waste of good food if you ask me!' I sighed sensing the red mist behind me. 'Come on girl, time to take you home!' I said, giving her one last lingering shake of the head. 'Think you've had enough, my friend!'

We were up early the next morning in search of a bar that was screening England's opening World Cup game in South Africa – which rather ironically had us pitted against the might of the United States. Should be an easy win then we both agreed, even Iran managed to kick their sorry arses in the last World Cup, we chuckled, as we entered the rather splendidly named Huck Finn's Cafe and Sports Bar on the edge of the French Quarters. Now Americans may well be a national humiliation when it comes to socccccccccer, but one thing they can deliver is a bloody great sports bar to watch it in. Truth is they don't know how lucky they are when it comes to watching live sport – in America you simply can't really go anywhere without noticing some kind of major league game being beamed out from every bar. They want to try catching a game in England, where thirsty patrons are often cast aside into darkened, cramped corners with nothing more than a solitary television set for company. Huck Finn's couldn't have been more different. A wall of plasma screens greeted our arrival, above the bar alone there must have been at least four giant screens showing the boys take to the field. It was still early morning, yet the place was absolutely rammed, buzzing with boisterous locals all clearly deluded on their teams faintest of chances. We pulled up our pews, ordered a portion of fries and tucked into our first round of Buds.

'This is the life, darling,' I said chinking our glasses.

'It certainly is, my friend,' Angie smiled. 'Now get the next round in, buster.'

'With pleasure, my dear, with pleasure,' I said looking for a vacant barman.

The game itself started brightly, although my cunning plan of covertly watching the game was immediately blown the moment Stevie G broke through the defence and slotted England into an early lead.

'Yeeeeeeeeeeeeeessssssssssss!' I screamed jumping off my stool and spinning around like some kind of demented madman. Now obviously this didn't go down well with the locals and my wild celebrations were greeted with jeers of... *'Sit down, you cheater!'* An unusually tame insult I'm sure you'll agree and one you'd definitely not expect to hear down any football ground in England; a *'Fuck off, you fucking Gooner wanker'* being a far more appropriate insult.

Anyway, my glee was short-lived as a few minutes later our second-rate keeper dropped an absolute clanger and the place erupted into a chorus of *'USA... USA... USA!'* and most of it directed towards me! Regrettably the game fizzled out into a dour draw and our hopes of glory would soon be crushed by another robotic German performance – sending our troops home packing before the tournament had really began.

On a positive note my wild celebrations were not totally in vain, as we got chatting to a couple of cool English girls, Kate and Ellen, who by sheer coincidence were also backpacking around the States. We instantly warmed to each other. The girls were probably the first backpackers we had encountered so naturally we had much to share, but in truth it's just nice to sometimes meet some of your own. Kate was taking a three month leave from her teaching work, while Ellen had had enough of the retail world and recently quit her job. They had hired a rental car from New York and were planning to drive around America for the rest of the summer. Like us, they too were in New Orleans for a couple of days rest before heading out west into Texas and Colorado.

'Wow!' Angie commented. 'You two are so brave. I can't believe you're doing all that on your own?'

'I know, it gets pretty hairy sometimes, especially at night,' Kate replied.

'All those dodgy motels, hey?' Angie replied knowingly.

'No, not the motels, all the driving. We take in in turns to drive through the night. Save on the motel accommodation.'

'Wow! Well I still think you two are absolutely nuts!' Angie screamed in amazement. 'Two young girls driving through the heart of the Texan desert. Must be well scary? My Jamie got scared driving through the quaint little villages of Vermont!'

'Yer alright babe, slight exaggeration, hey,' I said feeling the need to defend my manliness.

'We nearly ran out of petrol the other night,' Kate began. 'Really thought we were going to be stranded in the middle of nowhere.'

'Lesson learnt; always fill up whenever you drive past a gas station, as you never know when the next one will come along,' Ellen giggled.

'I'm not sure what's worse? Breaking down in the middle of the night or getting rescued by some creepy stranger a little too eager to help!' I laughed.

'Reckon you've been watching a few too many horror films on your days off, James. Don't worry, I'm sure we'll be fine,' Kate smiled.

And so the conversation flowed like we were catching up with old friends. Later that afternoon the girls introduced us to some of their American friends and we were soon necking back the vodkas, promising to see each other again. We never did meet up with Kate and Ellen again, our paths were just too different – we were getting ready to move north, and the girls were preparing to head out west. Shame, but that's the thing about travelling, for the briefest of moments you get the opportunity to cross paths with some of the most amazing, like-minded individuals you'll ever have the fortune to meet. You share a pint, put the world to rights and talk like you've known them for years, only to never see them again.

I spent the next few days gradually falling out of love with the Deep South. A combination of a crashing hangover and torrential rains ruled out any romantic notion of a Mississippi cruise, but in truth it was so much more. The simple fact being the longer we stayed, the more I wanted to leave. At first it was the constant harassment from beggars that ground me down, we couldn't go anywhere without being approached by random strangers demanding we hand them over money. At night it was particularly intimidating, even the short walk from the hotel to the French Quarters felt highly dangerous – while on one occasion a gang of youths deliberately crossed our path bumping into Angie as we tried to pass. There was a reason why the hotels employed military-like security guards upon every entrance. Matters weren't exactly helped when Angie suggested we should go and explore the real New Orleans, by insisting we jump on a local tram.

'Come on, baby, it will fun,' she giggled.

'Really? Anywhere particular you wanna go?' I replied, sensing trouble.

'I dunno, babe? That way!' She pointed in the direction of outta town. 'Let's just see where it takes us, hey?'

'Nice to see you've done your research again, darling?' I said clambering aboard. Although it didn't take long to realise it wasn't perhaps the brightest thing we'd ever done. My bulging rucksack proving so conspicuous I may as well have had a bunch of flashing lights requesting to be robbed. Entering the first township I turned to Angie and said, 'Nice one, babe. Is this what you wanted to see?'

'Not now, James, and why the hell you had to bring that stupid rucksack with you I'll never know?' she fired back. 'You're such a bloody tourist!'

Maybe she had a point, but how was I supposed to know we'd end up in the ghetto? We got off at the next stop deciding it probably best to walk back *Stand by Me* style immediately adjacent to the tram line. Safer that way, I thought.

It was fair to say I was ready to move on. It had been a stressful couple of days and my enthusiasm for the Deep South was now wearing thin, after all it was supposed to be a holiday not a survival exercise. The only dilemma now was which way to go? Did we head out west and follow the girls into Texas or catch the train north and head for Chicago, the official gateway to the Mid-West? Once again we were faced with difficult choices, as something would almost certainly have to give. In the end it came down to two simple options. A fifteen-hour overnighter to San Antonio in the heart of Texas or a twelve-hour ride along the great Mississippi to Memphis, home of Elvis and the legendary Graceland's estate? It was a tough choice as both were certainly very appealing, but I guess in the end there was only ever going to be one winner, wasn't there?

Memphis

It was close to midnight when we wearily disembarked our train on the outskirts of Memphis, as once again, the Amtrak had successfully achieved its corporate ambition in dumping us in the middle of friggin' nowhere.

'James, why do you always do this to me?' Angie grumbled. 'Are you trying to get us both killed?'

'Darling, you're a fine one to talk,' I said, remembering our recent ordeal in New Orleans. 'Look, it's not my fault they only have one long distance train each day. Take it up with Amtrak, not me.'

Angie was too tired to argue. It had been a long and fairly depressing ride up though the woodlands of Mississippi. The endless miles of cottonwood and pines only broken up by the occasional shanty town that would randomly pop up next to the line. Now *that* I certainly didn't expect to see and at times it was if we were riding through the world's poorest nation, not the world's richest.

Kate and Ellen had passed through Memphis a few days earlier and recommended we stay out of town as in their words '*It was a bit of a dump*' – so taking their advice we checked into a pleasant Marriott Courtyard on the outskirts of town. It also gave us time to take stock of the situation. We were now a month into our adventure, yet for the majority of time had used our rail passes to get by – which I must confess I kind of liked. OK there may have been the occasional midnight delivery to contend with, but that aside riding the railroad was perhaps the finest decision we'd ever made. The train was reliable, extremely cost effective and with its huge double decker super liners, it provided the perfect platform to take in the vast immensity of the great outdoors. The only downside being it tended to keep us locked inside the cities, as once delivered, we had little choice but to lug our things around in search of an available hotel. I wasn't complaining though, as at least we got to see places we might otherwise have missed. However, taking the girls' advice would mean we'd need a car again, which wasn't necessary a bad thing considering the security it offered, the Deep South wasn't exactly proving to be the most friendliest of places.

The next morning we collected our hire car from the rental salesman. 'Are you sure you don't want to drive something more comfortable, sir? You should really consider our premium range, sir? Stretch out those tired old—'

'Yes I know... Stretch out those tired old legs,' I interrupted. 'No need to worry, my friend, my tired old legs will be just fine, thanks!' I said grabbing the clutch of keys from the counter.

'You certainly told him, Jamie,' Angie smiled as we walked to the car.

'Well quite frankly I've had enough of all their sales patter. If I wanted a bigger car, I would have bloody well ordered one, wouldn't I? Do I look like a mug to you?'

A deathly silence prevailed and we were soon heading towards the city centre – and on first impressions I have to say Memphis was hugely disappointing. In its heyday it was once a thriving city. Its location on the banks of the Mississippi and accessibility to the abundance of cotton fields ensured much prosperity once flowed through the city – although sadly today its fortunes have somewhat reversed and rather like New Orleans before, Memphis is now considered to be one of the most dangerous places to live in America. Its sad decline was only too evident as we drove through its lifeless city streets, where the majority of businesses had long since boarded up and packed off elsewhere.

It wasn't all bad though and our spirits were soon raised the moment we entered the legendary Beale Street. Similar to Bourbon Street, Beale Street is the vibrant heartbeat of Memphis whilst widely considered to be the birthplace of American Rock and Roll. It was indeed in this very street that the young Elvis Presley would often meander to watch his favourite singer, BB King, perform his legendary Rhythm and Blues in one of the many open-air bars and nightclubs.

Finding a bar, we ordered some drinks and sat down by a huge open-air window that overlooked the street. Outside it was a hive of activity, the day had barely just began, yet the street was full of party goers, all mingling and laughing as they bustled between the bars – while in the background, the sound of jazzy blues and the familiar voice of Marc Cohan blasted out from every bar...'*And I was walking in Memphis, I was walking with my feet ten feet of the Beale*!' A wry smile crossed my face. *So this is the famous Beale Street they all sing about. I wonder how many times they must reel that one out a day?*

Utterly contented we could easily have stayed longer, but that would have meant missing out on our much-anticipated cruise on the Mississippi. So with that in mind we finished our drinks and headed to the riverfront where the majestic Queen Mary riverboat lay waiting. In hindsight we needn't have rushed, as like most things in the Deep South, we were kept waiting while the crew nonchalantly prepared the ship. Finally, after about twenty minutes the captain lowered the walkway to let the impatient crowds jostle aboard. Luckily for us there were only a few old wiry ladies to shove past and we managed to secure ourselves a fantastic position overlooking the rear of the boat. Getting comfortable we cracked open some beers, then watched with nostalgia as the beautiful old steamer chugged its way along the crystal-clear waters of the Mississippi. Not to be outdone the Captain grabbed his microphone and proceeded with his own running commentary... *'Did you know the Missisippppppppi is the longest river in America? Did you know that the Missisippppppppi is the 4th largest in the world? Did you know that we will be briefly crossing the state line into Arkansas?'* No quite frankly I didn't, but in truth I didn't really care either, I was just happy fulfilling my boyhood dreams in pretending to be Huckleberry Finn sailing along the mighty Mississippi. The scene was nearly set, the only thing missing now was a freshly cut piece of straw to chew upon.

'Angie... you didn't manage to pick up any straw on your way out did you, babe?'

'What? What you talking about, James? Why an earth would I pick up a piece of straw, you dummy?' she said looking at me with puzzled eyes.

'Yeah don't worry about it, it doesn't matter, darling.'

Where's that lazy layabout of a mate Tom Sawyer when you need him, hey.

After a few lengths of the promenade our boat headed back which was probably fortuitous considering I was as drunk as a skunk. Drinking in the afternoon sun has never been my forte. I don't know why as come sunset I can knock 'em back with the best of them, but give me a couple in the heat of the sun and I'm as good as ready for bed. They say your liver works slower in the day, but maybe we just drink twice as quick? Either way I was just happy to hit the sack early that evening as the next day was going to be a very busy day indeed.

I remember as a kid watching my mum pottering around the house doing her daily chores. Nothing exciting, spot of washing, bit of hovering, some dusting perhaps – come to think of it the latter must have been one her favourite pastimes as she was forever darting between the rooms poking her little feather duster around. One thing for sure though she certainly was one happy mother. Maybe it was her twice weekly coffee mornings where practically half the mothers in the street would come round for a natter? Although in hindsight I suspect she was just happily contented singing along to her favourite vinyls that would be playing somewhere in the background. '*Easy listening*' she once tried to justify it as, but the reality was some of her records were so appallingly bad that they've been etched into my mind ever since. Worst of the lot had to be Barry Manilow and his endless stream of seventies cheese. It was torturous stuff alright and the fact that now nearly thirty years later I can still recite '*When you're in love with a beautiful women... it's nice... everybody loves her... everybody knows her... everybody knows that she's been under attack'* is quite frankly rather worrying, and yes I'm not sure about that last bit either? Oh, the memories of childhood, but that was just the start of my introduction into the mind baffling world of easy listening. Even now I'm still trying to figure out just what the hell '*There's a brown girl in the ring tra la la la la'* was all about? Sounds like the poor girl's in a spot of bother if you ask me? Thankfully it wasn't all bad though, as in between all the dross, all the countless renditions of the Dolly Parton, the never-ending playbacks of Tammy Wynette and the daily grind of Cliff Richard, my mother would somehow find time to squeeze in a bit of Elvis, her favourite artist, and even though he would never know it, I can honestly say the great man saved an impressionable child from so many painful hours of Barry Manilow and his not-so-easy-listening chums.

My mother's fascination for all things Elvis did have its drawbacks though, mainly for the fact that my father was his absolute double and, on his day, could easily have been his twin he looked bloody similar. So, with the help of his tall, dark and very handsome looks, the aspiring young banker had my mother and practically every other woman in the neighbourhood completely wrapped around his little finger. Some days my mother could barely conceal her passion, she was so besotted, most notably when he used to return home from work all dressed up in his sharp pinstriped suits.

Watching her pounce on him like some lovesick teenager was particularly cringe worthy especially the times when she would drag him into the living room insisting he swing her around while she horribly sang out of tune *'We can't go on together... with suspicious minds... with suspicious miiiiinds!'* Worse was to follow though, as regular like clockwork a few hours later several rounds of hardened banging would inevitably be heard coming from the direction of the bedroom. There are just some things a child should never have to hear! *'Mummy, I'm scared, what's that noise?'* I would shout from my bed.

'Nothing sweetie, your Daddy's just fixing the bed. Don't come in honey, he's nearly finished!' she would cagily reply. He was certainly a good fixer my old man, that was for sure!

Yes, it's fair to say I was introduced to the King and his seductive ways from an early age, so it only appropriate that we visit Graceland and pay homage to the great man that used to sing to me all those years ago.

The next day we drove up Elvis Presley Boulevard to the entrance of Graceland, which rather surprisingly was situated immediately adjacent to the main highway. Overhead the weather wasn't looking too good, a clutch of dirty grey clouds were steadily moving in from the north. A storm was definitely brewing and could arrive anytime soon. The hairs on my neck began to sizzle as a strange lull come over. Out here in Middle America there is very little warning, a vacuum of air, a crackle of thunder then BOOOOOM as the ferocious lightning strikes, attacking everything in its path. Utterly merciless.

'I don't like it, Jamie!' Angie bravely declared to the world.

'Right, let's get in the queue, darling, reckon we'll be OK for the time being,' I replied, somewhat hopeful.

The whopping great entrance fee wasn't exactly cheap either *30 bucks a piece* but it didn't stop us handing over our hard-earned cash and hurrying aboard the bus for the ridiculously short ride across the road. Once on board, we collected our audible headphones then watched with anticipation as the coach headed towards the famed iron gates of the Graceland estate. Looking across it was surprising just how close the estate was located to the busy road. The familiar four column mansion we see in all the pictures could barely have been set back more than a few car lengths away from the heavy stream of traffic.

We waited a few moments for the iron gates to open then ascended up the main driveway. At the top, two marbled lions greeted our arrival as a tinge of excitement ran through me. Here I was standing outside the King's very own home and staring at the same front door he would have walked through every day of his incredibly talented life. Wow, my mother would be so proud. We followed the driver inside and were explained the rules – no flash photography, follow the guide at all times and definitely no wandering off piste towards his private rooms upstairs. Some of those rooms will no doubt remain off limits for evermore, for it was in that infamous bathroom barely a few feet above my head where he drew his final breaths. Not a place for prying eyes, that's for sure. Rumour has it that the upper rooms were permanently sealed immediately after his death and not a single item has been removed since – his underwear, his night gown, even his Brut aftershave still sits in exactly the same position where he last left it. Amazing, hey! We followed our audio cue as it guided us around the mansion. The house was both immaculate and lavish while also a testament to the flamboyancy of the seventies, the bright reds and garish greens reminiscent of fashions long since gone.

Yet as fascinating as it was snooping around the old place there was something very eerie yet strangely heartwarming about the whole experience. Following in his footsteps you could almost sense his presence watching over you, the longer we toured the closer we became, the ghost of Elvis so very much alive. We walked through 'the Jungle room' and out onto his shooting range. It was out here where he used to pass the time away firing his guns, his bullet holes still remain. We crossed the garden, the very same one where he would ride his buggies, and entered the racquet ball museum.

Today the museum proudly shows off much of his memorabilia, most notably his famed sequined jumpsuits that glittered overhead. In the background his glorious songs play on, whilst reminding you just what a legend he truly was. It was in this room where he played his last game of racquetball on the eve of his death, only stopping early to nurse a bruised elbow. A grand piano sits by the entrance, the same one where he would sing his final two songs 'Blue Eyes Crying' and 'Unchained Melody' before retiring to his quarters for the very last time.

However, despite all the wealth, the stardom, the trappings of fame, Elvis still died a relatively young, lonely and unhappy man unable to take any of his vast fortunes with him. So very sad. There aren't too many times in life that you can call life changing but this was certainly one of those times. To be allowed to catch a tiny, microscopic glimpse of how a true legend once lived is a truly remarkable experience and one I shall never forget. Visiting Graceland was incredibly moving and taught me something that will stay with me for evermore – it's not important what you do or don't do, have or have not, but what matters most is your health and happiness, as in the end it all gets left behind.

That evening we called a cab and had dinner in a fabulous American diner called Marlowe's. The theme for the night? Well I'm sure you can guess. Our Deep South adventure was coming to an end and without doubt it had been a roller coaster of emotions; from the Greyhound in Georgia, to the poverty in Louisiana, from the jazz of Bourbon, to the Blues in Beale Street. The Deep South, a place with so little wealth, yet despite all the hardships is a place with such incredible soul. Our visit to Graceland also represented a change in our own fortunes. For the first time in weeks I was beginning to feel positive again. Touched by something great I had found a new inspiration to continue with our own journey. We paid our bill and was about to leave when I noticed a small newspaper clipping on the wall. It was dated 17th August 1977. It read the following:-

'The king is dead...

A lonely life ends on Elvis Presley Boulevard. Elvis Presley the juggling jiving rock n roll king – lived just 42 years, seven months and eight days. It was an exciting but frustrating life which ended in Baptist Hospital, where Elvis was pronounced dead at 3.30 yesterday of a heart attack'.

And may the King of Rock and Roll rest in peace.

The Mid-West

Sunrise over the Plains

I was very much looking forward to our train ride from Memphis to Chicago. Our time in the Deep South had been highly eventful, but in truth it was only ever going to serve as the starters to the main course which would undoubtedly follow the further we headed west. I was also looking forward to our first overnight train journey and the prospect of waking up to an early morning sunrise over the Illinois Plains. What an introduction to the mid-west that would be.

But first the wait. The night train wasn't due to arrive until midnight and with Memphis not being the safest place after dark, we were again given little option but to hang around the station for much of the evening. This was the part I hated the most, the waiting, as once again we found ourselves loitering around another desolate station only to be told... '*I'm sorry but due to unforeseen circumstances on the line, the train will now arrive approximately an hour later than scheduled. Amtrak is sorry for any inconvenience this may cause.*'

'Oh, don't be sorry, my friend, just another hour of mindless torture watching the big hand slowly navigate its way towards the little hand. No inconvenience whatsoever my friend. Hey, why don't you come join us since we're having so much fun?' I mumbled aloud. The large clock above the counter read 22.55.

It was nearly 2 a.m. when we eventually boarded the train, and I have to say I was relieved to be aboard. We were safe now, no random strangers to worry about, no wanderers from the streets and definitely no strange men sitting uncomfortably close – just me, Angie and a whole load of other tired and weary passengers thankful to be onboard. Reclining my chair I leant back, tucked myself under the soft blue blanket and let the rhythmic sway of the carriage rock me to sleep.

That night I had a dream. I dreamt I was walking along the most beautiful beach in the world. Only I couldn't see the beach as the bright light of the sun was forever shining in my eyes. No matter where I looked or in what direction I was unable to shield myself from its blinding glare, and for the first time in my life I was blind.

I awoke the next morning with the bright Illinois sun beaming directly into my eyes. Shielding my face I scanned the horizon to see endless miles of nothingness, the only sign of life a lone tractor chugging away somewhere in the far off distance. It was a sight to behold that was for sure, the never-ending corn fields of the Illinois plains so flat you could roll a bowling ball over the top and watch it go on forevermore. Creeping from my cocoon I headed to the rear of the train to check out the view from the back. It was the most awesome sight that was for sure – and with the window down and air rushing through it was a sheer pleasure to watch the world pass on by. The next hour was mine and mine only. As the rest of the carriage blissfully slept – it was just me, the rising sun in the east and the vast Illinois plains to see in this beautiful Mid-Western morning. And what a wonderful welcome it was too.

Chicago

We arrived at Grand Union station shortly after nine, feeling refreshed, invigorated and not to mention slightly smug since we had managed to sleep the entire journey, while saving a whole load of cash on a night's accommodation in the process.

But most of all we were excited, excited to have finally arrived in Chicago in what many refer to as the Gateway to the West. As a city in its own right, Chicago is many things to many people. For some it represents the birth of the modern-day city, with its towering skyscrapers, thriving business districts and magnificent shopping, while to others it's the world class theatres, Chicago Bears and the official beginning of historic Route 66 that make it so special. Although to me, Chicago will forever remain in the Roaring Twenties, locked in a time where Al Capone was king and his seductive flappers his mischievous queens. It was the advent of prohibition that really livened things up in this town. Prior to this, the mafia had primarily operated out of New York, but following the introduction of the 'Volstead Act', the sale of alcohol was effectively outlawed, forcing them to review their operations. Chicago was perfect for them. Its location on the banks of the Great Lakes and relative proximity to the vast Canadian breweries was simply way too tempting for any wannabe smuggler to refuse. Quite why any sane government would wish to ban the lucrative sale of alcohol and forgo its huge tax revenues is itself beyond comprehension – but at the stroke of a pen a new economy was created – bootlegging. For the curious, the term bootlegging actually derives from the mid-19th century where crafty cowboys would conceal alcohol in their boots to avoid detection from local officials that were already implementing a strict ban on booze.

However, it was here in Chicago in the 1920s, and in the era of prohibition where bootlegging truly escalated to new levels. It was also the time where a man going by the name of Alphonso Capone would became the most revered and popular man in town – which is hardly surprising really when you consider he devoted his entire life in supplying cheap booze and loose women to a deprived and desperate nation. Much of Capone's dealings were done through the 10,000 speakeasies that were scattered around the district. To all intent and purposes the speakeasy was effectively an underground club run by the mob supplying the public with what they so desperately wanted. Legend has it that it was in these hidden dens where jazz finally found its soul, the faster rhythms providing the perfect beat for the daring hordes to swing their butts too. And so, with the authorities safely tucked inside his pocket, Al Capone was able to exploit the nonsensical ban for every last cent, it's just a shame he failed to have the foresight to employ a decent accountant! Oh well, at least he lived the dream.

The city's legendarily association with the mafia has long been depicted in many a movie. It was actually here in the centre of Union Station where they filmed that legendary staircase scene in *The Untouchables*. You remember the one? The one where that annoying mother and baby happen to rock up at the exact same moment when Kevin Costner is taking an absolute pounding from the bad guys. Poor old

Kevin, as not only was he completely outnumbered in the firefight, he had to take them down while chasing after that bloody pram in which *he* had accidentally knocked off the top of the stairs. I bet that was the last time he ever helped a damsel in distress. Anyway, luckily for him a few random sailors would conveniently pop up to take the brunt of the incoming – while who can forget his dashing sidekick, the young Andy Garcia, for heroically sliding under the pram and saving that little girl's life. Wow, what a scene and as I walked down the very same staircase I was half tempted to take a dive myself in a pathetic attempt to recreate the scene, but on the grounds of looking a complete fool I thought better of it.

We ventured outside the station as a cool breeze passed over.

'Ahhhh, so that's why they call it the Windy City, baby, what with it being so close to Lake Michigan and all those cold westerlies,' Angie proudly declared.

'Cor blimey, girl, cold westerlies, where did that come from? You been googling on the toilet again?' I said in a state of shock. 'Yeah I guess it's one reason, babe, but not sure it's the only one?'

'Oh really, well it's good enough for me,' Angie defiantly stated. 'So what other reasons are there then, Einstein?'

'Well the truth is no one really knows. Some say it's the lakes, while others reckon it's to do with the politicians bellowing too much hot air.'

'You what?'

'Well the story has it that a rival mayor got so pissed off when his beloved New York lost the right to host some massive trade event, he labelled Chicago the Windy City, basically claiming their politicians were full of shite, hence the bellowing of hot air, the windy city and all that jazz.'

'Well thanks for that, James, and by the way, if I wanted Chicago's life story I'd have gone and seen the bloody musical wouldn't I... *And all that jazz!* ' Angie began to sing. 'Now where's this hotel you've been banging on about?'

As usual it came down to me to sort the hotels. The reality being I had little choice what with our huge preferential differences. Me? I liked the plush, upmarket, downtown kind of hotels, whereas Angie didn't really care along as it was reasonably priced and had a recycling facility located somewhere inside the building; *she always was a bit of a hippy that one*! However, since it was our last major city before heading out west I managed to convince her – *'shall I get this one again, darling?'* – to stay in a swanky Renaissance hotel situated smack bang in the middle of town.

Feeling somewhat courageous I chanced my luck and requested a room with a city view. I was not disappointed; the views over Chicago were stunning. Granted, it wasn't quite the density and jaw-dropping awesomeness of New York, but what it did possess was a colourful array of beautifully designed buildings that are testament to evolutional design itself. From the early steel frame, Art Deco buildings to the contemporary tube structures typified by the new Trump building, Chicago really is a fusion of old and new that perfectly fits together. The city's long association with skyscrapers dates back to the late 19th century with the erection of the world's first skyscraper in 1885. The modest 10 story Home Insurance building has long gone, but it helped lay the foundations for the monsters we see today.

In a city that's always cherished its buildings it's no surprise then that Chicago lays claim to one of the tallest. At nearly half a kilometre high, the Willis Tower is said to house an impressive 117 stories, coming in at a monstrous 1,700 feet once the antennas have been added into the calculation. Although how any architect can seriously look anyone in the face and claim those ghastly metal poles that resemble a pair of devil's horns should actually be included in the buildings final measurements is beyond me? Kind of feels a bit like cheating if you ask me as have you seen the size of those bloody things protruding from the top? It's a bit like standing on your tippy toes, waving your arms in the air and claiming to be the world's tallest man. Exactly, people would think you're one sandwich short of a picnic wouldn't they. Anyway, despite my ethical concerns we would be mad to pass up the opportunity to visit the country's tallest building, even if the claims were a little dubious. I was also keen to try out the new 'Glass Ledge' attraction that had recently been added to the top floor observation deck, the thought of hovering out over the Chicago skyline a strangely appealing one.

The elevator ride to the top of Willis was one of the longest rides I can ever remember; in fact it was so long by the time we reached the top my ears had already started to pop. I don't know what it is about being so giddily high but for some reason it's always brought the schoolboy out in me, as once arrived, I wasted little time in rushing to the window to peer at the tiny human ants scurrying down below. *Ha ha... Look at those insignificant peasants! It's not my fault you're so small!*

'I think I see my dad? Son of a bitch is down there somewhere!' I commented.

'No, babe, he's in England, dummy,' Angie replied slightly confused.

'Yes, I know that, dear. I'm just quoting a line from *Ferris Bueller's Day Off*. They filmed one of the scenes from here. Don't you know anything?'

'No, Jamie, I couldn't really care. But now you come to mention it I always thought I was gonna marry Matthew Broadrick, oh he was such a babe,' she said with a mischievous glint of the eye. 'But I ended up with you instead. Life's such a bummer!'

'Take it from me, dear, he had a lucky escape. Now let's go and check out that ledge. I know how much you love your heights.'

'The ledge' is without doubt the star attraction of the Willis Sky deck. Recently bolted onto the side of the 103rd floor, the retractable glass box allows the foolhardy visitor the chance to walk out nearly 5 feet into the Chicago skyline. Quite frankly it was terrifying, well it was for Angie anyway, poor old girl could only muster enough courage to shuffle out like a sorry sloth sliding her arse across the glass floor. Oh, the shame.

'Is your backside actually trying to clean that glass or do you just need to go for a pee?' I enquired.

'I don't like it out here, baby?' Angie quivered, rather pathetically I won't hasten to add.

'Oh, come on, Angie, that's woeful. Stand up and grow some balls, will you, girl!' I said jumping on the glass to irritate her further.

'Look, it's perfectly safe.'

'Stop that James, the glass might bloody crack!' she shrieked.

'Oh darling, the glass is not going to crack. What da...? What da...? What da HELL...?' I screamed, sheer panic appearing across my face.

'What? What? What? What's wrong, James?' she said suddenly springing from the floor.

'Sorry, couldn't resist!'

'You... You... bloody idiot James, don't EVER do that again, OK!'

'Sorry darling, my bad, seriously though no more sliding around, it'll be a shame to miss out on all the fun.'

Eventually my brave little solider found her mojo and we watched with awe as the sun sank slowly below the horizon as day gradually drifted into night. At dusk the city is even more impressive, its sparkling buildings twinkle over the lake like a crown of coloured jewels.

Pleased with our efforts we ventured downtown for a quick pint in one of the many Irish bars that occupied the area commonly known as the loop. Chicago's long association with the Irish dates back to the 1800s when over 2 million people fled the ravages of the great potato famine to seek out a new life. Many of which settled in Chicago and by the time the 1850s came around it was estimated that one in every five citizens had originated from Irish descent. Today the city is so proud of its Irish heritage that on St Patrick's Day it even goes as far as to dye its river green. Now that's a bit much if you ask me, but Chicago isn't alone in its admiration for all things Irish – as come the great day virtually every other American city is awash with a ghastly green in some desperate attempt to demonstrate their questionable roots – even the major league sporting teams are keen to jump on the bandwagon, all donning the green and whites come the big day. Now the Boston Celtics I can perhaps understand, but the LA Lakers? Oh come on, that's kind of milking it, don't you think? I doubt we'll ever see such devotion on St. Georges Day? Oh well two more pints of Guinness please, Shamus!

I woke up the next morning with the hangover from hell. As partial as I am to the odd pint of Guinness, five pints of the black stuff has a tendency to knock me out for days. However, since it was our last day in Chicago I was determined to drag myself from my slumber to see some more of this fascinating town. First stop was the Magnificent Mile, situated a short walk across the river. The 'Mag Mile' as the locals affectionately refer, is a shopper's paradise with just about every major retail brand imaginable in its exclusive outlet stores. Unfortunately, our meagre budget of 200 bucks a day wasn't going to get us far, so after a quick stroll along the boulevard, we decided to head for the Millennium Park on the other side of town. We followed the river that snaked its way through the city to the shores of Lake Michigan on the southern tip of the Great Lakes. Standing to admire the sailboats, we then continued towards Millennium Park a few hundred feet from the shore. Now I must confess I wasn't actually particularly bothered in walking half the way across town to see yet another dreary attempt at a Millennium Park. Up until now I was a firm believer that once you've seen one lame effort you've kinda seen them all. Clearly the majority of governments were far too busy squandering our hard-earned cash in replacing all those dodgy IBMs that couldn't even tell you the time of day. And yes, the irony of that whole debacle should not be conveniently erased from history. Those IT bastards made a bloody fortune pretending those planes were going to crash and all that nonsense. In reality the only thing that probably crashed were the governments cash reserves for funding all their highly illegal cocaine habits! Wasn't it their cock-up in the first place that caused all the shit? Yes, I may be ranting, but post-university I had the misfortune of working alongside some of these supposedly IT hotshots and know exactly what they used to get up to. With names like Steve and Jon, those criminals were able to command hundreds of pounds an hour to basically switch over a hard drive in one hand while snorting copious of amounts of cocaine in the other.

An utter disgrace really, but when it comes to Chicago I should have known better. Unlike London's rather pathetic attempt of a Dome, Chicago absolutely nailed its challenge in delivering the marvellous 'Cloud Gate' sculpture that we see today. Nicknamed *The Bean* because its striking resemblance to the much loved vegetable, the giant stainless steel sculpture has to be one of the wackiest designs you will ever have the pleasure to see. Covered in mirrored panels, the curved sculpture is able to reflect both you and your surroundings in extraordinary crisp detail. Now that might not sound much, but get up close and it is as if you are standing next to some kind of futuristic spaceship so clear and defined your likeness is reflected back. Totally mesmerised by its hypnotic powers you find yourself unwittingly moving toward the mysterious object tentatively reaching out to touch you own reflection. *Oh my god is that what I really look like?* You know you're getting old when you look at yourself in the mirror and all you can see is your old man rather uncomfortably smiling back at you.

So that was Chicago. Our brief stay in the Windy City may have been coming to an end but our westward adventure was only just beginning. Ever since the conception of the railroad in 1848 Chicago has always been the main gateway to the west, its direct links to the gold rush states were not surprisingly some of the most popular routes of the day *'Yee haa... Show me the money!'* So it was only fitting really that we should begin our westward advance from here.

However, before we departed Chicago there was one more iconic landmark I just absolutely had to see – the one and only official start to Route 66. Completed in 1926, this much-loved road was the first highway to connect the eastern seaboard to the promised land of the west. The great depression and dustbowl droughts had convinced many to depart the east in search of a better life out west. Route 66 gave them an escape, provided direction, whilst also opening up new opportunities for many small towns along the way – the Mom and Pop shop a familiar and welcoming sight for any would be traveller.

Few will argue that Route 66 has evolved into a modern-day American icon. It may be old and tatty, take twice as long to drive, but ask any American what Route 66 means to them then you will likely hear the words – hope, freedom and opportunity. Standing at the junction of Adams and Michigan it was hard to believe I was afoot on the mother road of main street of America. In truth it was no different to any other busy downtown street, but then I saw the brown sign nailed to the post and my heart fluttered, if only for a moment.

It simply read – Historic Route 66. BEGIN.

Missouri

The next morning we departed Chicago's Union Station and within a blink of an eye were travelling through the most glorious grasslands of the Missouri prairies. And what a fantastic sight it was too.

It was shortly after lunch when we briefly stopped in St Louis, quickly grabbing a bite to eat before catching a connecting train to our next destination. It was a tough call missing out on St Louis, but on the grounds of being officially *citied out* we decided it was probably best to give it a miss and continue onwards with our journey to the small frontier town of Independence, on the outskirts of Missouri.

Regrettably then our time in St Louis was restricted to the time it took to disembark one train and clamber onboard another. Hardly the most thorough visit to a town once considered to be the most westward of frontier towns – which leads one to an interesting conundrum. When asked if we actually visited the historic gateway city, what does one say? *'Err kind of? Well technically yes? Does stepping out onto a station floor count?'* In truth I'm not exactly sure if we can

124

claim this one? Usually I like to take a walk, see the sights, and have a little interaction with the locals before claiming such a feat. It's almost as bad as stopping off in one of those rancid cigarette airport lounges then bragging to your friends you've seen the wonders of Bangkok, Hong Kong or Singapore. It simply isn't cricket, but I can guarantee that there's one who will always plot it on their pin board map of the world. I just hope that's not you?

So our time in St Louis may have been brief, but at least it gave us the chance to take in the stunning Gateway Arch, affectionately known as the 'Gateway to the West' that welcomes you to the industrial city. Arching its way up nearly 600 feet, the impressive steel monument proudly symbolises the historic discoveries of America's most famous pioneers, Meriwether Lewis and William Clark. For it was these two brave souls that led the historic 1804 Corps of Discovery expedition out of St Louis and into the vast wilderness of the American west. The story has it that President Jefferson had recently purchased significant territories from the French and was keen to discover a viable trading route to the lucrative fur markets off the Pacific coast. The expedition was tasked to follow the Missouri river and for the first time in American history, map a potential trading route along the unknown channels of the west. It was fair to say westward fever had officially begun.

For the next few hours we followed in their wake, only this time watching from the comfort of our *Silver Bullet* as our train snaked its way along the banks of the glistening Missouri. I can only imagine what they must have thought as they passed through the wooded waterways for the first time? Excitement? Trepidation? Or did they just look on in amazement at the lowering sun reflecting over the majestic river valley? Crossing over rickety old bridges we passed through several thriving towns along the way, Springfield and Jefferson being the most memorable. I watched with envy as every so often our train would casually fill up with a new load of passengers, secretly wishing that I too was as fortunate to live in such a charming and unassuming part of the world. The relaxed small-town community seemed a far more pleasant place to live then the mindless hustle and bustle of back home.

We were still a few hours east of Independence when it started to get dark – and I must confess the prospect of yet another late night arrival was hardly the most thrilling one. Luckily for us things turned out OK that night, but it did make me realise how naive and underprepared we had been. Did we really expect just to turn up and have our choice of awaiting taxis on tap? The train driver didn't exactly fill me with encouragement when he announced to a tired and weary carriage... *'That out of the twelve railroad stations located in the state, Independence had the 2nd lowest passenger traffic of them all!'*

Hardly then the most suitable place to set up your first Starbucks franchise then and even less chance of finding a cab, I thought to myself looking out into the dark. However, prior to our journey I had anticipated such an event and had rather cunningly programmed several local taxi firms into my phone. *You can catch me out once but never again* I thought as I chuckled to myself, a smug smile now beaming firmly across my face. Only natural then to remind Angie how clever I'd been, whilst assuring her that everything was going to be absolutely fine.

'Stick with me, kid, and you'll go far,' I said with a swagger.

'It had better be James, as don't forget it was your great idea to drop us in the middle of this shithole in the first place. I don't know why we just didn't go all the way to Kansas? You and your bloody trails!' she replied not particularly feeling the love.

'Babe, it will be fine, trust me, I got the numbers in my phone. See. What could possibly go wrong?'

'Don't, don't even go there,' she said frantically looking around for some wood to touch. 'I still haven't forgiven you for the last time you nearly got us killed, Mr. Stick with me, kid, and I'll show you some danger!'

'Yes, dear,' I replied checking my small collection of taxi numbers.

We arrived at Independence shortly before ten and under the cover of complete darkness. Rather worryingly we were also the only passengers to depart the train in what was quite possibly the most eerie of stations. Adding to our woes the surrounding street lights had been mysteriously switched off, leaving the immediate area so dark and moody I suspect that even a distant relative of Jack the Ripper may have felt some slight unease. It was the strangest, most peculiar feeling I had ever experienced, stuck on an invisible platform without the foggiest idea where to go next. I could barely make out my outstretched arm so dark it had become.

'Nice one, James. I don't suppose your iPhone can tell us where the EXIT is, can it? No? No, I thought not,' Angie sarcastically announced to the dark and creepy world in which we now stood.

'Don't panic, babe, I'll give the taxi a call,' I said dialling up one of the numbers I had preprogrammed earlier. I typed in the first number and waited for a voice. No response. Just the sound of a dead dialling tone informing me we could be in a spot of bother. I tried the next number, same again, no response. And the next, the same. Nothing. *Oh dear!*

'I take it you did tell your phone company that you were travelling abroad?' Angie said.

'Errr yeah? Guess so? Maybe? Did I have to?' I said, scratching my head trying to make sense of what she had just said.

'Of course you bloody have to, James. They need to unblock it, you idiot!'

'Really? You sure?' I grimaced.

'Oh great, so what now, Sherlock?' Angie said beginning to panic 'And my battery's completely dead!'

'Okay babe, calm down, we can still use the GPS on the maps application. I'll have to turn on the data roaming on to pick up the 3G though.'

'Oh babe, that's going to cost a flipping fortune.'

'I don't give a flying monkey how much it costs, Angie. We don't have a choice,' I snapped back switching on my data roaming and typing in Independence into the maps. A red pin dropped from the heavens onto the screen marking the centre of town. A flashing blue dot signified our position. *Phew*! It was just a case of following the blue dot to the red dot and hopefully finding a taxi in town.

'Piece of cake. Don't know what all the fuss was about?' I said trying to take control of the situation.

We crossed the tracks, heading towards a dim light in the distance – and it was all going so well until the blue dot rather sporadically decided to stop flashing, only for it to reappear, then suddenly shoot across the screen, repositioning itself on the other side of the map. 'Hang on, Angie, I think we're going in the wrong direction. It's telling us it's that way,' I said pointing the other way.

Turning around we started to walk, only for the blue dot to stop flashing once again. Freezing for a while, it then completely disappeared, reappeared, disappeared, before reappearing moments later in a completely new position on the other side of the screen.

'Hang on babe, think we're going the wrong way again?'

'Oh for Pete's sake, James, what's a matter with you? Can't you read a simple map, you fool?'

We continued in vain for another few minutes only to find ourselves back at the train station where we had originally began. My heart sank. We had officially been walking in circles and for the first time in my life I was hopelessly lost.

'Right, that's it, I'm going to knock on someone's door,' Angie said storming down the road.

'Wait a minute, babe!' I shouted trying to talk her out of it, but it was too late, she was already off marching down the driveway of the first available house. Deeply concerned, I could only watch from afar as eventually one old pop opened his door to see what all the fuss was about. Poor old boy probably had a heart attack seeing Angie peering back to him on the doorstep. It's not every night you open your door to see a crazed Latino staring back at you with a rucksack strapped to her back. I could almost see the whites in his eyes as he nervously agreed to her every demand.

'Everything alright, dear?' I enquired as she walked back down the drive.

'Yes, he's going to phone a taxi for us,' she replied looking pleased with her efforts.

I glanced over to thank the old man but he had already gone, and in record time too I must add, the sound of a dozen deadlocks breaking the night silence. We waited on the sidewalk for what seemed like an age, and then to our immense relief a bright yellow Checker Cab appeared on the horizon.

'Over here, over here!' we screamed like two lost shipwrecked souls seeing a rescue vessel for the first time in months.

A youngish looking fellow opened his doors.

'Where to, guys?'

'Residence Inn please,' Angie said with a smile.

Relived to be aboard, we spent the next ten minutes telling our driver what a wonderful man he was whilst leaving with the biggest tip our miserly budget could muster.

It was close to midnight when we finally arrived at our hotel. Turning to Angie I took in a deep breath and declared, 'Tomorrow my dear, we're getting ourselves a car!'

Independence

It's fair to say I liked Independence from the moment I awoke the following morning to the most glorious of sunshine's. Now I don't seek much in life, but for some reason I've always been drawn to the simpler things one has to offer – nothing flashy just good old-fashioned honest and reliable with a hint of something extra – which is kind of why I liked Independence. This warm, traditional, easygoing American town with its characteristic central square, gorgeously leafy streets and long green driveways appeared to offer everything a thriving small-town community could wish for. However best of all were the folk themselves. Never before had I encountered such a happy bunch of likeable *if not slightly simple* countrified folk on all my travels.

It's a tad unfortunate then that midwesterners have always been open to much ridicule. Curiously then over breakfast, I decided to Google it to see if there was any substance to all the scorn, and it didn't take too long to find my first piece of compelling evidence. For lurking in the shallows of YouTube was this fascinating clip of a young Barrack Obama coming to town during the last Presidential elections. It really was quite a moment as he marched through the streets announcing to dumbstruck residents '*Well, here I am*!' reaching out his arms and attaching himself to the nearest available stranger. '*Well, what a lovely town you have!*' He said shaking the poor man's hand, who could only stare back dazed and confused as to what he was now seeing.

So as I sat there laughing at Barrack's first real trip to the Mid-West, Angie was also up to no good, busily plotting away trying to regain control of our great travelling adventure.

'Right, James, so far you've had it all your way. I think it's time to do something I want to today. Is that Ok? Good,' she said, turning a piece of scribbled paper around so I could read.

'I have it all planned. First up we catch the bus outside the hotel, which will take us to town. Once we arrive, we wait ten minutes before catching the number 63 to the centre of Kansas. Shouldn't take too long, maybe half an hour or so. Once in Kansas we wait a little bit longer, say twenty minutes, before catching the airport shuttle, which I like to add is completely free, where we pick up the car, the compact one of course, then head back to Independence where you can do as many little trail museums as your heart desires. You happy with that, trail boy?'

'No not really dear. Personally, I'd rather take a cab and save all the faffing around, but do I really have a choice?'

'No, James, I'm afraid you don't. You had your day yesterday so today we do it my way.'

Angie would do anything to keep to her budget, even if it meant engaging in a pointless three-hour expedition just to save a couple of lousy dimes. Well at least it kept her happy though, which is never a bad thing I guess, and watching her skipping merrily around the bus stops was really quite entertaining *if not a trifle concerning!*'

A few hours later we picked up the rental car and headed back into Independence. Once again it was another scorcher, and with temperatures well in the nineties – just about every radio station in town was dominated by happy voices all reminding us that it really was the hottest summer they'd seen in years. Parking the car in the town square, we headed to the first available coffee shop for some much-needed caffeine.

'Oh, wow, I just luuurve your accent. Where you folks from?' the elderly Barista enquired from behind the counter. 'You folks from Australia?'

'Do I look Australian to you?' I said, shaking my head. 'I'm not *that* ugly, am I?'

'No, no, no, don't tell me!' the man continued. 'I know, I know... Iowa, ain't it. There's definitely a bit of Iowan in you,' he said, pointing his crooked finger right into the base of my nostril.

'No, sir,' I replied, retreating a couple of steps.

'Dakota?' he fired back. 'I definitely detect a bit of Dakotan!'

'Not even close, my friend.'

'Oh my goodness I know this one I really do,' he replied clearly not having the foggiest as to where we were from. 'I got it, I got it... Ireland? You folks from Ireland, aint cha.'

'We're actually from England,' I smiled hoping to put a lid on it.

'Oh, England, of course you are. I knew that! I just luurrrrve little old Engerland!'

'Ah, fantastic. Have you been there?' I asked.

'Nope,' he replied shaking his head, pausing for a moment before asking the inevitable... 'So have you met the Que—'

'No, no I haven't!' I interrupted, sensing the inevitable. 'But I bet you've met the President!' I smiled back.

'Yes sirrie, I sure have. Proudest day of my life when Mr Obamarama came to town. Well you folks from Engerlaaaaand have yourself a nice day and may God be with you,' he said, scurrying off to get our drinks. And to my amazement the rest of the morning followed in exactly the same pattern. Every time one of us began a conversation the locals would respond as if we were flaming royalty. '*Oh my goodness you're from England... that's amazing... You're amazing! Can I have your autograph, sir?*' We had only been in town a few hours and were already gaining celebrity status. After a while the attention got so much we had to take it in turns to fend off the questions.

'Right, that's it, Angie, I've had enough of all this nonsense. Your turn to get the drinks in next time!'

'Oh, Jamie, don't be such a grump. They don't mean us any harm,' she giggled.

And she was right. They didn't mean us any harm. Yes, they may have been a little slow and dopey at times, but that's the thing about midwesterners, you'll never meet a more friendly bunch of folk in your entire life. In fairness, it actually took a while to get used to, especially after recent experiences in the Deep South where the only ones who wanted a chat were the conniving, thieving little bastards who were most probably planning to rob us! *'Excuse me, boss... can I likkkkeeeeee have the time please!'*

Later that afternoon we visited the town's most famous attraction, the Truman residence, a few blocks down the street. The story of Truman is a fascinating one and one I knew very little about. From the humble beginnings of a farmer's boy to taking charge of a country at war, as a President, Truman was never far away from incident. Perhaps most notoriously was his decision to sanction the use of the first atomic bomb and thus bringing an abrupt end to the Second World War, effectively changing the world as we knew it. While domestically it was *his* policy that helped rebuild Europe in the aftermath of war. The $13 million Marshall Plan investment not only accelerated the development of Western Europe but also ensured sustainable American prosperity for years to come. However, despite all this though it's his private life that intrigues the most – as unlike his Presidential reign which was surrounded in controversy, his home life couldn't have been any more different. To coin a phrase, the life he led off camera was a world apart from the trappings of President.

The reality being he was a simple man who wanted nothing more than to return home to his quiet little cottage as often as his role would allow. After his wife's passing in

1982, the family house was donated to the state and opened to the public soon after, offering the visitor a fascinating insight into the former President's way of life. Truman himself passed away in 1972, and although his wife lived in the property for another decade it is believed she kept everything in exactly the same spot from the day he died. All his clothes remain neatly pressed in the upstairs drawers, while his black hat and duffle coat will forever be draping from the rack in the hall. Walking around the plain little house I was immediately reminded of my own childhood visits to my grandparents. From the flowery wallpaper to the neatly laid cutlery on the patterned table, walking through the Truman home was like walking into a bygone age, the musty smells and ticking clocks stirring long ago forgotten memories. It's hard to believe that such an unassuming place once belonged to one of the most powerful men in the western world, so simple a way he chose to live his life.

That evening we visited the local Applebee's steak house, located a short walk from the hotel. We had only been travelling a while, but I was already developing an unhealthy obsession for southern fried chicken wings and succulent baby rack ribs. Yummy, but as sad as it may seem our evening visits to Applebee's were fast becoming the highlight of our days. You see not only did the place serve up great American food smothered in sauces so tantalising tasty you could drink – it was cheap, had easy parking, and best of all, served ice cold Bud Lights on tap well into the early hours of the morning.

Every evening would follow a similar pattern.

'And what would you guys like for mains...?'

'Oooooo?? Ermm think I'll try the half rack of... no make that the full rack of ribs please, my friend,' I would reply with a satisfied smile. And as for my bulging waistline, well my obscene gluttony was beginning to take its toll. My recently acquired double chin combo wasn't exactly my most attractive feature on the table right now! I jest, but it's no wonder why our American cousins always appear to be on the larger side. When food tastes this good you can hardly

blame them really, can you? I swear I will never lay judgement on a chubby American ever again!

On that particular evening a friendly waitress came over and asked us for our orders.

'Hi there, folks, my name is Sara. I'll be your waitress for the evening. Have you guys decided on what you're having?'

'I most certainly have,' I replied eagerly. 'I'll have the full rack of ribs please.'

'Jamie!' Angie interrupted. 'You promised me you wouldn't be such a greedy pig this time. Too much more of this and they'll have to wheel you to the table!'

'You reckon? Come on I'm not that fat, am I?'

No response from Angie as she glanced down at my jelly belly.

'Yeah, ok, I get the message. I'll choose something else.'

I flicked through the menu and noticed the smoked chicken breasts looking rather tasty.

'The chicken looks good. Do you recommend it?' I asked the waitress.

'Well they're not the most humongous breasts in the world sir,' she began. 'But they're most definitely very soft and tender,' she said, arching her own little chest all over the table.

'Wow errr steady on girl, but I must admit they do look good, don't they. Ok I'll go for the fine pair of...I mean the chicken breasts then please.' I bumbled, wishing the ground would swallow me up!

On our final day we visited the National Frontier Museum to learn more of the westward trails that once departed from this fascinating town. For much of the mid nineteenth century Independence was considered to be *the final frontier* where folk would converge before venturing off into the unknown territories of the west. Commonly known as the 'jumping off point', a visit to Independence was the last chance many would have to resupply the wagons before embarking upon one of the three main westward routes – the Santa Fe Trail, the Oregon Trail or the California Trail. Each one offered its own unique challenge, while taking the traveller in a completely different direction. The oldest of the three, the Santa Fe Trail was a popular trading route with the Mexicans who still owned vast swathes of the Southern West. The Oregon Trail followed the paths of Lewis and Clark, offering unclaimed lands and fertile farming, while the California Trail promised untold riches after gold was discovered in the Sierra Mountains in the late 1840s. During this period it is estimated that over 400,000 trailblazers passed through Independence in what is still regarded as the largest human land migration ever seen. The California Trail was the most popular with over a quarter of a million hopefuls heading out west in the quest for gold. The challenges faced by these early pioneers were astounding. The Oregon Trail covered over half the continent, spanning over 2,000 miles of desert, dust bowl and the harshest of mountain terrain. A typical journey could take anything up to six months, and so stopping to resupply in Independence was a necessity if one was to make a successful crossing. Sadly though, many would perish along the way, through malnutrition, disease and fighting with the local Indians.

The completion of the transcontinental railroad in 1869 finally killed off many of the trails. What would previously take months would now take only days. Over the years the trails have gradually disappeared and with the improvements in infrastructure many of the trails have simply been concreted over and lost to history. What is left of these old trails is now protected by the government. The Santa Fe Trail ruts are now a national landmark, and at a length of over two miles, remain the largest visible stretch of trail to this day.

We finished the tour coming across an intriguing looking exhibition on the far side of the building. The exhibition was a small mock up of central Santa Fe, illustrating how it would have looked at the height of the trails. It was a simple depiction but one that caught the imagination. An antique wagon stood in front of a painted mural, while in the background an audio speaker provided the sound effects of the wagons as they arrived in the bustling town square. And it was from these very walls where I found inspiration for our own journey too. One by one I studied the routes, read the accounts, wondering what it must have been like to cross the plains in search of such hope. Then momentarily my gaze moved across to an old rail map where I noticed the railroad following the exact same path as the Santa Fe Trail. Starting from Independence, the line ventured westerly through the plains of Kansas and into Colorado. Turning south it straddled the southern Rockies before finally entering the barren desert on the northern fringes of New Mexico. Covering over 900 miles, the trail would take over three months on foot, but by train you could reach the city of Santa Fe in little over eighteen hours. *Hmmm...* And then it came to me. Excited I turned to Angie and declared my next intention. 'Guess where we're going, babe?' I said pointing to the painted mural behind the old wagon wheel.

Kansas City

The next day we headed into Kansas to return the car. The plan was simple – quick spin around the city, lose the car, and then back into town where we'd spend the rest of day chilling before catching the evening train out of Kansas. Yeah it was a bit of a faff, but we had little choice if we were going to continue our westward crossing by train.

Approaching the city I glanced at my map to note there were actually two Kansas Cities sitting exactly next to one another – one to the east of the river in the state of Missouri and the other to the west of the river in the state of Kansas? *How Weird?* 'Well, darling, looks like we have a choice on this bright and sunny morning?' I cheerily piped up. 'We can go to either Kansas City or we can go to err Kansas City? Any particular preference, my dear?'

'What? What are you taking about, Jamie? What the hell's the difference?' Angie replied trying to make sense of this crazy nonsense.

'I'm not sure, darling? I think the one in Missouri looks like the main one, while the one in Kansas despite actually being in Kansas looks like the cruddy one.'

'Cruddy? Now that's a word I haven't heard in a while,' Angie smiled. 'Although I still don't get it, baby? So you're telling me that the main Kansas City is not actually in Kansas but in Missouri?'

'Yep, that appears to be the case?'

'And that the Kansas City that is actually in Kansas is not actually the main Kansas at all?'

'Yep.'

'Well that's the most stupidest thing I've ever heard in the whole wide world? So why call it Kansas City then if we're not actually in Kansas? It doesn't make any sense?' she said scratching her head.

'No idea, baby? Maybe they had a big fall out, moved next door and christened it Kansas just to piss the other one off?'

'Who bloody knows but this is the Midwest after all?'

'Well then, which one did Dorothy live in then?'

'Dorothy? Angie, I have absolutely no idea? Didn't she live on some dodgy farm out in the sticks somewhere?'

'Thought she lived in Kansas?'

'Well she did for a while, darling... well at least until the tornado blew her away.'

'Maybe it blew her here... to Missouri? Toto, I have a feeling we're not in Kansas anymore!' Angie giggled clearly pleased with her linkage. 'And so the scarecrow named it Kansas to remind her of home.'

'Really? Do you really believe that?'

'Yes, Jamie, REALLY and the name has stuck ever since you see. It has to be? It's the only sensible explanation. Why else would you have two Kansas Cities sitting right next door to each another then Einstein?' she challenged back.

'Don't have a go at me, I didn't name it Kansas. However, your theory does have some logic to it. What about the Tin Man then? Where did he live?'

'In Kansas, stupid! The one in Missouri with Dorothy and the Scarecrow. Don't you know anything, Jamie!'

'Angie, you have one warped mind, my friend. But in the absence of any other sensible explanation, your mouse cheese theory is good enough for me!'

'Can we go and find Dorothy's house please,' Angie smiled.

'Right, behave, girl. She didn't really live here, OK. She lived miles away, somewhere else in Kansas.'

'Spoilsport. You always trample on my flower, James. I think I need to find myself a new man, one that lets me express myself, one that believes in me.'

'Yeah, yeah, whatever. Now shall we enjoy the rest of the day?' I smiled, shaking my head, not quite believing what we had just discussed.

We spent the next few hours driving around Kansas *the one in Missouri that is* and have to say on first impressions I kinda liked what I saw. Relaxed is the best way to describe it, as it certainly wasn't the most vibrant of cities I'd ever been – the main civic centre more neat and compact than consumer paradise and even now years later I'm still trying to figure out where exactly the main retail outlet area was supposed to be. Perhaps it was located on the outer fringes or hiding in the cool shade somewhere? Either way no one seemed to care much as they casually sauntered around the pedestrian friendly city. But don't for one minute think of Kansas City as small, oh quite the contrary, it really was quite the suburbia with its luscious green, immaculately presented neighbourhoods sprawling out for miles.

Dropping off the car, we caught the bus into town where we found ourselves venturing into the KC Power and Light district in what is effectively the new downtown. Costing a staggering 850 million dollars, the 8 block entertainment district is the biggest urban project ever undertaken in the Mid-West. What Kansas may lack in retail outlets it more than makes up for in trendy bars and restaurants. In its centre, lay an impressive outdoor semi-covered plaza, where a half moon of surrounding bars encircles the main stage like some kind of modern amphitheatre. Above the stage hangs the main attraction, a 250 square foot giant screen in what has to be one of the biggest televisions you will ever likely encounter – and with these huge comfy sofas spilling out onto every walkway it really was the perfect place to catch the game. We spent the next few hours slurping beers in the afternoon shade and watching the World Cup on the big screen – but our indulgence was about to be abruptly cut short due to a schoolboy error on my part – in temporarily leaving the complex, only to be intercepted upon my return by a miserable security guard who was adamant I would not be allowed back in. 'I'm sorry sir, we can't let you in,' he said, shaking his head.

'What? What do you mean you can't let me back in? I've been here all bloody day?' I responded in shock

'Sorry, sir, I can't let you in with that rucksack.'

'What? Rucksack? Well you did earlier?'

'That was earlier, sir.'

By now the security man was really starting to annoy me.

'So you could let me in earlier with my rucksack but not now?'

'Correct, sir.'

'Well that's absolutely ridiculous, isn't it?'

'I'm sorry sir, it's the rules. Can't let you in with a backpack after five.'

'Well why the hell not?' I said, frustration beginning to take over.

'Because it's the rules, sir.'

'Ahh come on mate, my girlfriend's in there waiting for me. You can search through it if you like, I got nothing to hide. Do I look like a terrorist threat to you?'

'That won't be necessary, sir...'

'Good. Well I'm glad we finally see sense then...'

'Because you're not coming in, sir.'

I was beginning to understand why so many Americans frequently use the term 'bonehead'. If there ever was a stereotypical version of bonehead then this was it – a rather unpleasant, slightly unsanitized, balding, no nonsense of a security man. He had his rules and by heck he was going to stick to them no matter how idiotic they may have been, miserable bloody sod!

So, with hours to kill and nowhere to go we found ourselves wandering around the main railway station in the hope of finding something entertaining to do before our overnight departure across the plains.

Now Union Station at Kansas – *Yes I know yet another Union Station I hear you cry.* You'd think they'd come up with a more original name for a train station once in a while? I can only imagine the suspense and intrigue they must have encountered during the official naming ceremony... *'I hereby declare that this brand new, state of the art, transcontinental railroad terminus shall be named... the Railway Station.'*

But this Union Station was far from common and without doubt one of the finest stations you'd ever have the fortune to see. Built at the outset of the First World War, the grand old station had me captivated the moment I walked through its huge stone archway at the front of the building. Inside it was even more impressive – the shiny white marbled floor being the most grandest of entrances – while high above, the giant clock and three magnificent golden chandeliers that used to govern this old hallway really were the most spectacular of sights. *Timeless.* But despite all the grandeur, it was a small picture on the far side of the wall that intrigued me the most. The image itself was a black and white photograph depicting the Grand Hall's waiting area way back in the day. There must have been close to a thousand passengers waiting for their trains that day. I was immediately intrigued. Never before had I seen such a picture that so perfectly encapsulated the railroad spirit of the time. One central hub leading to an infinite of possibilities. From the old couple sitting patiently on the benches, to the seductive women standing alone guarding her bags – the smartly dressed man with a twinkle of the eye, to the small child skipping along merrily in the clasp of her mother's hands. Each and every one of them were about to embark on their own epic journey. It really was the most wonderful picture. In its heyday in the early thirties, nearly one million passengers would have annually passed through this bustling station. Today it is quiet with only a handful of services operating each day. Walking along the marble halls there was not a soul to be heard. The only sound being the pitter patter of my footsteps marching along the station's marble floor. The once thriving waiting room has now long since gone. In its place a splattering of restaurants, cordons of red tape and a soulless exhibition centre with nobody around. We collected our tickets and were ushered to a small waiting area at the rear of the building. The drab plastic chairs and greying walls a far cry from the glamour of this once great hall. Pulling up a chair I gathered my thoughts. Waiting for a train at such a late time is always a surreal encounter. The endless hours of stranger-watching a common yet most absorbing experience. A scratch of the nose here, a twitch of the eye there, these things suddenly become all very absorbing when there is nothing very much else to do. Occasionally someone would get up, stretch out their tired old legs and head off to the lone vending machine to break up the night – only to return minutes later with a packet of crisps that you so desperately wanted to eat.

A few hours later word got around that they were experiencing problems out east. The information was sketchy but it appeared there had been a crash somewhere near Illinois. A chorus of sighs broke out as the news quickly filtered around the waiting room. It was going to cost us at least another couple of hours we all reckoned.

It was approximately a quarter to three in the early hours of the morning when our train eventually rolled in. In total the delay had cost us over five hours. One by one we gathered our things and silently boarded the train. Not surprisingly then it didn't take too long to settle down, which in hindsight was probably very wise; you see, the next day was going to be another very long and testing day indeed!

The Great Plains

I awoke the next morning tired, confused and a little disorientated. I looked out the window to see we were riding through the wide-open prairies of the Great American plains. Checking my watch I noted it was 8.45 a.m., barely six hours into our eighteen hour epic journey across the continent.

'Where are we, babe?' I asked, noticing Angela had already awoken from her sleep.

'I dunno, babe? Kansas, I think? All looks the bloody same out there!' she replied.

'I gathered that, darling. Any idea whereabouts in Kansas we actually are?'

'No not really, James?' she replied with a nonchalant shake of the head. 'Think the driver last mentioned a town called Hutchinson, but that was ages ago.'

'You sleep much?' I said rubbing my eyes.

'Yeah like shit, thanks, James. That's the last time I ever let you bully me into buying one of those all singing, all dancing cross country rail pass, my friend. Departing at three o' bloody clock in the morning. What's all that about, hey?'

'All part of the experience, my girl. Look at that,' I said pointing outside the window. 'The Santa Fe Trail. One of the most famous trails in American history. There would have been an endless stream of wagons out there. It would have taken them the best part of three months to cross these fields. And you think lugging your rucksack around town is hard work!'

'Well Mr great *plain* in the arse, you can always carry my rucksack if you feel like a challenge, my friend?' she smiled.

I glanced at my map to check the next station. Next stop Dodge City. A tinge of excitement ran through me. There are many towns in America that lay claim to their Wild West heritage, but few can compare to that of Dodge City. Widely regarded as the last frontier town, Dodge City's lawlessness was stuff of legend. The excessive gambling, widespread prostitution and drunkard gunfights certainly put the wild into the west, but it was its real life characters like Wyatt Earp who will be forever championed in their attempts to install some kind of law and order to this wild and crazy outpost. Founded in 1865, Dodge City was created to serve the needs of her sister town, Fort Dodge. The Fort was one of many military outposts created along the frontier to provide rest, shelter and much-needed protection for the tired and weary wagons. Its location on the river banks provided ample drinking water, while its military guns fended off the advancing Indians that would regularly skirmish into the area. Although it was the advent of the railroad in 1872 that really enabled Dodge to truly thrive – this, coupled with the much-needed demand for local bison, helped propel Dodge into one of the most prosperous cattle towns in the west.

The origins of the cowboy is an intriguing one, but one that is fraught in sorrow. At the time over a million bison roamed the central plains and with demand for their hides reaching insatiable levels, the newly installed railroad offered the perfect outlet to trade these commodities back east. Sadly, within less than a decade the entire supply of North American bison were virtually wiped out in what has to be one of the most savage tales of species elimination ever played out.

With the bison gone, demand for cattle spiraled, most notably that of the Texas Longhorn which very quickly quadruped in value. Word soon spread to the southern ranches where teams of cowboys were hurriedly assembled to escort their newly found *cash cows* to Dodge. These annual cattle drives quickly established Dodge City as the main boomtown, soon becoming known as Queen of the Cow towns. The era of the cowboy had officially begun.

Over the next few years money flowed throughout Dodge as the town grew to accommodate the massive influx of Texan cowboys. Watering holes, gambling dens and numerous brothels quickly sprang up to serve the needs of the ravenous traveller. Drunken disputes were commonplace, often spilling out into the streets. The law of the gun now ruled the day. However the fun and games came to an abrupt end in 1885 when the Kansas State authority outlawed the sale of the Texas Longhorn, fearing the 'tick' that was present in the animal would spread to other livestock. This imposed quarantine forced many out west to seek their fortune elsewhere and thus ending Dodge's brief status as the cowboy capital of the world.

Our train pulled into Dodge to collect the next batch of passengers. The rail station was located slap bang in the middle of town. To the north, lay the famous Front Street or what's left of it since it burned down in 1885. Today only a car park stands in its place, although an outdoor 'Disney style' reconstruction does its best to recreate the old salons and whorehouses in what is known as the Boot Hill museum. A few yards away sits the legendary Boot Hill Cemetery, and final resting place for many a dead cowboy. Legend has it that Wyatt Earp finally restored some kind of law and order by drawing an imaginary line from the railroad, banning the transportation of guns on one particular side of the track. It was said that if you had any business to resolve then you'd be wise to do it the other side of the line.

A short while later we were back on our way and about half way into our journey the driver announced some bad news over the tannoy. *'Excuse me, folks, but due to unforeseen weather up in Raton, we shall be terminating our rail journey in La Junata, where a collection of coaches will be waiting to transport you to Albuquerque. We're sorry for the inconvenience and hope you have a great day!'*

The news was not good and greeted with a loud crescendo of groans from just about every seat in the carriage. 'I'd rather walk, thanks!' Angie shouted aloud. A round of applause soon followed, but it didn't hide the fact our journey had suddenly just gotten a whole lot more complicated.

We arrived in La Junata station shortly before noon, disembarking onto a baking hot platform, where we were quickly ushered towards a line of waiting coaches. Always the gentleman I offered to carry Angie's bags *and was doing a bloody good job of it too* until I hastily threw one of them to the ground not realising she had recently loaded it up with two bottles of her favourite champagne. A dull clunk echoed from the bag. *Oh dear.* I retrieved the bag hoping she wouldn't notice but regrettably the crunch of broken glass had alerted her attention.

'What? What was that, James?' she said.

'Nothing dear, just the sound of the train gearing up I think?'

'Oh, I don't bloody believe it! You haven't done what I've think you've done, have you?'

'No, dear, absolutely not, dear,' I said trying desperately hard to conceal the wet patch that was now rapidly expanding from the bottom of her bag.

'I can't believe you've just done that!' she screamed, grabbing the bag to frantically search through what was now becoming a small pond. 'You just don't care do you, James? You don't care about my things. You're so bloody selfish. All you care about is yourself!'

'I'm really sorry, babe, it was an accident,' I said.

'I can't deal with this anymore. I've had enough. I'm going home!' she replied, tears now streaming down her face.

'Angie, you can't do that, we're in the middle of friggin' nowhere, you know!'

'I don't care, James. I'll hitch a ride... do anything just to be away from you right now!'

It was fair to say I was not a popular chappie that afternoon. Truth was we were totally exhausted, both mentally and physically. The long tiring days on the trains were finally beginning to take their toll. What would often seem like a short journey on paper would inevitably prove anything but just. We boarded the bus barely saying a word. The deathly silence only broken by Angie's occasional mutterings... *'That's the last time I listen to you'*... *'This was all your idea'*... *'Next time I'm in charge.'* Before finally declaring... *'I was looking forward to that wine, you bastard!'*

Deciding it was perhaps best to not say anything; I rested my head against the glass and watched the terrain change from a grassy green to a dusty gold – the farmlands of the prairies gradually evolving into the unforgiving barren scrublands of the Colorado Plains. The change in landscape also signifying our time in the Mid-West was well and truly coming to an end. In a little over a week we had ventured through the corn fields of Illinois, discovered Chicago, passed through the gateway cities of St Louis, Independence and Kansas City, before following the great trails along the high plains of Colorado. In truth, I had learnt more about the American spirit in a week then I had in a lifetime back home. We often mock Americans for having such an over the top, positive 'can do' attitude. We consider it fake and irritating but in most cases we don't really understand it at all. However spend a few days in its heartlands and you soon learn that the passion they have for life is very real, almost infectious, as you too discover the meaning of the words hope, dreams and opportunity. Maybe it's the vast open space that opens the mind or the promises of wealth and fortune on the other side of the mountains? I'm not too sure? But one thing for certain, you'll never see a more happier bunch of people then the ones you'll come across in the many mid western towns of America.

I pondered that thought and then through the corner of my eye I caught a glimpse of it. Tiny at first then it steadily grew.

The nearer we got the taller it became, this vast, impenetrable, towering barrier stretching out as far as the eye could see. Quite simply it was one of the most awe-inspiring sights I had ever seen. I had read so many books, seen so many pictures but nothing had prepared me for what was now staring me straight in the face. Spanning the horizon like a wall of fluffy clouds, sat the majestic Rocky Mountains, aka The Rockies. Stretching over 3,000 miles from the far reaches of Alaska to the deserts of New Mexico – the Rocky Mountains is one of the longest, continuous mountain ranges on the planet. It is the backbone of North America separating east from west. It is *the* continental divide where on one side its rivers flow to the east and the other towards the west and the waters of the Pacific Ocean. Comprising over 100 separate mountain ranges, its lofty peaks can soar an almighty 15,000 feet into the sky. In Colorado alone there is said to be fifty-four peaks over 14,000 feet, or fourteeners as locals like to say. At its widest the Rocky Mountains can cover an astonishing 300 miles, housing a varied of wonders from mighty canyons, bubbling mud pools and stunning waterfalls – while also offering refuge to some of the most spectacular wildlife you will ever have the fortune to see.

I wanted to see as much of this great spectacle as I possibly could. I wanted to drive it, climb it, and stand on top of it to view the sweeping plains down below. But to fully understand it we'd have to eventually cross it. So the plan was set. We would hire a rental car from Albuquerque and drive along the southern edge from its humble beginnings in New Mexico to the eastern rim in Colorado. Catching a train out of Denver we'd cross the heart of the Rockies, checking out the states of Utah, Idaho, Wyoming, and Montana, before eventually reaching the majestic wonders of Yellowstone in the North West.

Sometime later that evening we rolled into the dusty town of Albuquerque. Wasting little time we hired a cab to the car rental, picked up our Jeep and drove off into the warm desert night. Our Rocky Mountain expedition was about to begin.

The Rockies

New Mexico

When looking over a map of America it had always intrigued me as to why on earth Route 66 passed through the city of Albuquerque? Fancy having the most famous roadway in America going through a town you could hardly spell, barely even pronounce properly? I wonder how many navigators have looked down at their maps and decided to give it a miss solely on the basis they hadn't the faintest idea how to articulate it to the driver? *'Right, mate, up ahead is the town of errr....Al? Albur? Über queer key? Oh sod it, shall we just drive to Williams instead then, shall we?'* So to all readers whose Spanish is as poor as mine it's perhaps better if I break it up for you – Al-bur-ker-key.

However, I must add since writing this piece, I have since invested in a very reasonably priced Netflix monthly subscription; where binge watching American television shows has become the norm. One show in particular, *Breaking Bad*, had me captivated from the very beginning. And the location for the series? You guessed it, the desert town of Albuquerque. Oh, how I've missed watching our unlikely heroes, Jessie and Mr White taking on those evil drug cartels in what was arguably one of the greatest television shows ever produced.

Anyway, in answer to my previous ignorance it soon becomes apparent that Albuquerque sits at the very bottom of the southern Rockies, therefore being one of the most logical places to cross the great divide. Why go through all the trouble of building a road through the mountains when you could virtually bypass them altogether. Its location on the southern fringes also proved to a suitable home for the Pueblo Indians, an advanced native tribe that has inhabited the area for thousands of years. These busy little fellows were an industrious bunch who specialised in building magnificent Adobe houses that were sound enough to house entire communities. These impressive flat roofed structures were derived from whatever resources they could find – usually a combination of clay, stone, dried straw and about as much muck as they could possibly lay their hands on *literally* to mould it altogether. Nice, but despite its somewhat dodgy ingredients, the end product looked nothing short of fantastic – it's irresistibly smooth, chocolatey like surface looking so good you could almost wrap it up and eat it. The early Spanish explorers also took an instant liking to the area. It was close to the banks of the Rio Grande, provided good wood source and irrigation, but perhaps more importantly offered ample protection from the disgruntled natives they had only so recently displaced. Over the years the old town *as it's now known* changed hands several times, before entering the Union in 1848 when the Mexicans were finally defeated. Keen to learn more of this fascinating city, we hit the central plaza early the following morning. A handful of old Indian ladies greeted our arrival, ushering us towards one of the four shady verandas that surrounded the main square. One in particular gestured us over, making a point to show us her huge array of trinkets that she had carefully laid out onto a blanket. Angie immediately sprang into life, her eyes lighting up the moment she caught sight of the hand-woven beads and shoddy looking handbags. A smile crept across my face. She had always been a fan of her cheap rubbish, ever since her first trip to Pisa, where she was more contented in skipping around the tacky souvenir stalls then she was actually climbing the Leaning Tower itself. '*Bring it on*' she had once declared – be it key rings, mugs, or plastic pens – she didn't care as long as it was bright, tacky, had the city's name on it, or even better, had her name plastered all over it as well. Not surprisingly then Angie rushed over for some serious negotiations the moment she caught her first glimpse of the shiny plastic bracelets.

'Excuse me, how much for the bracelet?' she enquired to one of the ladies.

'Very good bracelet. I give it to you ten dollar. Very good price,' the old lady replied.

'Oh, I'm sorry that's like waaaaayyyy too expensive,' Angie politely responded pretending to walk away. She had clearly done this before, a bit of an expert some might say.

'Ok, Ok I give you for seven dollar. You breaks my heart, lady.'

'Oh, I'm not sure about that?' Angie grimaced.

'Come on, babe. If you like it, just go friggin' buy it. It's only a few lousy bucks!' I chipped in rather impatiently.

'I don't know, James? Think I need to see a few more first,' she said before whispering into my ear. 'I think I can get it cheaper!'

Turning our backs the old lady shouted.

'Ok, Ok, Ok, I give you for five dollar. Five dollar very good price. You breaking my heart, lady!'

Sadly for the old girl her time in the spotlight had passed, for Angie was already poking around another stand adamant she would find herself a better deal. In the end she settled for this rather tasteless Route 66 cane handbag, an absolute bargain for seven dollar, but a sure fire certainty to fall apart within days. Pleased with her new purchase she opened her bag, dropped in her branded Route 66 pencil case and announced rather proud. 'Didn't I do well!' And you know what, it was the happiest I had seen her in weeks. Bless!

We were heading back to the hotel when disaster so very nearly struck. While Angie was busy admiring her new pencils, I was struggling to navigate my way through the city's gridded streets. For reasons unbeknown, the local traffic authorities had decided to do away with traffic lights and replace them with these random intermittent 'STOP' signs on the corner of every other street. The rule of the road was simple. If you could see a stop sign then you must slow down at the junction and let the oncoming car pass. If you couldn't see a stop sign then you're fine to continue *just hope and pray that the other driver cutting across you caught a sight of his first!* It didn't take long for the inevitable to happen. We must have been nearly halfway across the junction when I noticed the bright red truck hurtling towards us!

'Oh my GOD!' Angie screamed as I slammed on the brakes. 'Slow down, James!'

And so for a brief moment our fate was sealed. Paralyzed with fear, we could only watch on as our car skidded across the road and straight into the path of the oncoming lorry. Pumping the brakes one final time I closed my eyes and braced for impact. 'Fuccccccccccckkkkkkkkk!' I screamed as the world around me began to slow down like some random scene from *The Matrix* – although somewhat miraculously our car came to a juddering holt barely a gnats fart away from the onrushing vehicle. 'You bloody idiot. You could have bloody killed us!' I shouted, but the truck had already gone, totally oblivious to the pandemonium it had so nearly caused.

Restarting the car we chugged back to the hotel but it was clear something was wrong. Every so often a massive pulling sensation would tug from beneath restricting our speed. This was not good, there was definitely no way I was taking this heap of junk up those mountains and how much damage *had* we really done? It wasn't limping like this before? No, we were left with little choice, the car had to go back and go back fast.

'No, mate, honestly it was like this when we got it,' I said with the straightest of poker faces to the man at the rental counter. 'Reckon the last lot must have buggered it up coming down the mountains.'

'I'm sorry, sir, there's absolutely no way we can accept the car in this condition.'

Angie interrupted. 'I'm actually really disappointed with the quality of your cars. You advertise yourself as a premium service, only to supply us with a complete bomb. I'm sorry, I need to escalate this to your manager and log a formal complaint. My consumer rights have been totally violated. Can I have your name please as I will need to report you immediately?' she demanded pulling out one of her multi-coloured Route 66 pencils. Angie's serious demeanour had clearly scared the life out of the young sales executive *hell even I was scared* and we were soon handed another set of keys for a shiny new upgrade.

'Good work, Angie,' I said strolling up to our glimmering Jeep Cherokee. 'Never thought you'd pull that one off, my friend!' I chuckled. But Angie didn't bite, not this time anyway.

'Jamie, let's get one thing straight shall we. Today I'm in charge. Do you understand?' She smiled. 'A glass of the finest pink champagne will do me nicely, thank you very much. You work for me now.' She nodded as we drove off into the late afternoon sun.

The next day we drove up into the Sangre de Cristo foothills to complete our own Santa Fe Trail. It had taken the best part of a day to get there, but the leafy courtyard plaza that welcomed our arrival was well worth the wait. Sitting at over 7,000 feet above sea level, the city of Santa Fe is said to be the oldest State Capitol in America and it's fair to assume very little has changed over the years. A mouthwatering mix of Pueblo style structures flank the main square, while these huge, chunky, vertical beams support the most fabulous looking verandas you'll ever likely to see. It was as if we had entered a western movie set, so wooded and rustic our surrounds.

Overlooking the central green sits the Palace of Governors, the oldest occupied building in America.

157

Constructed in 1610, the impressive Adobe building once served as the official residence for the Spanish, Mexican and American administrations. Over the years the mansion has been impeccably preserved, while recently being converted into a delightful museum. Inside, magnificent wooden struts overlook a vast array of artefacts, each one chronicling the towns diverse cultural history. In the absence of any gold, the early settlers utilised the town's central location as the main trading point between the two Americas. Chinese vases, Mexican pottery and gold jewellery were just a few of the items that were exchanged along the trail.

As the west expanded, Santa Fe's status as a frontier town grew – sprouting its own legends along the way – most notably that of Billy The Kid, arguably the most famous Wild West legend of them all. The museum had a whole section dedicated to 'The Kid' – detailing his various exploits and numerous skirmishes with the law. The story of Billy The Kid is a fascinating one and dare I suggest one of the greatest tales in American history. For not only is the hero young, dynamic and extremely charming, it encapsulates a time when the American frontier was arguably at its wildest. William H Bonny, as he was formally called, moved to Santa Fe with his dying mother in the summer of 1872. Within a year his mother was dead and 'The Kid' was being shipped off to various foster homes in and around the state of New Mexico. Keen for a way out he joined a varied of gangs, and quickly developed his shooting skills in which he would later become famed for. His reputation as a skilled marksman flourished and at the age of eighteen was hired by John Turnstall, an English merchant who had recently set up a cattle ranch, much to the disdain of local rivals. The cattle game was big business and the arrival of new competition directly threatened the cosy status quo that was very much prevalent in the area. Tensions rose and the dispute escalated when Turnstall was gunned down in what would become known as the Lincoln county wars. 'The Kid' and his men were so outraged they vowed to hunt down the perpetrators and seek their revenge – but unfortunately this would mean taking down a sheriff in the cold light of day. Billy The Kid was now a wanted man and would spend the rest of his life as a fugitive until he was eventually tracked down and killed by his old friend, Pat Garrett. He was barely twenty-one years of age. After his death various accounts of his exploits have fuelled his legacy – Pat Garrett even having the cheek to write a book detailing their early exploits together. But above all it was his wit and humour that will forever endear him. While serving time in a Santa Fe jail, the judge of the day declared that he would hang until he was '*dead dead dead*' – The Kid famously replied '*And you can go to hell, hell, hell.*'

Years later much controversy still remains. To this day we cannot be sure exactly how many men he killed? Who he had killed? Or whether Pat Garrett actually killed him at all on that fateful summer's evening? Experts still cannot decide if he was left-handed, right-handed, or even locate the whereabouts of his grave? One thing we do know is that only one genuine photograph of him remains. As I looked at this reproduction hanging from the wall it was hard to believe that I was looking through the lens at the great Billy The Kid. He didn't look much of a warrior. He may have been standing outside a saloon proudly sporting his trusty rifle, but with his oversized chin and freakishly buckteeth he looked more like a goofball then a warrior to me. However, despite my concerns it didn't stop the tiny photograph measuring a modest 3x2 inches from being sold at a recent Denver auction. Folklore suggests Billy The Kid used to taunt his victims by claiming he would make them famous before shooting them. Whether that is true or not we will never really know. Although one thing's for sure, with the sale of the photograph fetching a whopping 2.3 million dollars, his abiding memory really did make his proud new owner a very famous man indeed.

Colorado Springs

We were up bright and early the next morning in preparation for our first major road trip along the base of the Rocky Mountains. Our plan was simple – hit the interstate and drive around the southern tip of the Rockies all the way to Colorado Springs, some 80 miles south of Denver. Firing up my laptop I clicked onto the online distance calculator that I had bookmarked a few weeks earlier. This recent gem of a discovery was fast becoming my favourite travel website – as not only did it measure the distance between two different destinations, it also gave you an estimated journey time depending on how fast you travelled. Typing in Santa Fe to Colorado Springs, I was quickly informed it would take a little over four and half hours to cover the estimated 235 miles. Not the longest journey in the world but certainly not one you'll want to be running out of petrol on. You never know whose eyes are watching from those hills? Yep you've seen that creepy movie too then, hey? Somewhat rather cautiously we rolled out of Santa Fe and headed straight for the nearest petrol station.

'James, is this really necessary?' Angie bemoaned as I pulled onto the forecourt. 'We've still got nearly half a tank left of petrol. This is completely ridiculous,' she sighed, shaking her head.

'Yes, Angie, it is necessary. It could be ages until we come across another and you know what happened the last time,' I said referring to a previous time we nearly run out of gas whilst driving through the rolling hills of Chianti. 'I seem to remember *you* shouting at me saying it was all my fault and that I should have filled up in the last town! Do you remember that, darling?'

Angie sat in silence. A clear sign that she *was* remembering and had nothing further to add.

'So this time I'm not going to let the tank fall below half...'

'Yeah yeah whatevvvvvver! Oh, you do bang on, don't you, dear,' She smiled, trotting off to get some snacks for the journey. 'What do you want to eat, babe?' she shouted.

'A can of Dr Pepper, some chocolate and two packs of Cheesy Cheetos, please, sweetheart,' I replied.

'I've only got a twenty, you sure that's going to be enough, mister I'm too scared we're going to break down?' she giggled.

'Yes dear. Fifteen bucks for the gas should be plenty.'

I briefly paused. When was the last time I had made such a comment back home? Fifteen bucks would barely get you out of the red these days what with petrol being so ludicrously expensive. It couldn't have been more different out here in America and with half a tank of fuel costing you less than a twenty, gasoline was effectively cheaper than water. Now that's a steal in anyone's language but rather ironically most Americans aren't particularly happy with the cost of their gas. You only have to turn the radio on to hear some old codger complaining about the rising costs of fuel and how it's affecting his livelihood and all that nonsense. The fact of the matter is though most middle-class Americans simply don't know how good they have it. You see it's not only the fuel that's cheaper but just about everything else.

Your weekly shop in Walmart, your Friday night visit to TGIs, or that brand new iPad beckoning you in from the shop window. On average Americans can pay up to 30% less than what you'd expect to pay back home and that's just a conservative estimate. I was looking at the real estate when we were travelling through New England and I couldn't believe how affordable their homes were. A luxurious four bed cottage sitting on 3 acres of prime woodland was less than $125,000. One hundred and twenty-five grand! I nearly fell of my stool reading that one. You'd be lucky to get a garage in London for that kind of price. But then I guess it's all relative really. We get accustomed to a way of living and then we want more. What we have is never enough. It's only when you branch out and see how others truly live, you really start to appreciate how lucky some people are.

We spent the next few hours driving up the interstate and what a surreal experience it was. To the east laid the vast open space of the Colorado plains, while to the west sat the hypnotic frontal range of the Rocky Mountains. I was in absolute awe, unable to avert my gaze from the magnificent structures such was their towering presence. I was also looking for one peak in particular, Pikes Peak, and arguably the most famous mountain of them all.

Discovered by Zebellion Pike in 1806, the mountain was thrust into the limelight when Pike famously quoted '*No human will ever ascend that pinnacle!'* after his expedition's quite lame and unsuccessful attempt to climb it. Sounds a tad bitter if you ask me. However, it was the Colorado Gold Rush in 1858 that really cemented the mountain into the hearts of the nation. Located at the very edge of the frontal range, the mountain was the first visible sighting of the Rockies from the eastern plains. The snowcapped 14,000-footer being so prominent it could be seen from over 100 miles. Its distinct peak being so recognisable it was also used as the main marker in directing the wagons to the alleged mines. At the time the slogan *Pikes Peak or bust* was a common sighting scribbled across many a wagon as gold fever rapidly spread across a feverish nation.

Unfortunately for many, the majority of the early finds were located upstream west of Denver and it wasn't until much later when substantial deposits were eventually discovered in the Pikes Peak area. The lack of gold however didn't stop new towns springing up all over the region. The towns of Colorado City and Colorado Springs quickly prospered, both operating as the major supply hubs to the more lucrative mines in the north. Colorado City was originally a mining town full of the usual saloons and brothels, while its sister town Colorado Springs was considerably more refined, prospering as a result from the newly invested wealth.

We rolled into Colorado Springs shortly after lunch and were immediately taken back by its beauty. There are not too many places where you can fall instantly in love with but Colorado Springs was certainly one of them. Set among the backdrop of the spectacular Pikes Peak, the town is pure picture postcard, its small stretch of city skyscrapers completely dwarfed by the immensity of the great west behind. We took a walk along Main Street in what had to be the most perfect afternoon; its thriving, unassuming downtown was an absolute pleasure to walk down. We ambled for a while watching the local townsfolk quietly going about their business – a group of joggers said hi, a young family laughed and chattered as they passed us by, I pondered for a while then smiled *this is how life should be*.

We found ourselves a table in one of the many open-air bars and restaurants. Looking across the street I noticed a small family cycling on the other side the road – Dad and Mum upfront with three little siblings holding up the rear. I watched them goofing and giggling as their long lingering shadows gradually faded into the early evening sun. A simple but surreal moment nevertheless. The image of that happy family riding off into the sunset rather fittingly summing up the wonderful small-town community vibe I was currently feeling. Perhaps it's the fresh mountain air that brings out the best in people, or the 300 days of glorious sunshine they apparently receive in these parts. Either way it's no surprise to learn that Colorado Springs and its neighbouring towns are annually voted the most desirable places to live in America. Colorado Springs was recently voted best small city to live in by *Money* magazine, coming out top on job prospects, housing, schooling, entertainment and just about every other key indicator you could imagine. Only right then we should stay for a few days to sample such a cherished lifestyle. I flicked through some marketing flyers that were sprawled across the bar. Tomorrow we would go to Pikes Peak, the most famous peak of them all. Tonight we would sit outside drink lots of beer and watch the lowering sun dip below the majestic Rocky range. *How much are the houses here again?* I wondered as I supped on yet another ice-cold beer.

The next morning we departed promptly for the long haul up Pikes Peak. Earlier at breakfast I had rummaged through my marketing leaflets to determine which route we would take - of which there were three simple choices – we could climb it, we could drive it, or we could train it. Climbing was obviously out of the question. If Mr Pike himself couldn't even manage it then what chance would a couple of hungover backpackers have? That left us a coin flip between driving to the summit or hopping aboard the Cog mountain railway. The train would be the easier option; involving a three-hour round trip, although the problem being you only got to spend thirty or so minutes on the summit itself. The car on the other hand would offer us far greater flexibility, but also came with its perils, most notably negotiating a 38 mile stretch of sandstone road, death defying bends, very few safety barriers and a girlfriend insistent upon driving. After a short deliberation it was decided we would take the car option on the sole proviso that I would be the one doing the driving.

A short while later we reached the main highway and were soon ascending our way up the mountain. The first ten miles being relatively tame as we drove through the sun-drenched Aspen forests that surrounded the lower region.

Stopping for lunch at a memorable lake, we found ourselves a charming little picnic spot overlooking the turquoise waters. Up on the shoreline an elderly couple fished for trout, while in the shallows a sprinkling of children clambered over a cluster of rocks, occasionally dipping their feet into the chilly blue waters. On the other side of the lake stood the impressive Pikes Peak. Its snowcapped summit and alpine reflection dazzled like a peacock in the early morning ripples. Finishing our sandwiches we continued our journey and were soon travelling above the tree line. From that point on it was second gear all the way as we switchbacked our way through a tight series of bends. A short while later the road turned to gravel and things got a whole lot more scarier when we momentarily slid into a sharp, unprotected bend rather uncomfortably named 'The Bottomless Pit'!

'I don't like it!' Angie screamed. Always the brave little soldier.

'Sssshhhh, just let me concentrate on the road, you big baby,' I replied eyes firmly glued ahead. 'Anyway, I thought you wanted to drive?' I said before shouting, 'Look, no hands wahooooooo!'

The obscenities in which she replied are unprintable, but it's fair to assume my one-hand-off-the-wheel gesture didn't go down too well.

We continued cautiously in what was the toughest part of the drive, taking the best part of an hour to crawl our way to the top.

The views from the summit were simply breathtaking.

We parked the car and clambered over some rocks, finding a secluded little spot on the mountain's outer fringes. It was from this vantage point where famed writer Katherine Bates was once inspired to write the anthem 'America the Beautiful'. Looking out over the golden plains below, she later declared she'd found the gateway to heaven – and who was I to argue looking down from our lofty position to the beautiful world below. I cracked open a beer and scanned the horizon. To my right and practically all around sat the marbled coloured Jewels of the Sangre Christo Mountains. To my left I could just about make out the distant high rises of Denver. Down below the sleepy town of Colorado Springs glistened in the afternoon sun, while beyond that a huge mass of nothingness except the vast open space of the Colorado plains rolling gently away into the far-off distance.

The high Colorado plains are said to be over 8,000 feet high, although from our vantage you'd never believe it so infinitively flat they appear from afar. I sat in silence wondering how it all became. It is as if two worlds have collided, the flat world and the rocky world. Nature's very own barrier where one world's evolution is dramatically halted by another far more almighty one. It was a wonderful moment and one I will always go back to in search of inspiration. There may well be higher mountains, there may well be more spectacular mountain ranges, but few will be more contrasting, more thought provoking and more inspiring then the one I was lucky to be standing upon on that early summer's afternoon.

After a while we made our way back down, but not before checking out the local tack in the mountain's solitary gift shop. The most notable of which being the selection of T-shirts proclaiming 'Guardrails are for wimps' in reference to safety work that had recently being carried out. Call me a big girl's blouse but I'd take the protective guardrails every time, thank you very much.

We began our descent down the mountain and if anything, it was even more hairy than it was going up, in that our immediate survival was now entirely dependent upon the durability of the car's braking system. Large signs frequently encouraged one to drive in lower gear, while resting your brakes every few minutes. Half way down we were required to pull over for a mandatory brake inspection from one of the Rangers.

'Well they've certainly taking a bit of a battering, sir, but I think they're holding up. Maybe next time you should go for the Mountain Jeep, my friend?' the Ranger jested as he patted the car.

'Yeah maybe?' I replied. 'But next time, I think we'll get the train. Safer that way I reckon!'

We arrived at our hotel shortly before sunset and once again found ourselves sitting on the lawn watching the sun sink slowly behind the majestic Rocky Mountains. It was our last night in Colorado Springs and in truth I wish we could have stayed for longer. Regrettably this was not to be, as for the first time in weeks we were now working to a ridiculously tight schedule. The Californian Zephyr was due to depart from Denver in three days' time in what promised to be an unforgettable train ride across the mountains. Denver would require at least a day's visit, the Rocky Mountain National Park another, but before that there was one more place I just absolutely had to see.

The next day we departed Colorado Springs and headed to Fort Collins, some sixty miles north of Denver. Rumour had it that there was a little bit of magic to be had in this town. The rumour being that the town's historic district was once used as the main inspiration to create a very special place – and if these murmurings were true then we'd be in for a very special treat indeed.

Fort Collins

Up until recently I had never heard or ever had any intention of going to the college town of Fort Collins. Then one day over breakfast I came across a very interesting article where the town of Fort Collins was gleeing over its recently awarded accolades. The roll of honour was impressive, ranging from 5th best metro area to live, top 10 town for real estate opportunities, 5th most educated town in the country, and so the list went on. All very well but it was actually something else that caught my eye, right at the very bottom of the page in a tiny reference to the town's unique fairytale style architecture. Apparently, many of the buildings in the downtown area had been used as the inspiration for several of the buildings that can be found in and around Disneyland's Main Street. Disney's City Hall, Central Bank and Main Street station are all allegedly exact replicas of various buildings that can be found in and around Fort Collins.

Now this was interesting, you see as a boy Main Street Disney was technically the first American downtown I had ever walked through. OK, it may only have been a theme park, but its quirky little shops and friendly charm was a world away from my own grotty little high street in central Slough. It was love at first sight that was for sure and arguably the very moment when my American love affair truly began. I sat there reminiscing for a while as the distant memories of that first American trip came flooding back. It was also the first time that I'd ever experienced a real-life holiday romance. Well it wasn't exactly love and come to think of it I didn't even know her name? What I do remember is that we were both staying in the Disney Village and that our paths would often cross. My big chance would finally arrive one afternoon on the hotel's top floor observation deck overlooking the vast greenery of the Disney estate. I turned to my left and there she was, this stunningly beautiful girl standing right next to me. Nervously I began to introduce myself, but couldn't think of anything sensible to say, so could only manage a garbled sentence. *'Hi my na... na... name is Ja... James... Wh... wh... who are you?'* I spluttered before scurrying back to my room, hopes totally crushed. However, all was not lost, as over the next few days my new found friend would go out of her way to acknowledge me, even occasionally throwing me a cheeky smile once in a while. Sadly, our budding young love didn't progress beyond the *'Alwright*?' stage. Rubbish, I know, but some say it's better to have loved and lost than to not have loved at all!

We returned home from that holiday and my fascination for America spiralled. I had tasted the American Dream and now I was going to live it. Television would never be the same again. In the evenings I would accompany my mother for our weekly fix of *Dallas*, while at weekends it would be *Bonanza* reruns and spaghetti westerns on the sofa with my father. I developed an unhealthy passion for the NFL, studying its rules and staying up late to watch the Chicago Bears thrash the New England Patriots in the UK's first ever live Super Bowl. At one stage I even contemplated setting up a basketball court at the back of the garden, so obsessed I was now becoming. In hindsight it's amazing how one brief walk down one simple street would have such influence over a young boy's childhood. Twenty-five years later the passion still burns, so when the opportunity finally did arise to actually walk down the *real* Main Street, it was one I would most certainly take with both hands.

The drive up the interstate to Fort Collins had a very familiar feel about it. The jagged mountains to my left so recognisable it felt like we were driving alongside an enormous can of Coors Light, which in a way we kind of were, since the brand's logo resembles the exact location where the beer is brewed in the small town of Golden, just west of Denver. It was late afternoon when we hit the outskirts of Fort Collins. Struggling with my bearings I turned on my sat nav to let the sweet lady's comforting voice steadily guide us in. *Although our dippy digital friend clearly hadn't the foggiest idea where she was going either* – to be fair at least she didn't keep us in suspense – it only took her the best part of three minutes to completely send us in the wrong direction, dumping us in the middle of some random, run down alley somewhere in the back of beyond.

'James, you sure this is the right place? It looks kinda... dead?' Angie quizzed, winding up the windows.

'I'm not sure, darling. The sat nav reckons it's the next turning?'

We turned into 'Main Street' only to discover a sad and desolate place. A few rundown, dirty wooden houses were all to be seen.

'Well, baby, I think it's your sat nav who's taking the *Mickey!* As there's no way this place was the inspiration for that goody two shoes of a mouse. It's a complete dive!'

'I don't get it? Why call it Main Street if there's nothing here?' I questioned.

'No idea. Perhaps it's a trap to lure in gullible and deluded Disney lovers like you?' Angie giggled. 'Maybe a whole bunch of disgruntled Disney employees secretly set up base and now they're gonna torture you, dress you up as Cinderella and make you watch endless hours of fluffy girly films. *So you still love Disney now do you, my little princess*?'

'Yeah alright babe, that's some warped imagination you've got there.' I laughed. 'Come on, let's get the hell out of here. Looks like the real downtown is a few miles back,' I said turning off the sat nav to follow my nose.

'Do you think they have a tram here?' Angie piped up a few minutes later.

'Hope so,' I replied

'What about a gift shop?'

'Maybe.'

'And how about a magical light parade with dancing chipmunks?' she chuckled

'Yeah alright, girl, now you're clearly taking the piss, aren't you?'

'Sorry babe, I couldn't resist,' she smiled.

A few minutes later we found ourselves in Main Street, but something just didn't feel quite right. It just didn't feel like Disney and it certainly didn't feel we were walking down my favourite street in America. A couple of the buildings may have looked familiar, but if I hadn't been told it was the inspiration for Main Street USA then in truth I never would have guessed. Something was missing... *And no, it wasn't Cinderella's bloody castle, before you ask!*

The problem with this Main Street was that it had evolved. Where once there would have been a horse and carriage clip clopping down the street, there was now a dull pedestrianised zone in its place. Walking down this Main Street was like walking down any other typical outdoor shopping centre. I was disappointed that even my beloved Main Street had sadly moved on with the times. What would the late Walt Disney have made of these changes? I doubt this was part of his utopian vision for America? Perhaps someone should grow some balls and tell Disney their park doesn't reflect the real America anymore. Maybe I should write and propose they build a new park, one where its Main Street reflects the trials and tribulations of the modern day and not some fluffy idealistic version of the 1950s. It should be run down, drab and soulless, full of estate agents, dollar shops and closing down sales. All the rides should be located on the far outskirts of the car park in the newly established Walmartland - a land of convenience where people drive through the attractions because they can't be arsed to walk anymore. In this modern-day Disney, Fantasyland shall be renamed Viceland and house only the finest strip bars and Casinos. While Tomorrowland should be dubbed The Hood, and feature real life gangsters, Mexican drug barons, and a dramatic night time shootout as the new electrical light parade. OK, perhaps I am being a little harsh as Fort Collins is actually a rather pleasant and amiable place. My problem being I had so many expectations riding on this town, I was expecting a Main Street full of nostalgia and inspiration yet all I got was a paved over vision of the future instead.

The next day we drove into the Rocky Mountain National Park, a short drive west of Fort Collins. Designated a national park in 1914 and covering over 400 square miles, the park is widely considered to be the crown jewels of the American Rockies. In comparison to other national parks it is fairly small, but what it may lack in size it sure then makes up in content. Home to over seventy *12 thousand footers*, lush meadows and an abundance of wildlife, the park is blessed with a diversity of natural wonders just waiting to be explored.

Luckily for us the park has a custom built super highway, the Trail Ridge Road, a 42-mile paved highway that traverses the craggy peaks. Ascending to heights of over 14,000 feet, the Trail Ridge Road is officially the highest stretch of continuous roadway in North America, a third of which is above the tree line in the cold and windy Alpine zone. Conditions on the mountain are notoriously harsh so the road is only open a few months of the year. Every Spring, a specialised rotary snow plough requires an estimated forty-five days to drill a pathway through the 20-foot-thick blanket of snow that covers the road. Even in the summer there can be huge fluctuations in weather, so as the sun shines brightly in the forests below, cold frosty winds will frequently batter the highs. We made our way to the Alpine visitor centre, the road's highest point, where we stopped off for lunch overlooking the heart of the higher Rockies. A range of snow-capped peaks spanned the horizon. In the far distance the familiar diamond shape peak of Long Horns was clearly visible. One of Colorado's famed *55 fourteeners,* the mountain is popular among hikers and although frequently conquered it is not without the occasional tragedy. Several people fall foul to the mountains each year with lightning strikes being the common cause of death. After Florida, the Rockies are the second most prone area in America for lightning strikes – its high altitude, low cloud structure and warm Gulf Streams ensure the mountains continently get peppered each and every summer. Strikes are commonplace above the tree line, and in a world where *you* are the giant it doesn't take much to figure out that you are the most obvious of targets. Only recently a hiker was struck by lightning as he descended from the summit. He was found a few days later dazed and disorientated but miraculously still alive; the only thing he could remember was his hair standing on its end moments before the attack.

We continued our journey and followed the roadway across the mountains. Occasionally the world below would open up revealing drops so deep you wished you'd never looked down – at one stage the trail width narrowed to such an extent we could see both sides of the mountain sloping directly beneath us. You certainly wouldn't want to be puncturing a tire up here! *Maybe that rather annoying car rental salesman had a point after all?*

We completed the main loop then headed back to the visitors' centre. It had been another wonderful day, exhilarating at times, if not a little hairy. We drove back down the mountain pulling over frequently to digest the immense views. At each overlook a variety of hiking trails would enticingly present itself. Following one, we found ourselves walking through the woods heading for a hidden lake somewhere half way down the mountain. It was beautiful, serene, and perhaps even spiritual being all alone out there with only the birds and the trees for company.

'Come on, Jamie, keep up. Let's go this way. I want to see what's up there!' Angie said, skipping merrily ahead. In an American national park even the simplest of things can become exciting as you eagerly turn the next corner in the hope of discovering something new.

We followed the trail until the light began to fade. An eerie silence fell upon.

'Come on darling, time to go back,' I said looking to the skies. 'We have got a busy day tomorrow.'

That evening while we watched our laundry do its final spins we discussed our next moves. Tomorrow we would drive down to Denver, and then catch our train the following day. According to the Amtrak it would take approximately twelve hours to cross the Rockies by train. We would need supplies – food, drink, something to read and of course, a camera. You see if the reports were correct then it was going to be one of the most spectacular crossings of all.

Denver & the Rockies

The next day we headed back down the interstate to Denver, the capitol of Colorado, in what was to be our last stopping point east of the Rockies. Denver, like many towns on the frontal range grew and prospered during the mass influx of the Pikes Peak Gold Rush. It quickly became the most popular destination in that many of early discoveries were found in and around the adjacent foothills – and where there's a thirsty gold miner there's usually a high demand for whorehouses, gambling dens, saloons and a whole host of other questionable establishments willing to feed the need of the ever hungry gold digger. Don't you just love the way the Wild West evolved?

Today things aren't quite as sleazy, with Denver evolving into *the* commercial heartbeat of Middle America. Its central geographic positioning makes it an ideal location for many a business hub to operate from. As a result, the city has become a natural magnet for freight, distribution, telecommunications, as well as the more traditional energy and mining businesses.

The city's marketing department has also been busy too. Standing at a height of 5,280 feet, the city is exactly one mile above sea level – and you can't go anywhere in Denver without being constantly reminded that you are now officially standing in '*the Mile High City*'. In fact the city is so proud of its mile high heritage that they've even gone as far to carve an official marking onto the eleventh step of the Capitol building – which is said to be exactly a mile high – well it was until 1969 when some young, hot shot of a super grad noted that the exact spot should have actually been carved four steps higher, and then again in 2002 when they discovered the city was also three foot higher then originally first thought. And the city's official response to this disastrous calamity? *'Well take your pick – but one of them is assuredly one mile high*!' Now that's one hell of a relaxed attitude and it doesn't take long to figure out why everyone in the city is apparently so chilled. It's common knowledge that living at a high altitude is good for you, but it's only until more recently that scientific studies have collaborated with this. According to the University of Colorado, living at a high altitude can increase your life expectancy by up to three years. The combination of long sunny days, high doses of vitamin D and low oxygen levels is believed to reduce the risk of both heart disease and many types of cancers. It's no wonder why everyone walks around with a smile on their face. However, living at altitude does apparently come with the occasional risk. When visiting the city you are advised to double your intake of fluid, as according to locals the surrounding air is dryer then that of the back of a camel's arse. Never forget to pack your sunscreen, as with an alleged 300 days of sunshine, there's more sun to be had here in Denver than there is in the city of Miami – and finally you're advised to watch your alcohol levels as drinking at high altitude supposedly gets you drunk twice as quickly. Now I personally can't see any problem with any of that, and if I was dithering beforehand, I'll certainly be coming back again very soon.

Keen to explore our new favourite city, we hit the centre of town for a spot of dinner in one of the many outdoor restaurants that lined the leafy streets. As downtowns districts go, 16th Street in Denver has to be one of the finest I have ever seen – the long, lingering avenue of trees, is the undisputed star attraction in this most pedestrian friendly city. Pulling up a pew we supped on a beer and watched the vibrant district come to life. It was the evening of the 4th of July and the town was packed full of visitors all out in preparation for the late-night fireworks. Buskers were out in their droves busily entertaining the crowds; while in the very centre, a collection of beautifully crafted grand pianos lined the streets in readiness for the occasional musician that would randomly plonk themselves down to blurt out a tune. I was half tempted to have a go myself but didn't think the locals would appreciate my somewhat rather depressing cover of Alfred Hitchcock's notorious 'shower scene'. I didn't want to put a damper on things, what with the evening being so young.

I was about to order the food when Angie dropped the bombshell. 'James, have we got time to go to Canada as well?'

'What? What, dear?' I said spluttering my drink. 'What on earth made you think of that?'

'Well I'm kinda getting used to this mountain lifestyle. Kate reckons it's supposed to be real nice up there. A bit like Denver perhaps?' she replied. *For the record, Kate was one of Angela's best, and highly influential chums back home. What Kate said, Angie unquestionably believed!*

'I suppose so?' I shrugged, secretly cursing the advice. *And what's it got to do with her anyway*?

'We could go to Vancouver, Calgary, Toronto, Montreal, Quebec. It will be so fun,' Angie continued.

'Woooooe... steady on, girl. I'm sure it would be lovely darling but don't you think we're cutting things fine already?'

'There you go again James, always trying to talk me out of the things that I want to do!'

I was stepping on dangerous territory here, but Canada was the last thing on my mind at this stage of the trip.

'Why have you gone quiet? You don't want to go do you, James?'

'No, it's not that babe, but there's so much more we need to do in America first, darling. Can we think about it for a while?'

'Well I think we should go. And I think you should do what I want to do for a change,' she smiled.

I wasn't pleased with this, any of it, as it would mean rushing around for the next couple of weeks trying to fit it all in. There was no way we would have time to see all the cities. A compromise was definitely on the cards. 'Well, maybe, baby. How about we visit a couple of places in the last week when we're back on the East coast?' I proposed.

Angie looked at me, not sure what to make with my swift compromise.

'I don't know, Jamie? You'll only try and talk me out of it.'

Damn it! This girl knew me all right, she knew my motives, and she knew my every move. The worst thing was I knew I had absolutely no chance of talking her out of it. But right now I was too tired to care. The last few weeks had been hectic. Not only had we whizzed through much of the Mid West, but we had also covered a fair bit of the southern Rockies as well. Tomorrow we would finally cross the great divide and head to Salt Lake City in the heart of Utah. After that, California, and we still had to check out Vegas and the Grand Canyon as well. My only hope was to try and minimise any Canadian trip to a few days, maybe Montreal? Perhaps even Quebec? But for now Canada would have to wait. Tonight was all about enjoying ourselves and celebrating freedom. And so while the rest of the country toasted their independence – we too thought about our newly found freedom and the life we'd left behind.

The next morning we gathered our rucksacks and headed to Union Station – *Yes, I know, another Union Station!* – to catch a ride on what many believe to be one of the greatest railroad journeys in America. Departing from Chicago and arriving in San Francisco some fifty-two hours later, the Californian Zephyr is said to be one of the longest rail routes in the entire continent. Crossing over a total of seven states and covering over 2,500 miles, the Californian Zephyr embarks on a journey through some of the most diverse and unspoiled landscapes in the American wilderness. By the time it's reached Denver it has already whisked its way over the rolling plains and is now preparing to ascend through the Rocky Mountains – and then out into the vast deserts of Utah. We arrived at the station a little early so sat ourselves down on a wooden bench while we waited to board. Then from the corner of my eye I noticed them, a middle-aged couple introducing themselves to the rows of waiting passengers.

'Hi, my name is John,' the friendly man opened. 'And this is my wife Sheila. We're volunteer Rangers from the National Park Service and will be your guides for the day.'

'So if you have any questions then please don't hesitate to join us in the viewing deck at the front of the train,' his wife Sheila chipped in.

'Ah yes and did I mention that our services are completely free of charge? So don't be afraid to come up and ask any questions you may have.' The old man winked before moving on to introduce himself to the next passengers.

'Best get some change, hey darling. Looks like they'll be around with their begging bowls later,' I muttered.

A short while later our huge double decker silver liner rolled into the station. Ahead of the field, I raced onto the carriage making myself cosy under the impressive glass domed viewing deck.

The train soon departed and John wasted little time in beginning his commentary.

'We will soon be approaching the continent divide where we will pass through the Moffat Tunnel, America's largest mountain tunnel measuring a staggering 6.2 miles. It is believed the tunnel cost an estimated 25 million dollars to build.'

'Yes, it may well be expensive, honey, but at least it saves us the ordeal of a 176-mile detour around the mountains,' Sheila chipped in.

'Worth every cent then, Darling,' John quipped back.

And so the banter continued, John opening up and Sheila closing and a right old little double act they were too.

A short while later the conductor called out our names, instructing we go to the restaurant carriage as lunch was about to be served. Excited to be dining aboard we gathered our things, quickly finding ourselves a perfect window seat.

'And would sir like any wine?' the waiter at the table requested.

'Yes please,' I replied. 'I'll have a glass of white.'

'And for you, madam?'

'Ohh I'll have two please. One red and one white please, thank you very much,' Angie enthusiastically replied.

'Steady on, girl. You'll be hammered before dessert.'

'I don't care, Jamie. I'm having fun... and I can have as many glasses of wine as I like, thank you very much,' she replied somewhat defiantly.

Crossing the Continental Divide we ventured deep into a series of ancient canyons, a deathly hush prevailing as we gazed out at the enchanting landscape that was rapidly unravelling before our eyes. Some time later we entered the spectacular Glenwood Canyon where we followed the ferocious Colorado River for the next few hours.

'The river in these parts is affectionately known as Moon River,' John smiled. 'And before you ask it has nothing to do with Audrey Hepburn or the dazzling moonlit sky, but more for the cheeky little greeting you get from the white water rafters the moment they spot a passing train.' He continued as another group of rafters bent over giving us the notorious 'moon' welcome.

Angie responded by raising her glass only to spill half of it down her pristine white T-shirt. Clearly the fresh mountain air was having an immediate impact on her already questionable tolerance levels.

The terrain gradually changed from greenish brown to orangey red as we entered the multi-coloured and alien world of Utah. John stood up and instructed us to focus on a small sandstone structure immediately to our right, where a small engraving marked the borderline. It read – Utahcolorado. No state line, no border control just a simple chalk dusting engraved into a stone. We were officially in the wilderness but on what planet? For the deep red boulders we were now passing through were more reminiscent of a Martian landscape then anything I had ever seen before on this planet. The desolate landscape reminding me of a specific moment in my student days when I woke up to watch the world's most expensive Mars probe, The Rover, taking its first mechanically controlled steps onto the Martian surface. To this day I will never forget that low hazy sun setting away in the far-off distance. One by one my housemates would silently enter the room, curiously watching our robotic friend prodding and poking his way around this strange new world in which we now stood – and for one brief moment we were all there with him, armchair pioneers exploring another world. Now here I was years later travelling through the deserts of Utah now seriously doubting that Martian mission ever existed, so similar was the environment in which we were now in.

The landscape opened as we exited the canyons. In the distance a small town stood out alone.

'We are now approaching the ghost town of Cisco,' John informed us.

'And over to your left you may recognise the Sweet Grills Cafe and Gas Station which was featured in the film *Thelma and Louise*.'

A brief pause swept through the carriage as we all desperately tried to recall what part of the movie this rundown shithole had apparently appeared in.

'Was that the cafe where Brad and Geena had it off then?' Angie said turning towards me.

'Not sure, honey. The only thing I remember is them driving over the edge of the Grand Canyon,' I shrugged.

'The movie not only won an Oscar but was widely credited for launching the career of Brad Pitt,' Sheila purred. 'Next year it will be celebrating its twentieth anniversary. Seems like only yesterday, hey folks... and Brad looks as good today as he did back then, hey ladies,' she smiled with a twinkle in her eye.

A chorus of applause ripped throughout the carriage.

'Well that's it from us today, folks,' John announced over the wolf whistles. 'The next stop is ours. So on behalf of Sheila and myself we hope you all had one swell of a time with us today. Please remember we don't get paid for our services so any donations will be gratefully accepted.'

'Bloody hell, he's not backwards in coming forward, is he, babe? And I was just beginning to warm to him as well,' I said reluctantly searching for a dollar bill.

The Rangers departed at Green River, the last major stop before Salt Lake City. A hushed void fell upon the carriage as the lowering sun sank below the ruby coloured sandstones. It was slow going from there onwards, the growing darkness clouding any chance we had of a decent view.

A while later the horizon lit up as we entered the outskirts of civilisation. The journey through the outer suburbs was long and laborious, never before had I seen such an endless mass of urban sprawl. But then where else could they all live; the Mormons that is. You see Salt Lake City is to a Mormon what the Vatican is to a Catholic – home. And so, for the first time on this trip we had entered the Bible country, aka the Bible Belt and official Head Quarters to the Church of the Latter-day Saints. So what are the chances they'd be in when we come a knocking on their door?

Salt Lake City

Many years ago I remember a knock at the door and turning around to see my mother panic like she had never panicked before. There she was shivering before me, eyes wide apart and sweating profusely.

'*What is it, Mummy? What's wrong*?' I asked watching the colour drain from her face.

'*Don't answer the door. Stay away!*' she shrieked. '*It's a bloody Jehovah Witness. Get down or they'll never leave us alone!*'

My mother was so frightened she insisted we spent the next twenty minutes hiding behind the sofa, camouflaged, so they couldn't see us when they peered through the windows – which they inevitably did as it was very common for *the knockers* in our neighbourhood to hang around for ages once rejected at the door. They would usually come in pairs; two middle-aged women wearing these big, clumpy, ugly shoes which according to mother they needed to wear to jam open the doors with. However, despite my mother's fear of being trapped on her own doorstep she one day decided to confront her demons and inform the knockers that she was in fact a Catholic – which of course was complete nonsense. Unfortunately for Mother they obviously caught her on a bad day and she was soon seen passing over a sizeable donation in exchange for some light bed time reading, a Bible study magazine rather ironically named '*Awake*'! Although on further research it appears my mother wasn't the only one who would rather squander their hard-earned cash than listen to their drivel. According to global statistics over 42 million copies of the Watchtower, their sister publication, are printed every month, ensuring the magazines status as the most widely circulated publication on the planet. Now that's impressive in anyone's language, especially when you consider there's officially only a total of one million true believers. Now that either tells me that each believer buys a staggering forty-two copies a month or those knockers must be on one *hell* of a commission if you pardon the pun 'Ok, Ok, Ok... *If I sign up you promise to never set foot on my property ever again?*'

It's fair to say the general public is a little sceptical when it comes to people preaching on one's doorstep. There are reasons why we stick those 'sorry no salesman' stickers up on our windows – we simply don't like being sold to especially in our own home. It's a principle thing, I guess. It's alright for them to come knocking on our doors trying to peddle their dreams, but I bet they'd be really annoyed if I rocked up on their doorstep, peddling a load of *Amway* cleaning product, insisting they come and join *my* pyramid? I rest my case and by the way pyramid selling is definitely not the future either. However, I'm pleased to say not all religious groups are quite as persistent as our Jehovah friends. I seem to remember a practicing Mormon ward located on the other side of town and never really recall them harassing my mother on such a frequent basis. Although in hindsight perhaps we were the lucky ones, as over the pond the Mormons have built up quite a fearsome reputation for turning up rather uninvitedly. They can't be that bad, can they, I thought as we departed our train. Mitt Romney's a Mormon and he seems perfectly normal, doesn't he? Well kind of? Anyway we were about to find out for sure and where better place to start then a brief visit to Temple Square, world HQ and spiritual home to every practicing Mormon sect on the planet.

The story of the Mormon faith is a fascinating one, almost heroic once you accept its rather dubious beginnings. It all started back in 1830 when founding father Joseph Smith was sent a message from a mysterious angel to uncover an ancient Indian box at the top of a nearby hill. Legend had it that he retrieved this box to discover a set of golden plates hidden inside, each one inscribed in ancient carvings allegedly concealing hidden messages from God. However, by sheer luck Smith also possessed a rather unique talent which allowed him to decode these ancient messages by staring into precious stones. This particular talent involved placing a precious stone at the bottom of an upturned top hat, then rather like an ostrich burying his head inside the hat to reveal its magical powers. Absolute bloody genius if you ask me and why anyone else didn't think of that is beyond me? Yes, he may have looked like a complete tool in the process but this ingenious method seemed to work for our friend Joseph, as by sheer coincidence he was able to conjure up the exact translations and convert them into what is now commonly known as the great Mormon Bible.

Undeterred by its somewhat fluffy conception the Mormon religion has since flourished. Today it is estimated that there are over 15 million worldwide members, which is pretty impressive really when you consider it started out barely 150 years ago from the bottom of a sweaty hat. It's not all fluffy clouds though. The book of Mormon basically instructs its disciples to lead a good, healthy, and peaceful lifestyle, devoting one day a week to worship with an ultimate desire to form a new and harmonious kingdom of Zion, a kind of modern-day Israel. The strict Mormon code forbids followers indulging in many vices – the banning of alcohol, coffee and pre-marital sex being the most common. However, it's the faith's acceptance of plural marriages that has caused the greatest concern among non-believers. The *if I can't have sex before marriage then I'll just go and marry the whole bleeding clan* attitude didn't go down well with the do-gooders of the east, and as a result the Mormons were effectively banished from society and driven out to the western frontiers. Salvation didn't last long and after much harassment they were left with little choice but to cross the treacherous Rocky Mountains in what was known as the expedition of the Mormon Pioneers. Led by the inspirational Brigham Young, over 70,000 disciples followed, traversing the mountains to find a safe haven in what is now Salt Lake City. Quite remarkable really; they then proceeded to build their own flourishing community in the remotest of valleys, with little help from the outside world. The crowning jewel in their new society was the creation of Temple Square, which took over twenty laborious years to complete. The square itself is located on 1st Street, overlooking the city from the north. Each subsequent street ascends in number while also serving as a handy reminder in telling you how far you've strayed from the nest.

Disappointingly we arrived at Temple Square to learn that the main church, Salt Lake Temple, was officially out of bounds as only fully-fledged members of the faith were allowed to enter. It wasn't all bad news though as immediately opposite was the South Visitors' Centre. I looked at Angie for approval?

'What do you reckon? Shall we brave it and have a look around?'

'Why not, Jamie baby. When in Rome or shall I say when in Salt Lake...' she began before bursting into a fit of laughter.

'You going to finish it off? I have a funny feeling what's coming next.'

'I can't, it's too complicated. When in Salt Lake and do as a Mormon does? It just doesn't quite cut it does it, Jamie?'

'Best leave the humour to me, my friend. Anyway, you need to pull yourself together now. Could be pretty brutal in there, you know. If you show any signs of weakness they'll be all over you like a bad rash.'

'Oh Jamie, I'll be fine.'

'We'll I've warned you, Angie. They'll have their Mormon army in there that's for sure. On a commission to save our souls and all that nonsense. Don't be lured in by their warming smiles. If they come near just look away, pretend you haven't seen them.'

'Yes, dear,' she replied, blissfully unaware that we were about to enter the lion's den of what is widely considered to be one of the most persuasive and proactive religions ever known to man.

I opened the large glass door of the exhibition centre and a tinge of excitement ran through me. This was going to be fun, I thought with a wry smile. Surely only a matter of time until one of us was spotted, and in a weird way I was kinda looking forward to a game of holy hide and seek. Walking into the exhibition centre was like walking into some kind of weird parallel universe and on first impressions it was as if we'd walked straight into Salt Lake's very own impersonation of Madame Tussauds. Only this time the waxworks weren't exactly that of Michael Jackson or Marilyn Monroe, but of their gallant Mormon leader Brigham Young guiding his young disciples across the Rocky Mountains. To his right, a large flat screen depicting the moment where he looks up to the skies, hears a message from God, and declares to his followers... '*Right, bugger this for a living, I'm bloody knackered, looks like this soulless valley will have to do*!' Ok, Ok, Ok that's not exactly what happened as he obviously played up on the dramatics a bit more. The TV documentary showing him coming to a juddering halt, looking up to the sky, outstretching his arms in full *Platoon* cinematic style – before turning to the crowd to announce. '*This is it. This is the place where we lay down our tools and build our kingdom.'*

All very impressive but personally if I had just lumbered my entire contents over the almighty Rockies for the last three months I would quite happily have bought into the I'm-bloody-knackered speech just as easily. We progressed into the main hallway where a small queue of people were hovering over a miniature replica of the Salt Lake Temple, a teaser of sorts, showing you what you could have seen if you were a fully paid up member of the faith. An orderly line formed as we waited in turn to have our chance to peer through the tiny glass box at what could have easily been mistaken for a shoddy wooden dolls house. Looking through the glass I immediately sensed the danger. On the other side of the box I clocked three young women smiling back at us, watching our every move. One of them retreating back to a nearby desk to collect a handful of leaflets, while the other two shuffling forward ever so subtlety in our direction.

My heart raced as I looked around for a pillar to duck behind, but it was too late, one of the women caught my gaze and attempted to draw me in.

'Hello there.'

'Err hello,' I replied

'Do you have any questions you'd like to ask us?' she said, pointing in the direction of her two smiling companions.

Errr yeah? Like ever seen The Stepford Wives? 'Err no, I'm fine thanks,' I replied, backing away.

'Phew that was a close one wasn't it, Ang... Angie?' I said turning to see her being slowly escorted away to a nearby seat, a lamb to the slaughter if ever there was one. It was painful to watch, seeing her wincing and squirming as a wad of unwanted membership flyers were uncomfortably stuffed into her hand.

'Go on, you know you want to,' one of the ladies insisted. 'We can give you a guided tour of the temple if you like?'

I watched the colour drain from her face. The prospect of a guided tour was clearly a step too far and just like my mother many years before, she was left with little choice but to frantically rummage through her purse in a desperate attempt to secure her freedom.

'You alright, girl?' I said as she trudged back to the pillar I was hiding behind. 'Not like you to put your hand in your pocket.'

'Thanks for saving me there... mister where's my hero when you need one,' she said with a shake of the head.

'Sorry about that. My mother told me never to talk to strangers. And they were a little scary, weren't they? What did they say?'

'They said why is your boyfriend hiding behind that pillar? Does he think we can't see him over there?'

'Really? They said that, did they?'

'No, darling, they didn't. They were too polite but it was bloody obvious what you were doing. I was so embarrassed.'

'Sorry, darling, looks like I owe you a drink to make up, hey.'

'Yes, several, I think. Come on, I've had enough of this. All these wandering eyes are making me paranoid. Let's go and find a bar.'

And so we headed for a bar, which in Salt Lake City is no mean feat what with drinking establishments being a little on the scarce side to say the least. I suppose it's only to be expected really, when you enter the world HQ of a faith that strictly forbids the consumption of alcohol. The rules in Utah are so strict that up until a few years ago you had to be a specific member of a club to be allowed to have a beer in a public place; even then you were forbidden to have a glass of wine with your meal inside a restaurant. It's no wonder why tourists cheekily refer to it as the 'Zion Curtain' rather then the Zion heaven.

Today things are a little more relaxed but if you do manage to find a bar, then by law, they are only allowed to serve you low alcoholic beers not exceeding 4%. Late night bars are only allowed to serve you one drink at a time and if you do fancy a shot of something then the barman has to watch you neck it before pouring you another. Prague and Dublin it certainly is not and I can't really see them hosting too many hen parties here in the immediate future.

Anyway, after much searching we eventually stumbled upon an American sports bar in the recently developed Gateway District, a large open air shopping mall on the edge of town – but unlike the main city centre which had been eerily quiet, this place was a hive of activity. Built to service the 2002 Winter Olympics, the multi-million-dollar complex is an outdoor shoppers haven. Centred around the old union rail station, the outdoor mall offers its 750,000 annual visitors just about everything that the old city centre does not. Lively bars, restaurants and coffee shops spill out into the squares, while designer retail outlets encircle a cluster of fountains providing much-needed water squirts from the relentless midday sun. Kind of ironic really that in such a religious town the only place to have any soul was the 21st century shopping mall. I supped on my beer watching the shoppers go by and a sobering thought crossed my mind. Once upon a time we used to go to church to follow a faith. Not anymore. Now the consumer is king and the mainstay of his community is the suburban shopping mall in which he now shops. With much of downtown closing down and moving to the perimeters it can surely only be a matter of time until the main town centre is affectionately referred as the 'old town' so quickly things change these days. Evolution before our very eyes.

We finished our drinks and headed to the hotel pool to contemplate our next moves. Tomorrow we would be taking the I-15 north, past the Great Salt Lakes and into the mountain wilderness of Idaho and Wyoming. Our journey through the Rockies was nearly complete but there was one final wonder I just absolutely had to see.

America has always had a love affair with its national parks. And in a land of so many beauties it's no wonder why conservationists are so keen to protect it. According to the National Park Service there are currently 401 specific areas of protected land covering over 84 million acres, 47 of which have been officially classed as wilderness areas. Now that's a fair amount of wilderness to get through, so where better place to finish our Rocky Mountain journey than a visit to the nation's first designated national park – the one and only Yellowstone Park – home to the great Grizzly Bear and arguably one of the greatest wilderness areas of them all.

Yellowstone

The next day we collected our car rental and headed north to the small Mormon town of Rexburg on the southern fringes of Idaho, a good day's drive away yet still eighty miles short of the west Yellowstone entrance. Don't worry we weren't suddenly becoming all religious and seeking out every Bible town in the valley, but in truth we were given very little choice; the Yellowstone area isn't exactly blessed with an abundance of affordable and available hotels.

It was close to dusk when we eventually arrived at our reasonably priced Residence Inn on the outskirts of town. Tired and hungry, we grabbed whatever snacks we could find and retreated to the comfort of our one-bedroom studio apartment to plan the next day's activities. Now I have to confess that prior to our trip I'd always been a little bit sceptical about visiting Yellowstone. This uncertainty was in no way connected to a lack of interest in the park itself, quite the contrary, for I had heard many enchanting stories of its stunning wilderness, deep lying canyons and abundant volcanic geysers, so naturally I was very intrigued. However, what did concern me was the possibility of bumping into a great big hungry bear along the way. It would be just my luck to be merrily wandering through the woods only to find myself surrounded by a pack of salivating bears looking for a feed. A frightening thought I'm sure you'll agree. But the bears you'd likely encounter wouldn't be just any old bears, but the fearsome, uncompromising grizzly ones with an attitude and personality that more than lives up to their names. Quite frankly the thought of wondering around a park unprotected and at the mercy of one of nature's fiercest creatures was a tad frightening, even a little maddening to say the least. Standing over 7-foot-high and weighing an almighty 800 pounds, the Grizzly Bear is to the animal kingdom what the SAS is to the military world – the dog's bollocks, or perhaps bear's bollocks being slightly more appropriate in this case. Able to reach speeds of up to 30 mph, they can outrun an Olympic sprinter, have the intelligence and dexterity to climb trees, and come equipped with a set of paws so sharp that even Freddy Krueger would be left shitting in his pants. So if you really are one of life's unfortunate sods and happen to stumble across one of these fearsome beasts then you're likely to be in a whole heap of trouble. The official advice is not particularly helpful, instructing to you remain perfectly calm – *yeah right* – and once you have come to terms with the fact that you are now eyeballing one of nature's fiercest creatures, you are advised to retreat cautiously whilst talking to the beast in a perfectly clear, polite and rational manner! Really? *Morning Mr. Bear, splendid day, isn't it. Care to join me for a spot of lunch, old chap?* Somehow I just can't see that, although whatever you do you must never look them directly in the eye – *oh shit* – and for Christ's sake don't turn your back and run for the hills as that will only encourage them to hunt you down like the dog you really are. So if the unthinkable does happen and you are actually attacked, then the only way to survive a near certain death is to close your eyes, dramatically fall into a ball and hope your pathetic submission is good enough to convince the beast that you really are dead and not just lamely offering yourself up for lunch. Yeah, well good luck with that then.

Yet despite our inherent fears, bear attacks on humans are extremely rare. Each year only a few are ever recoded, most of which can be attributed to overprotective mothers being taken by surprise by passing hikers. You can hardly blame them really when you consider that over time man has hunted them down to near extinction. When the first settlers arrived it is estimated that there were over 100,000 Grizzlies roaming the plains. Today less than 1% are left, with the majority of these now residing in the Yellowstone area. After much deliberation I finally decided to do the right thing and pay the park a visit. To miss out on Yellowstone because of my obvious cowardliness would have been completely unforgivable. How do you explain that one away when you get back? It's hardly the actions you would expect from a seasoned traveller now and besides it's not often you get the chance to visit the alleged eighth wonder of the world, is it?

I flipped open my laptop and scanned the web for any crumb of knowledge I could find, quickly learning that what drives this wondrous place is not the immense scenery or indigenous animals that you see in all the brochures, but the powerful super volcano lurking just beneath the park's mysterious surface. Considered by many to be one of the most powerful and active volcanos on earth, Yellowstone Park sits neatly inside a massive Caldera *which is basically an incredibly large crater* that was formed from the remnants of the last major explosion some 650,000 years ago. It may have been a while since we last saw any action but don't be fooled into complacency just yet. The Yellowstone volcano is well and truly plotting its next moves, for barely a few miles below, lurks a massive boiling reservoir of pressurised larva slowly creeping its way up to the ground. The evidence is everywhere and it's this intense thermal activity that fuels the spectacular bubbling mud pools, hot springs and sprouting geysers that we see today. Experts suggest we should enjoy the show while it lasts, as one day in the very near future things are going to get a lot more violent in the Yellowstone area. It is not a question of *if* but *when* the Yellowstone volcano will eventually erupt in what now is considered to be a vastly overdue cataclysmic explosion. And if the unthinkable does eventually happen? Well let's just say most of North America will be completely wiped out, while the rest of the world is likely to be covered in a thick layer of volcanic ash for many years to come. However, we needn't head for the hills just yet, as the experts who regularly monitor the volcano, reckon we're safe for at least another century – which is all very reassuring when you're being chased up a tree by a humongous great bear!

Sorry, I'll let the bear thing go now. Grizzlies aside though, Yellowstone Park has always held a special place in American hearts ever since the first explorers stepped foot onto its alien landscape all those years ago. Its bewildering surface activity eventually persuaded the US government to declare it as America's first national park. This recognition was largely due to one man, Ferdinand Hayden, who was convinced that unless protected, the westward migration of the time would eventually destroy the land's mysterious wonders for evermore. Prior to Hayden's famous expedition, many passing fur trappers had earlier documented their experiences but their accounts were deemed so ridiculously farfetched they were immediately dismissed out of hand. In order to convince the doubters, Hayden brought along a team of scientists, artists and photographers to prove such a place existed. These findings were used to lobby Congress in passing a bill that would preserve the park in its natural state. Finally, in 1872 the area was cordoned off and the first official national park was formally opened to the public.

The next morning we drove through Idaho, briefly skirting into Montana, before joining the back of the queue at the westward entrance on the outer fringes of Wyoming. Three States in half an hour, we were living the dream. Paying the $20 gate fee, we collected our park guide and unravelled the map to reveal five distinct areas – The Geyser Basins in the south of the park, the lake and Hayden's Valley to the east, Mammoth Springs to the north and its very own Grand Canyon further east. An ironic smile crept across my face as I explored the varied landscapes. Yellowstone may well have been the first national park but with so many natural attractions you could argue a case it was also the first unofficial theme park as well. Who needs Mickey Mouse when you have nature's very own Mountain lake-land, Grand Canyon-land and Serengeti plains-land all rolled into one. And it wouldn't surprise me if a certain Mr Disney got some of his themed inspirations after a quick visit to the Yellowstone area? I tucked the map into my pocket and headed for the main attraction, Old Faithful, the biggest and most reliant Geyser propelling its boiling waters high into the sky every ninety minutes. The famous old Geyser is one of many that occupy the south side of the park. Thoughtfully park officials have constructed a network of handy wooden boardwalks overlooking many of the bubbling Geysers or Geyser-land as Walt would have most probably called it.

'What time's the next eruption?' I enquired to the nearest park ranger.

'Well sir, the last one was twenty-eight minutes ago, so if my calculations are correct, which they usually are, sir, then the next one should be in exactly sixty-two minutes, sir,' the Ranger dutifully replied.

'Is that enough time to get to Morning Glory and back?' I said looking out into the distance to see if I could see the parks second most visited attraction.

'Well, sir, how fast do you walk?'

'Well I'm pretty fast, mate, although I am carrying a little extra baggage today,' I said giving Angie a cheeky wink.

'Yes sir, I understand, sir. If you hurry the lady up then you might just make it back in time, sir,' he knowingly nodded.

'Come on, girl,' I said turning to Angie. 'If you get your skates on we should catch the next showing.'

'Yes, dear, I'm doing my best,' she replied. 'You wanna try walking in these friggin' heels. I can't win, can I? I'm damned if I wear them and not sexy enough if I don't. There's just no pleasing you men is there?' she said while attempting to place her foot on the wooded panel without her heel slipping into one of the many grooves.

We hurried along the platform, stopping every few minutes to admire the bubbling mud pools and fiery geysers that were spouting up in every direction. A smiling Ranger greeted our arrival, huddled us together then proceeded to explain why the Morning Glory was so called. 'Hey, guys, the pool was originally called Morning Glory because its once striking sapphire colours were reminiscent of the Morning Glory flower. Sadly though folks, the natural whirlpool has turned a murky shade of green due to idiotic tourists thinking it was some kind of wishing well and clogging up its heated vents with rocks and coins,' he continued with a disgusted shake of the head.

'Hey, best put those quarters away, you naughty boy,' Angie giggled, provocatively rattling my pockets to alert the Ranger.

'Yeah alright, steady on dear, you trying to get me in trouble?' I said slapping her hand away.

The Ranger then went on to inform us that over the years the water temperature had dropped nearly 25% from an insanely hot 200 degrees to a just a burning hot 150 degrees. Now that may not sound much, but it's significant enough to kill off much of the bacteria that were responsible for the water's unique bluely colours. 'However, folks, don't be fooled into thinking you can now take a quick dip,' he continued. 'The water temperatures may have cooled ever so slightly, but the hot pools are still more then capable of killing a human or two. Over the years a total of twenty humans have been scalded to death, eighteen of which died in valiant yet ultimately vain attempts to rescue their poor little doggies who couldn't quite resist a quick dip into the inviting waters.'

'Silly mutts,' Angie muttered.

'And I was looking forward to donning on the old Speedos,' I smiled back.

Conscious of time, we tipped the Ranger and rushed back to catch the next eruption of old faithful. Although unfortunately every other person appeared to have the same idea and shuffling our way back through the human traffic was about as productive as a Friday afternoon joyride on the M25. We got about half way round when in the distance *and on time* Old Faithful erupted to a series of whoops and cheers from the excited crowds. Typical, we had a whole hour to prepare yet still managed to miss the showing. Regrettably though our strict time frame wasn't going to allow us to wait around for another showing, so we rejoined the ring road and headed anti clockwise towards Hayden's Valley, Yellowstone's very own Serengeti plains and grassy home to the last free roaming herds of bison in North America – and if you're really lucky you may even spot the occasional Grizzly as well. My previous concerns were now clearly evaporating as I desperately scanned the horizon in the hope that one would suddenly appear *from the comfort of the car of course.*

We lunched on the balcony of the Lake Yellowstone Hotel, and then paid a visit to Yellowstone's very own Grand Canyon in the north side of the park. In its own right the Grand Canyon of Yellowstone is a mightily impressive attraction. The flowing waterfalls and rocky terrain are an intriguing combination of Niagara Falls and the real Grand Canyon all rolled into one. The lower falls themselves are said to be twice the height of its more famous cousin over the Canadian border.

Keen to explore more, we ditched the car and took a hike along the canyon rim – whilst once again finding ourselves alone in the great American wilderness – just me, Angie and... 'What the bloody hell was that!' I shouted hearing a large twig cracking behind us. My heart racing as I turned round to see a small bird fluttering out from the leaves. *Phew!*

'James, it's getting dark can we go now please,' Angie demanded.

I looked around to assess the situation? *What on earth are we doing here? Where the hell does this path take us? And where the bleeding heck is everyone else?* It was amazing to think that only yesterday I thought it completely mad to be scouting around bear country, yet here we were twenty-four hours later faffing around the woods with only a muddy footpath for protection. What were we thinking?

'Right, let's get the hell out of here,' I insisted.

'About bloody time,' Angie replied.

And so our brief walk in the American wilderness came to an end. And in hindsight I'm thankful we got out in one piece, as only a few days later it was reported that three campers in the Yellowstone area were attacked as they slept. One of which, a middle-aged man was dragged over 25 feet from his tent and savaged to death by a mother and her two cubs. The incident made the national news. The women survivor describing the moment she was bitten. *'I screamed, he bit harder. I screamed harder, he continued to bite. I could hear my bones breaking. I told myself, play dead. I went totally limp. As soon as I went limp, I could feel his jaws get loose and then he let me go.'*

Yellowstone is full of campsites and despite the inherent dangers it's amazing how many of these camps are sold out during the summer months. We all take a risk when we venture out into the woods, somehow believing that if we stick to the trail we'll be safe. It seems madness to put yourself in such danger – but that's the thing about the backcountry, slowly but surely it sucks you into its immersing woody world. Enticed by its beauty and aroused by its danger there's just something about the American wilderness that makes the hairs on your neck stand up and take notice – and for a brief moment you really do feel truly alive once again.

The Grand Tetons

I recall several years ago picking up a copy of the *Sunday Times* Travel magazine from one of my local newsagents. Now it's not every day I get suckered into purchasing one of those all-singing, all-glossy magazines, but I seem to remember being drawn to this intriguing image of a lonesome cowboy directing his cattle as the fading sun sank below the jagged, shark tooth mountains in the background. It was such a raw, iconic image and perhaps one of the finest depictions of the American West I had ever seen. For there he was, this strapping young cowboy sitting bolt upright upon this stallion of a horse, one hand holding the reins, the other holding a rolled-up cigarette as the early evening shadows drew a long and lingering presence over the darkening valley. It really was a magnificent picture and left me wondering what it must have been like to be riding alongside that lonesome, rugged cowboy. Now here I was years later driving south out of Yellowstone, most probably down the very stretch of road where that cowboy once rode, watching in awe as the sun dipped below the magnificent mountains of the Grand Teton National Park. It truly was a wonderful experience.

'James, will you concentrate on the bloody road please!' Angie shouted in my ear.

'Sorry, darling. I can't take my eyes off them,' I responded referring to the imposing peaks that dwarfed the surrounding valley. 'They're just... likeee... so beautiful...'

'Yeah alright, whatever darling, and when did you turn into such a nature loving hippy anyway?'

'I can't help it they're just incredible, aren't they?' I said looking to my right once again.

'It's getting late, James, so you can stop milking those bloody mountains and concentrate on getting us home please. We're in the middle of friggin' nowhere, you know!'

'Yeah, Ok babes, I heard you. You haven't seen any cowboys riding around have you?'

'No, James, I haven't.'

'Perhaps they've all finished for the day and hit the saloons up in Jackson Hole,' I said pointing to the flickering lights in the distance.

'Maybe they have? Maybe they haven't? But quite frankly my dear...'

'Yes, Angie, I know you couldn't give a damn,' I interrupted. 'But this is proper cowboy country, you know. They may have even filmed your favourite film out here?'

'And what's that then, my darling?' Angie smiled, sensing what was coming.

'Don't you play dumb with me girl you know the one I'm referring to. *Did You Hear About the Morgan's?* I think it was called? The one with your best mate in?'

Her smile broadened as the penny dropped.

'What is it with you girls anyway? Why do you all love Sarah Jessica Parker so much? Every character she plays is exactly the same – sad lonely girl forever searching for her Mr Right? Personally I think she's a bit of a loser if you ask me?' I added with a shake of the head.

'Yes, well I haven't asked you, have I, darling, so you can keep your opinions well and truly to yourself and just concentrate on getting us home please.'

It was understandable why she was so keen we drive home. It was only moments earlier I had belatedly informed her we had to cross the Grand Teton Pass in order to get ourselves home. I have to say I too was a little concerned about crossing the mountains – with it being so late – but the opportunity to drive alongside the legendary Grand Tetons was just too good an opportunity to miss.

With time against us, we skipped through the cowboy town of Jackson, filled up with gas then headed for the mountain bypass. Fortunately our crappy little rental managed to summon just enough energy to chug its way over the mountains and lead us back into the farmlands of Idaho. The remainder of the journey was quiet, eerily quiet in fact; actually, it has to go down as one of the longest and loneliest night time drives I can ever remember. For the next sixty miles or so, our car cut a lonely swathe through some of the most desolated farmlands of rural Idaho. It was so dark you could barely see the road, the only lights to be seen were the occasional spooky headlight creeping up behind in my rearview mirror. It was times like this I wish I'd never ever watched the film *The Hitcher* as even when the nightmares subsided, the fear of being hunted down and cut into pieces by a psychopathic lunatic will forever haunt me. One car in particular tailed us for some time. Cautiously I slowed to let it pass, sensing the piercing eyes of a stranger peering back though the side of my window.

It was close to midnight when we finally rolled into a lifeless Rexburg.

'Well done baby, you did us well,' Angie commented. 'Time for bed I reckon.'

'You're not wrong there, babe,' I said pulling up into the car park, glad to have survived the ordeal.

I awoke the next morning feeling somewhat travel weary. After two long weeks of driving, we had finally completed our comprehensive tour of the Rockies. I opened my map, glanced across the laminated page, and traced my finger over the long bendy spine that dissected the huge continent. Looking at an American map will never be the same again. For what may often look like a gentle, meandering range of mountains on paper, is actually a mightily enormous, unforgiving, living breathing landscape entirely of its own nature. There are just some things in life you simply have to experience yourself to fully understand, and crossing the great backbone of America is most certainly one of them. I pondered for a while coming to a swift conclusion – *I conquered you, you bastard!*

It was now time to plan the next stage of our adventure. I sat on our bed for the next few hours, plotting every possible westward route. Another dilemma quickly presented itself. By now I was running on empty, so very much favoured heading south through the deserts of Utah, and then onto Vegas for some much-needed rest and relaxation. Angie, on the other hand, had suddenly found some new energy and was adamant that we should complete our crossing by rail.

'Come on James, we've come this far and it would be a shame not to finish what we started,' she insisted.

'I don't know, babe?' I sighed. 'We haven't stopped for weeks. We could be relaxing by a pool in a few days' time!'

'I can't believe you want to give up now. We're on the verge of doing something very few people ever get the chance to do and all you want to do is go and blow it for a game of friggin' cards! Are you some sort of idiot? You'll regret this, I know you will.'

And she was right, I would regret it. It would be a tragedy not to complete what we had started. To come this close only to give it all up at the final hurdle would have been ludicrous. A diversion to Vegas would almost certainly mean the end of the line for our railroad adventure. Why go through all the trouble of following the great westward trails if we weren't going to complete our mission in full. And what would I say to our future kiddies? *'Son... we nearly did it... we nearly followed the route to the old American west... but your mother got lazy and let us down!'*

And so it was settled. The next day we would phone the Amtrak to book ourselves onto the next available train from Salt Lake City to Sacramento, the heart of the Californian west and final destination for many a gold-digging cowboy.

Idaho

The next morning I passed Angie my laptop to complete what should have been the relatively simple task of booking our seats onto the next available train. Unfortunately it proved to be anything but simple, as what should have been a relatively straightforward task of picking a day and choosing your seat was sadly not the case. You see out west they reckon there's more chance of catching a fleeting UFO sighting than there is a passing Amtrak train. A little harsh perhaps, but with only one late night departure meandering out of Utah I was certainly in no mood to disagree. Now the midnight trains I could just about handle. Over the last few weeks we had become very accustomed to the ridiculous scheduling and despite sometimes living on the edge I'd somehow managed to convince Angie that it really was all part of the adventure. What I couldn't stomach was the fact we had splashed out over $1,500 on a rail pass that still couldn't guarantee us a seat – quickly learning that the Amtrak had these crazy rules where only a set amount of pass holders were allowed to board each train at any given time. Rather typically then it was just our luck that the next few trains had already reached their quota and we now had to pay an additional admin fee to secure our seats.

'If they think we're paying an extra 25 bucks then they can go shove it where the sun don't shine, my friend!' Angie immediately declared.

'Alright dear, calm down,' I said shielding her from the mouthpiece. 'I'm not happy with it either but we'll just have to wait my friend.'

Feeling robbed and cheated we were left with little option but to book ourselves onto the next available quota free train.

Unfortunately this also meant hanging around Rexburg for another couple of days, which wasn't exactly one of the most exciting places we'd ever been to. So with nothing better to do we agreed to do something we should have done a long time ago and catch up on some much-needed chores. Once again our trusted chain of Residence Inn's didn't let us down. The onsite laundry facilities were certainly very convenient, but perhaps even more impressive was the brand spankingly new basketball court in which they had recently built alongside it. A handy distraction we both agreed, as all we now had to do was unload our washing, collect a ball from reception and throw in a few cheeky hoops while we waited for our washing to finish.

Which brings me on to another enigma: American sports. Now to the vast majority of the outside world, American sports are a tad bewildering to say the least – and I was very much of the same opinion – but after being exposed to nothing else but ESPN for the last couple of months, I was now in a position to reconsider my opinion and submit my half term report on all sports American.

Baseball. D-
Quite simply this is one sport I will never understand. It may have history and all that, but any sport that calls its national finals a World Series event where only one country participates seriously has an identity complex. And yes, I'm sure it can be argued that the winning team is the best in the world... but quite frankly, who gives a shit. I was once the

school champion of Kingy so does that make me a world champion as well then? Maybe I should disclose that on my CV and note the strange looks I get from prospective employers as they read down my list of sporting achievements. 'So, Mr. Taylor, world champion of Kingy, hey? Are you sure about that, sir?'

And for those of you who don't remember what Kingy was all about? Well, shame on you. Tennis balls? Squares? King, Queen, Jack, Nut? Special gloves to help you skimmer the ball across the surface to knock out your opponent? Oh, the memories of the playground.

NASCAR Racing. F-
NASCAR racing is just a crappy version of Formula One, so the least said the better.

American Football. B-
American football is ok, actually I kinda like it. Watching them chuck those Hail Mary throws from one end of the field to the other is really quite exciting. Gridiron as some like to call it, is considered the national game by some distance, it's just a shame no other country in the world can be friggin' arsed to play it. But then again you can hardly blame us really, when you consider an average NFL season lasts barely a third of the year. If they can't be bothered to play it properly, then why the hell should we?

Soccer. D-
Soccer? Football? whatever they wanna call it. Don't get me started on that one!

Basketball B+
Now basketball on the other hand was one sport I was beginning to take more than a passing interest in. The common perception back home is that one team gets the ball, runs up the other end and scores. Other team gets the ball, runs up the other end and scores. Which is kinda true, but despite the ridiculously high scoring there are two things I

have grown to admire about the sport. First, the home team nearly always wins. I have absolutely no idea as to why but even the most formidable teams can turn into quivering wrecks when playing on an opponent's court. And secondly, there always has to be a winner. So if it's a tie after four quarters then overtime has to be played until someone bags a winner. Therefore, not only is every game an enjoyable contest to watch, it is also *the* game to wager the occasional flutter on. And may I add unlike English football, where the home favourite can often infuriatingly slip you up – 'Arsenal 0 Coventry City 0' – in basketball this rarely happens, every 'home banker' really is a home banker and there can surely be no greater desire to cheer on a team when you've got a few easy quid riding on it.

The truth was I'd never felt more American than I did right then, surging past Angie and shooting some hoops on that empty basketball court. 'Watch this, Angie,' I shouted as I demonstrated my newly discovered running jump shot, slam dunk move that I had recently honed to perfection.

'Yeah, that's really great, baby. I think the washing's nearly done?' she replied clearly not in the slightest bit interested. Women can be so cutting sometimes, can't they?

Domestics sorted we headed into town to pass away the rest of the afternoon. Not that there was much to do, the town of Rexburg was hardly the beer swilling, door swinging saloon town in which we had driven through the night before in Jackson. Much to my disgust we couldn't even locate one drinking establishment in what was quite possibly the dullest Main Street we had encountered so far.

'Right, Angie, swear you'll never ever let me book a hotel in another Mormon town ever again. You promise me that?'

'Yes, dear, if you say so, but why are you so suddenly desperate for a drink? It's not even midday yet,' she smiled back.

'Well there's nothing else to bloody do is there!' I shrugged.

'Look there's a grocery store up the road... and also a hairdresser. You could do with a bloody good tidy,' she smiled, looking at my hair.

For the record, my haircut in Rexburg was my first and only haircut of the trip. It's a strange thing when travelling but for some reason you always seem to remember the place you got your first haircut in. Thing is I've never really liked getting my haircut anyway. It's always one of those jobs I've tended to put off. I'm not sure what's worse? Smiling uncomfortably in the mirror for twenty minutes as you stare back at your chubby chins *it must be the way they tie up that apron?* Or being subjected to the usual barrage of mindless conversation the hairdressers usually churn out. Personally I couldn't give two monkeys if they have to work every Saturday, are forced to take every second Tuesday off, or it gets really busy in the lead up to a Christmas. I just wish they'd all stop bloody moaning and get on with the job in hand.

We entered the salon and within a few moments I quickly realised how naive and sheltered the majority of these small-town folk were.

'Hello, sweetie, my name's Joannnnnnaaaaa and what can I do you for, Mr?' the young hairdresser said directing me to my chair.

'Can you shave it all over please?' I said looking at my overgrown mop. 'A grade 2 on the sides and a grade 3 on top should do it.'

'Err ok, honey? If you insist?' the young lady replied, scratching her head.

'Everything ok?' I asked

'Err yeah I guess? I've just never had a request like that before?'

'Really? You're kidding, right? What do they normally ask for around here then?'

'It varies, I guess? Some like it kinda spiky on the top and longer at the back.'

'Ahhhh, as in a mullet? Seen a few of those around here, haven't we, darling,' I said looking at Angie's smiling reflection in the mirror.

'A mallet? Sorry, sweetie, never heard of one of those. What in God's name is a mallet?' she replied, now completely baffled.

'It's what you just described. Short at the front and long at the back. It was very big back in the eighties,' I chuckled.

'Oh, I get yer... As in hockey hair.'

'Hockey hair?'

'Like the ice hockey players. Folks sure love their hockey hair around here. Yes sireeeee!' she smiled, now fully on board.

Yes, it was far to say my new found friend wasn't the sharpest tool in the box. This was further confirmed a few minutes later when I innocently asked her what the state capitol was.

'Err oh my goodness. I should know that, right? It's been a while since I've been outta this town, honey. Tina, what's the capital of Idaho, sweetie?' she said, shouting to her friend.

'I dunno, honey?' Tina replied. 'It's that funny one, ain't it?'

It is fair to say neither of them had a clue as to what or where indeed their state capitol was. In their very own words, they didn't get out much, but then Idaho isn't exactly blessed with an abundance of places to visit either. On last count there were only five towns where the population exceeded 50,000. Compare that to the 200 or so towns in Britain then you begin to appreciate just how sparse things can be out west. Our day in Rexberg will never go down as the most eventful one we'd ever experienced, but it did at least offer a fascinating insight in how the majority of Americans live out their daily lives – rarely venturing afar while living in total oblivion to the outside world. Bless them.

Our Rocky Mountain adventure was now officially complete. We packed our bags and drove south to another Residence Inn in the heart of Salt Lake City – where we would wait until evening before catching our overnight train to Sacramento, in what would be the penultimate leg of our railroad adventure. Saying goodbye to the car was never going to be easy, especially out west where the wide-open spaces tended to lend themselves towards the open road rather than the rail. Not that I didn't enjoy the train but the car was made for the west and nothing compared to driving down an empty highway towards that never-ending horizon. Sometimes there is just that sense of freedom that you can only ever experience in a car. Although I must confess the stunning views weren't the only thing grabbing our attention – the extensive array of roadside diners were proving to be a very welcome distraction indeed.

'Oh look baby, there a Denny's over there. Shall we get ourselves some kwoffee?' Angie would say in her best New Yorker accent.

'No, no wait, look at that!' I would eagerly reply pointing to a branded billboard. *'There's an Applebee's, two miles ahead. I fancy some chicken tonight,'* I would say clucking my arms like a fool.

'Cracker Barrel alert!' she would say while patting her stomach.

And so the jovial banter continued. Every time we passed a town we would turn into excitable kids as we marvelled at the vast array of eateries that can be found along the American highway. To this day I still wonder why we both got so galvanised by the sight of these large roadside billboards. One thing was for sure though, the food was cheap, plentiful, absolutely delicious and I would challenge anyone to find a better value for money option than there is to be found in an American roadside diner. But as much as I loved the freedom and food of the road, the main reason I was reluctant to give up the car was the security it offered. Venturing into the unknown never feels quite as terrifying when you're safely locked away in the cocoon of a car controlling your own destiny – and the thought of compromising again on our security whilst hanging around another dimly lit station was hardly the most appealing one on the menu right now.

It was approximately quarter to eleven when we departed the hotel to walk the last few blocks towards Grand Union station. An easy journey on paper, although little did we know it was going to be another long and very challenging evening ahead.

The West

Way Out West

And so we headed west, where once again we would join the Californian Zephyr to embark on what many consider to be one of the most beautiful journeys of all – watching from the comfort of your carriage as the railroad cuts a swathe through the old American West. It was going to be another epic journey. Departing at midnight, we would pass over the great Salt Plains of Utah, before entering the desolated scrublands of northern Nevada. Once through Reno we would begin the long ascent over the majestic Sierra Nevada Mountains, the highest range in the lower forty-eight states, then onwards to California and ending our journey in the golden cornfields of the Sacramento valley. But first we had the little matter of waiting for our train to arrive.

So with nowhere to go and absolutely nothing to do we had little choice but to decamp at a nearby Residence Inn, a few blocks north of the Salt Lake City railway station.

It was close to eleven when I eventually shuffled out of my chair and asked the receptionist, 'Is it safe to be walking around this time of night?'

'Yes, sir, it's completely safe,' she replied. 'It's only a short walk to the station. You'll be absolutely fine,' she smiled.

'I told you we will be fine,' a familiar voice blurted from behind. 'You never listen to me, do you?'

'I don't know, darling? Why don't we just call a cab? It is getting a bit late don't you think?' I said still not entirely convinced.

'Oh, come on James, it's not exactly the Bronx out there, is it now? What are they gonna do? Demand we hand over our Bibles? Keep it real for Pete's sake!' Angie laughed much to the amusement of the receptionist.

'Fine, we'll do it your way darling. But don't come crying to me if...'

'Yeah yeah, you do bang on, don't you, James? We'll be fine. Look, even the receptionist thinks you're being a big girl's blouse!' Angie giggled, clearly delighted I had succumbed to her reason.

Assured it was perfectly safe, we set off only to immediately stumble upon Salt Lake's very own equivalent to *woe betide* the bloody Bronx! Out of all the places in this apparently safe and Godly-like city we had managed to come across the only street where the local cops refused to patrol. A tremor of fear alerted me to immediate danger in which we now found ourselves in. On one side of the street sat the druggies rolling their papers around a makeshift campfire, while on the other, the twitchy no good-for-nothing loafers lurked in the shadows with dangerous intent. A hushed silence fell upon us. Turning back was no longer an option as our path was now completely blocked by a gang of tricky youths.

'Right, that's the last time I listen to you, Angie,' I murmured under my breath.

'Oh, bugger off, James,' Angie shouted down the street. 'It was your idea to take us down this fucking hole in the first place, you idiot! What was wrong with the main road?'

Days of pent up frustration suddenly spilled out into the streets.

214

'Oh shut it, woman. If you weren't such a bloody airhead we would have got a taxi and be safely at the station now!' I roared back.

'Yeah and if you could read a map properly we wouldn't bloody be here right now, would we?' she screeched at the top of her voice.

'Fuck you!' I said giving her the big birdie. 'Not my idea, Angie!'

Angie glared at me nostrils flaring. Never before had I wanted to wring that little neck so much. What a sight we must have looked shouting and screaming, blaming each other for our misfortune – which in hindsight may well have been our saving grace. For I can only assume our deranged outburst must have confused the hell out of them. You see, not one person approached us, enquired about the time, or sought dodgy directions to the station that evening. But then no one likes a madman, do they? You're never quite sure what you're gonna get? A valuable lesson learnt though nevertheless. And I can tell you now the next time I find myself in a spot of bother I certainly won't have any hesitation in randomly twitching out my arms, crossing my eyes and squaring up to the invisible fucker standing next to me.

Anyway, to much of our relief we turned the corner to see the huge neon sign of Grand Union Station shining brightly before us. Somewhat regrettably though, the once mighty railroad station had long since been converted to a museum. In its place a rusty outdoor bus shelter lay in wait for disgruntled Amtrak passengers. Not exactly the most pleasant place to be waiting for your midnight train; therefore, it left us with little option but to take refuge in the adjoining Greyhound bus station. Now I naturally was a tad apprehensive about the Greyhound. My only previous experience being a gruelling eight-hour journey sat alongside a bunch of agitated prison convicts through the American Deep South. Hardly the best introduction to the Greyhound, and within moments of entering the station I was immediately reminded why I'd previously sworn never to chance it again. For reasons unbeknown the Greyhound brand always seems to attract the more unscrupulous members of American society, and tonight was no exception. We found a bench and almost immediately felt a disturbing presence hovering from behind. I leaped from my seat to see a crazed loon staring back at me, eyes glazed, clutching a black bin liner barely a yard from my head.

'You alright?' I nodded, wandering what the hell was in *that* bin liner!

'Ex... ex... excuse sir, is there likkkkkeeee any sec... sec... security around here?' he stuttered

'I sincerely fucking hope so!' I quipped back.

'Wh... wh you saaaaayyyyy?'

'I said I dunno, mate,' I replied, crossing my eyes and twitching my arms wildly.

The man held his gaze for an uncomfortable moment before turning his back to another couple sitting behind me. Fearing the worst I remained standing, eyes firmly fixed on his wandering hands ready to intercept at any given moment.

A few minutes later a woman in security piled through the double glass doors.

'C'mon Edward, I told you not to disturb the passengers. I've made your bed up over there,' she said, pointing to the collection of pillows she had hastily put together on the far side of the corridor. Poor guy was homeless and that bin liner I was so scared of was the entire contents of his sole possessions. Did I feel bad for being so judgemental; however, the reality of the situation is that you can never be so sure. Barely a few minutes later another man entered the waiting room, but unlike Edward before, this fellow was clearly up to no good, pacing the area for any unguarded luggage. I remained standing. One eye on my rucksack, the other firmly on the little fucker who had now sat himself down on the adjoining bench. *I'm watching you, you little shit!* Although he seemed to get the hint, quickly moving on to harass another couple.

It was well after one when the train eventually rolled into the station and in all my years I'd never seen a group of weary

216

people leap up so quickly from their slumber. It was certainly a relief to be on board that was for sure. What the Amtrak may lack in official security, it more than makes up by employing the meanest looking bunch of train guards you will ever have the fortune to meet. Behaviour on the train is therefore immaculate and any disturbances are swiftly dealt with onboard – while their tough, no nonsense, take no shit philosophy is wholly admirable. Maybe they've overloaded on too many Westerns and think they're expressmen escorting a cache of gold? Or perhaps it's something more deep-rooted? Like a natural instinct inherited from their railroad ancestors *'Must protect the train!'* but more fool you if you think you're getting away without paying for your ticket, a good slap at the back of the carriage being a far more likely outcome. It's not called the Wild West for nothing, you know.

The train pulled out of the station and drifted on its way. Tales of the Old West had always fascinated me. To be an expressman back in the day was perhaps one of the most dangerous jobs of them all. Charged to protect the cargo, they were the only ones on board who knew the combination to the safe. They were fiercely patriotic and would often end up sacrificing their own lives rather than giving up the code. However, with the advent of dynamite their resistance would likely be in vain; bandits would simply blow up the safe to retrieve the hidden treasures. Famous train robbers included Jessie James, Butch Cassidy and the Sundance Kid, but perhaps the most notorious of the time were the Reno Brothers. These guys were the first bunch of bandits to successfully rob a moving train. Not contented with that honour, they went on to officially hold the record for the first three train robberies ever recorded in American history. It was these daring heists that bought them worldwide notoriety inspiring a string of copycat robberies across the American West. Their fame though was somewhat short-lived, as despite netting their largest ever haul in the summer of 1868, they couldn't evade the advancing forces of the Pinkerton's, a private army hired by the State to hunt them down. Within a few months all had been captured, imprisoned and eventually killed.

The story of the Reno Brothers fascinates me because it encapsulates the westward spirit of the time – new frontiers, daring robberies, hired muscle, and of course the never-ending gun battles that would undoubtedly follow. Like many of these great western tales, the events have subsequently been played out in numerous movies. In 1953 a rising young singer auditioned for his first movie role and was given the part of Clint Reno, the youngest member of the gang. The movie was originally to be named *The Reno Brothers* but at the last minute the name was changed due to the supporting actor's debut single sweeping to the top of the charts. The new title would be called *Love Me Tender* in what would be Elvis Presley's first major motion picture. I closed my eyes and pondered for a while, remembering our recent time in Graceland – his house, his cars, his suits, everything... and how it all gets left behind.

Nevada

I awoke the next morning to discover we had crossed the state line into the deserts of Nevada. It was the strangest of places. To my left, and no more than a few car lengths apart, lay the empty highway of I-80. Nothing else just a barren Interstate and ageing railroad travelling in unison through the endless miles of rocky terrain. For the next few hours I would look out my window watching the occasional car pass us by. I was glad to be on the train that was for sure. We may have been the slower of the two, but it wouldn't have been much fun breaking down in this forgotten outpost. In Northern Nevada, towns are a premium. Apart from Reno on the Californian border I couldn't recall any other we passed that day, so insignificant they all must have been. It's fair to say that the I-80 is a very lonely road, but believe it or not there are lonelier roads in America. That honour officially goes to Route 50, a parallel highway a couple of hours south from where we were now travelling.

The Nevada stretch is particularly lonely. Dubbed by *Life* magazine as 'the loneliest road', travellers were advised not to venture out unless they possessed suitable survival skills. Down there it really is another world and for over 300 miles you'll see nothing else but sagebrush, mountains and endless miles of barren scrubland. Signs of civilisation are few and far between and in the land of vastness, Jerry Cans suddenly becomes the order of the day. When leaving the town of Eureka in northern Nevada, you are advised to stock up as you won't pass another one until you reach the navel outpost of Fallon Station some 200 miles later. It was indeed down this lonely stretch of expanse that the Pony Express cemented its place in Western folklore. Operating out of Missouri on the frontier borders, riders were enlisted to carry mail across the deserts on horseback to Sacramento, the newly formed capitol of California. Prior to this it would have taken a stagecoach weeks to cross the country. The introduction of the Pony Express changed all this, revolutionising frontier communication and cutting travel times to less than ten days. The job itself was considered highly dangerous. If the inhospitable terrain wasn't challenging enough, then the regular confrontations with rogue Indians most certainly were. Ambushes were frequent, leaving riders with little choice but to shoot their way out of trouble. There cannot be too many careers that come with the following job description as was once advertised in a local paper:

'Wanted young skinny wiry fellows not over 18. Must be expert riders and willing to risk death daily. Orphans preferred.'

It was exactly noon when we passed through the gambling town of Reno. A clutch of high risers suddenly appearing on the desert horizon – and quite frankly the thought of hitting the self-proclaimed 'Biggest little city in the world' was more than a little appealing.

'I know what you're thinking, Jamie,' Angie whispered into my ear. 'And it ain't going to happen. So you can hold your wild horses and wait until Vegas before you completely blow all our money away!'

'Come on, baby, just a little flutter, it won't hurt anyone. We may even get lucky?' I smiled.

'Yes, James, and more than likely we probably won't. These grand palaces you see before you weren't built on kind donations, you know?'

I stared back blankly.

'And besides, we haven't budgeted for this. If we lose all our money now, the rest of the holiday will be ruined!' she continued.

It was hard to argue in the face of such reason. So reluctantly I said my goodbyes to Reno wondering what might have been.

We continued westwards and were soon ascending into the Sierra Nevada Mountains, the final hurdle before reaching the promised land of California. A short while later the conductor summoned the first group of lunchers into the dining cart. Being our penultimate ride we had decided to splash out and book ourselves a top table overlooking the mountains.

'Ahh look baby, they've got white table cloths on all the tables,' Angie smiled, pointing gleefully around.

'Yes, darling, how civilised and look they've even been so kind as to provide us with forks so we don't have to eat like savages,' I smiled back.

'Don't be getting smart with me, buster. It's not my fault you've got a gambling problem!'

'Me, a gambler? Never! I should sue you for slander, my dear. And besides, what would my boss say to such vicious and unproven rumours?'

'Sweetie, you ain't got a boss. You're unemployable, remember,' Angie giggled.

'Yes, darling, thanks for that, rub it in why don't you.'

The waiter ushered us to a table and presented us with menus.

'Bloody hell, have you seen these prices? Hope you've bought your credit card with you, girl?'

'No way, baby, this was your idea so you're treating me, my friend,' she said scanning the menu. 'Hmmmmm? Think I'll have the largest glass of red considering you're paying. You may get lucky tonight.' She winked.

'Yes, darling, and may I add that your negotiation skills are indeed very admirable. Ever thought of becoming a buyer for Tesco? You'd be a perfect edition to their charming buying team!' I replied, feeling for my wallet.

A wide smile beamed across Angie's face. Someone was clearly looking forward to her free lunch. I gazed out of my window towards the lakes below and found myself once again drifting into thought as the train chugged its way along the rim of Lake Donner. How ironic to be tucking into lunch from the comfort of our carriage, while only a century or so ago this intriguing spot was the exact site where forty ordinary people would ultimately starve to death, in a valiant but ultimately unsuccessful attempt to cross the snowy mountains. This tragic tale would later become known as the notorious Donner Party expedition and for its very scruples would catch the media attention of the world. Stranded in the high Sierras and at the outset of winter it took a rescue party over four months to reach the group's makeshift cabins. What they found shocked a nation and for the first time in living memory America had to deal with the dilemma of mass cannibalism. I guess the surviving members of the group had little other choice? Unlike the poor Donner Party a hundred years before, our journey through the high Sierras passed without incidence. The only choice we had to make was whether the warm chicken should be enjoyed best with a glass of red or a glass of white? Oh, how the world has changed.

It was early evening when we entered California's sun-kissed Central Valley. The green and fertile lands were such a pleasant contrast you could be forgiven for thinking we were once again rolling through the wide-open plains of the American Midwest. *So gold really does come in many guises!* Now I must confess that prior to our trip I'd known very little about Sacramento, actually it will be fair to say that I hadn't even heard of the place. If someone had asked me to name the capital of California, then like many others I would have hedged my bets and ignorantly plumped for either San Francisco in the north or LA in the south. Little did I know that Sacramento was once *the* thriving centre of the expanding west. It wasn't until we reached the mid-western town of Independence that I would actually learn of Sacramento's pivotal role in the development of the frontier. You see in 1848 at a place called Sutter's Mill, a small yet very significant discovery was made – gold. More discoveries would soon follow, with word quickly spreading of the fortunes to be found in and around the Californian Mountains. Situated on the confluence of two major river systems, Sacramento provided the perfect means to escort the gold, offering both an inlet to the mountains to extract it and an outlet to the Pacific to sell it. As a result the town prospered, quickly becoming the major stopping point to gather supplies. What was to follow was the biggest westward migration in American history. Excitement was at fever pitch and within a few years over 300,000 hopeful prospectors, known as the 49ers, would pass through Sacramento on their way to the mountain foothills. We chugged along for another hour passing numerous corn fields along the way. It was hard to believe such a fertile oasis still existed this far out west. And so after nearly two months of non-stop travelling it felt like we too had entered the homeward stretch – and so where better place to stop off than the epicentre of the old west and spiritual home to the great American Dream.

The Old Town

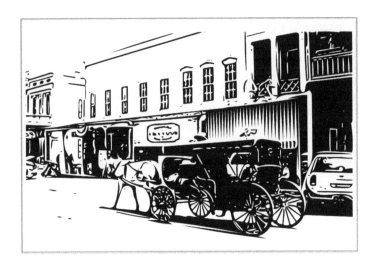

It was late afternoon when the train rolled into a shady Sacramento station. Outside it was as pleasant an afternoon as one could possibly wish for – the sun was shining, the temperature was high and every so often a cool breeze would flutter in the wind. Perfect and what a wonderful welcome to the Golden State it was too.

We departed the station, flagged down a taxi and on the driver's recommendation headed to a plush courtyard hotel on the other side of the river.

'I'm sorry sir, we are fully booked,' the lady on reception regrettably informed us upon our arrival.

'Oh wait, there's been a late cancelation. I have one room left, sir.'

'Well how about that then. What an amazing coincidence that turned out to be?' I smiled with a hint of sarcasm. 'Do you mind telling me how much it will cost to secure this very special room?'

'Well, sir, as I said it is our last room. Let me just check for you... *tap tap tap*... just give me one moment... *tap tap tap*... OK then... *tap tap tap*... yes, the best I can do is $279 a night. How many nights will you be staying, sir?' she said rather presumptively.

'Two hundred and seventy-nine bucks, are you sure? At that price not bloody many?' I said looking at Angie *the boss* for any kind of steer.

'I don't know, James? It's a bit expensive maybe we should look elsewhere?'

'It does come with a poolside room, sir,' the receptionist intervened.

'Sorry? Did you say poolside room? It actually comes with a poolside room you say?'

'Oh yes sir, right outside your room.'

'Oh, now you're just teasing me,' I said pausing to ponder. The thought of crawling straight from my bed and into a cool, refreshing pool was highly appealing. And besides I had just saved us a fortune by sensibly forgoing the temptations of Reno. Angie could easily have blown all our money on those Pokies. She does like a cheeky gamble that one.

'Done! We'll take it. Two nights please!' I said slamming my credit card on the counter.

'Good choice sir, you won't regret it,' the smiling lady nodded, sounding more and more like a skilled saleswomen with every comforting word.

Not wanting to miss out on the fine weather we grabbed a couple of beers, slid open our new patio doors and meandered through the long grass towards the pool. Perfect, well at least it was until I caught a glimpse of the two tattooed meatheads busily crunching cans of beers beside their sun loungers. Don't get me wrong I have absolutely nothing against meatheads, but given the choice I'd rather not have to engage in any polite conversation with them. Therefore it was only inevitable then that the uncomfortable silence be broken the moment we ventured into the pool.

'Hey, heard your accents, you guys Australi—' the larger of the two began.

'English, actually. We're from England,' I anticipated, slightly irritated.

'Oh wow, England. We sure love you English guys. What are you folk doing in Sacramento then?' he continued.

'Travelling, mate,' I responded. 'Quit our jobs and decided to come and explore your wonderful country.'

'Oh, cool, that's amazing,' he responded with a genuine interest.

'Well, you only live once I reckon. So why not, hey?' I said.

'Absolutely, my friend. If you get the chance you gotta go ahead and do it,' he replied.

'Nice to meet you. My name's James,' I said shaking his hand, already warming to his southern drawl.

'Hi, I'm Sean and my friend over there is Jacob. We're in the Marines,' he said, pointing towards his mate.

'Bloody hell, that's amazing!' I said still in a state of shock, amazed I was actually having a conversation with a real life Marine. The closest I'd ever been to a Marine was watching them get their sorry arses kicked in the Oscar winning film *Black Hawk Down* by a bunch of Somalian street kids!

'No worries my friend, anytime. We're just doing our job,' Sean replied.

It didn't take long for Angie to find an excuse to strip off. My only surprise was that it took her a whole five minutes to do so.

'Sure is hot here, fellas. Hi, my name's Angie,' she said, smile beaming, and eyes slightly glazed. She never could handle her drink much.

We spent the next hour sipping on beers, putting the world to rights and I have to say both men were extremely charming, if not also slightly mad!

'Yeah, Afghanistan can be pretty mental,' Jacob reiterated. 'The Taliban are clever little fuckers.'

'It's all about the law of engagement,' Sean chipped in. 'They know the rules and milk it for what it is worth,' he said, looking frustrated.

'I've heard they all pretend to be farmers,' I replied, pleased I was actually contributing something meaningful into the conversation.

'You're not wrong there, my friend. They come up close, plant their IEDs and the moment they're spotted they wave their little shovels around pretending to be noble citizens,' Sean continued. 'The law says we can't touch them. Rules of engagement – they have to shoot at us first.'

'That's outrageous. So even when you know they're up to no good you can't do anything about it?' I questioned.

'To make it worse they usually have a cameraman sitting in the mountains filming the whole fucking thing, just in case we do open fire,' Jacob said with a shake of the head.

'The cheeky little bastards. That's hardly bloody fair is it?' I said angrily.

'Yeah, it's a bummer, my friend, so sometimes we just shoot the guy filming instead. That usually does the trick,' he said with a devilish wink of his eye.

'Fair play, mate. I'm with you on that,' I smiled.

'Well I think Baghdad sounds like a nasty old place if you ask me,' Angie chipped in blissfully unaware she was referring to another war.

'Err... I wouldn't know ma'am, I've never fought in Iraaaaq,' Jacob politely replied.

'Well, whatever the war I'm so... so proud of you boys,' she stuttered, alcohol clearly having its effect. 'And I think we should all go out later to celebrate.'

'What we celebrating, dear?' I said smiling.

'Fr... fr... free... freedom,' she said, raising her glass above the pool.

And so we arranged to meet later that night. Only it was never going to happen. For all Angie's good intentions it was a sure fire banker she would be sleeping like a dog within the hour, and as much as I enjoyed their company the thought of hitting the town with a couple of nutcase Marines was absolutely terrifying.

We retreated back to our room and on cue Angela was away with the fairies the moment her head hit the pillow, leaving me the unenviable task of politely informing the Marines that we wouldn't be joining them for dinner. *Thanks Angie, knew I could rely on you, pal!*

The next day we hit the town in search of the Capitol Building. It wasn't too difficult to spot. Located smack bang in the centre of town, the domed rotunda cast was a striking resemblance to the one we had previously seen back in Washington. Finding a bench we sat in silence to admire its beauty.

'Do you think Arnie's around?' Angie questioned, referring to Arnold Schwarzenegger, the incumbent State Governor.

'I'm not sure, honey, think he lives in Hollywood, doesn't he?'

'Well that's a bloody let down then, isn't it? We've come all this way and he can't even be bothered to be here!'

'I don't think he's ever lived here, darling?' I said, vaguely remembering an article I had recently read.

'Well so much for false promises, Mr. *"I'll be back"* cos he clearly wasn't referring to Sacramento, was he, babe? Couldn't wait to get the hell out of here, I reckon!' she ranted rather irrationally.

'No dear, clearly not,' I said, still laughing at what was quite possibly the worst Arnie impression I could ever remember. 'But you can hardly blame him, can you, darling? It's not exactly LA around here, is it?' I replied noticing the surrounding streets bore about as much life as my beloved Arsenal's new multi-million pound football stadium back home in London. You can hear a pin drop in that place, what with it being so bleeding quiet. It's no wonder why rival fans mockingly refer to it as 'the library'.

Downtown Sacramento was clearly lacking something as well, but I couldn't quite put my finger on it? Couple of decent shops perhaps? A few bars maybe? Christ, even a few grumpy office workers skulking around the neighbourhood wouldn't have gone a miss. Anything to break the eerie silence; it was supposed to be the capital city after all. I was about to give up on Sacramento, when in the corner of my eye I noticed a brown sign saying 'old town'.

'Come on darling, let's give this a try,' I said pointing to the sign.

A few minutes later we found ourselves in the old town and what an unexpected gem of a discovery it turned out to be. Once the thriving centre of the American West, then left to rot for decades, Sacramento was once known as '*the worst skid row outside of Chicago*'. Things changed in the 1960s when an extensive restoration program radically transformed the old town back to its former glories. Today the old town is effectively an outdoor museum dedicated to all things west. The historic district still boasts many original buildings, but the majority have been either remastered or revamped, leaving you with the feeling that you've once again entered into another Disney interpretation of the Wild West. Few could argue that the *new* old town is much more 'Frontier-land' then the authentic Wild West – its polished floors and freshly painted wooden sidewalks surely bare little original resemblance. But I didn't care, Frontier-land was always my favourite one anyway and Angie was just pleased to fling open a bar door and strut her stuff like she was some sort of bad ass cowgirl.

We ambled around the streets checking out the tacky western gifts, but the highlight of the day was definitely our visit to the old town museum.

To be brutally honest I was never one for museums. All those boring school trips to the Victoria & Albert Museum in central London had seriously put me off. In hindsight I can only assume that the museum's curator must have really hated kids, as what other miserable bastard would insist in showcasing his finest Tudor ruffs behind an impenetrable glass fortress in the first place? What's the fun in that, hey? What's the point of having a museum if you can't have a little touchy feel with the ancient artefacts? The only thing I used to look forward to on our annual pilgrimage to London was tucking into my mother's penny-pinching jam sandwiches on the bus journey home.

A Western museum on the other hand is an entirely different proposition altogether – as barring the odd gold nugget or loaded revolver, everything else is completely up for grabs. If wagons are your thing, then go right up for a feel, my friend. Ever fancied a fur trader's hat? Then why not go and give it a good old stroke. Old torches, coins, pickaxes it's all there, you can even go and read a dozen or so articles written by folk from the moving wagons themselves.

Now that's a proper learning experience and in the past few weeks I'd learnt more of the westward trails then I had in a lifetime of reading books back home. Walking around the museum also gave me a little time to reflect upon our own westward journey. Somewhere along the line we had been lucky enough to stumble upon the trail, visiting three of the major westward museums along the way. The first in Independence, the famous tipping point to the west, the second in Santa Fe, one of the main frontier trading routes, then finally and somewhat fittingly ending up in Sacramento's historic district next to the old Pacific railroad – end of the line for some, but hopeful beginning for so many. On reflection the museum in Sacramento was perhaps my favourite of them all. Its stories of the Californian gold rush were particularly captivating. Not only were there crinkled old maps showing you where to find the gold, there was ancient footage telling you how to extract it. In the early days it was basically a free-for-all, the lucky buggers could literally sieve it up from the river it was so plentiful. More sophisticated measures were soon needed though, the firing of water cannons into the side of the mountains being the most common method. The introduction of the 'Sluice' quickly followed, which was basically a man-made channelling system used to catch the watery debris on its slippery descent – while eventually dynamite would have to be used to extract the nuggets from deep within the mountain itself.

We ambled around learning of the flash floods that so nearly wiped out the city, but as fascinating as it was I found myself wandering back and forth to the gold rush exhibition located on the second floor. I stood there for a while casting my eyes over the golden trinkets that lay on display. The watches, the bracelets, the golden tooth plucked from a dead man's jaw. Only now was I truly beginning to understand the westward fever from all those years ago.

The next day we caught the westward train for the final time. In a few hours' time we'd hit the west coast of San Francisco and would have officially crossed the continent by rail. It may not have had the uncertainties of the past but even today it still represented a major accomplishment. The sad thing is that few people ever really get the chance to undergo such a journey. They either don't have the time or in most cases the desire to undertake such a challenge. Why go through all the hassle of crossing it when you can just fly over it instead? In truth we hadn't exactly planned it either, but the further we progressed the more it seemed the right thing to do. Our railroad experience across the American continent had taught me one thing: Travelling is more then a book, a map, or a set of directions, more a common desire to follow a path and go explore a land you never knew existed.

It was only a short journey from Sacramento but as the train rolled into eyeshot of the Golden Gate Bridge a strange sense of anti-climax came upon me. It was difficult to explain. Here we were on the verge of completing a journey that very few people ever get the chance to do, yet here I was filled with a bewildering sense of emptiness, not a heroic euphoria as one might have expected. My mood probably wasn't helped by the fact that we weren't technically in San Francisco, but in Oakland, its rather less glamorous sister town on the other side of the bay. Although it was more than that – as even though we'd only just arrived it somehow felt like the beginning of the end of our long and fabulous westward adventure. You see that's the thing about travelling, the best bit is always the getting there bit, the in-between bit, the journey itself. You know where you are, you know where you're going but you have absolutely no idea what or who you're going to meet along the way. But once you get there it's a whole different story.

As our train slowed into Emeryville station I looked at the sun setting below the derelict high-rises and an unnerving thought crossed my mind. *What the hell we gonna do now?*

San Francisco

There are three reasons why we travel to new places.
The first is to learn of the historic events that shaped what
exists today. The second is to experience a place's cultural
vibe, to see the sights, hear the sounds, and to gain a better
understanding of how its people live today. While the third is
our overwhelming desire to seek out new opportunities in the
hope of a more prosperous and successful return.

Right that's enough of the philosophical bullshit. Clearly I'd
been spending far too much time staring through rose-tinted
carriage windows of late. However, the fact remained, we
now needed a new plan, a plan that would allow us the
freedom and flexibility to explore the west, but also a plan to
get us home and on our flight in a little under three weeks'
time. I unfolded my map and began to plot a path through the
Californian west.

'Right, James, I think we should go to Calgary, Montreal,
Quebec and we gotta do Niagara Falls?' Angie said looking
over my shoulder.

'What the...? Babe, I thought we discussed this already? That will take ages to do and there's still so much to see here in America. We've barely even set foot in California yet!' I replied, somewhat alarmed.

'Yes, I know, James, but Kate did insist we must go to Canada, and you promised me back in Denver, don't forget!'

'I know darling, but this is *our* holiday remember! I'm sure Canada is lovely but what you're proposing will take us weeks to cover and we've only got a few left,' I replied, sensing some kind of compromise was needed.

'There you again James, always trying to talk me out of what I want to do.'

'No, it's not that babe, but there's still so much more to do here. Ok how about this then. We focus on America for the time being, then give ourselves enough time, maybe a couple days at the end to check out Montreal and Quebec if you like?'

'Mmmmm... I guess that sounds ok. But we're definitely going to Canada this time. No more excuses, buster! Oh, I'm so bloody good to you, Jamie. I really hope you appreciate how wonderful I am? There's not too many like me, you know!'

'Yes, darling, one in a million I reckon. How did I ever get so lucky?' I replied.

'I don't know, Jamie? Reckon you must have caught me on a bad day. Think I must have felt sorry for you?' Angie replied, affectionately kissing my cheek.

We spent the rest of the evening plotting the next few weeks' activities from the comfort of our hotel room. Tomorrow we would drive into San Francisco and be done with Oakland forevermore. After San Francisco, we'd head north up through the wine valleys then into the Redwoods. After that, we'd head back south along the coastal road to LA. Time would be tight so depending on the mood we'd hit either San Diego in the far south or the desert town of Palm Springs, before finally arriving in Vegas for the big blow out. Oh, and we couldn't come all this way without a quick detour to the Grand Canyon – so that would have to be squeezed in somewhere, before catching our flight east in a little over two weeks' time.

The next day we collected our Jeep and crossed the iconic Golden Gate Bridge into San Francisco. A moment I'd never forget, although not for the glorious memory of passing over one of the seven wonders of the modern world but for the simple reason we couldn't see a bleeding damn thing, barring a thick layer of cloudy fog. And as for all those familiar panoramic images of a bright red bridge basking under deep blue skies? Well I can only assume they must all be taken in the month of September, as for the rest of the year the Bay area is permanently covered under an impenetrable layer of white fog that has slowly drifted in from the Atlantic. They say San Francisco is America's natural air vent and looking at the size of my rapidly expanding goose bumps I was in no mood to disagree.

There are apparently two reasons for the city's famous fog. The first is San Francisco's unique geographical position – where the warm sea winds of the west coast collide with the chilly waters of the Bay. Now chemistry was never my thing, but according to experts, when the two collide a natural layer of chilly fog is immediately created. Just to rub it in, all the other areas in the surrounding valley are constantly basked in glorious sunshine. Unfortunately for the sun lovers of San Francisco, this hot air in the surrounding valleys is constantly rising, leaving behind a massive pressurised vacuum that literally sucks the fog into its void, covering much of San Francisco in its path. As a result, wind speeds on the bridge itself can reach 100 mph, with Bay waters often dipping well below freezing. Temperatures in the area can be so cold that even the ever-optimistic Mark Twain once commented *That the coldest winter he ever spent was the summer he spent in San Francisco*!

All things considered it comes as no surprise that some bright spark in the 1930s thought it a wise idea to convert the military fort of Alcatraz into a maximum security prison. *Yes, they may be mad, but they can't be that mad, can they?* And so for the next thirty years the island known as The Rock proved inescapable even for the likes of the great Al Capone. Incidentally, in the island's brief time as a federal prison there were over thirty daring escape attempts, although official reports suggest no man ever found his way to freedom. Most were either recaptured, shot dead, or lost at sea in the freezing waters never to be seen again. So it is hardly the ideal location for your next all-inclusive beach holiday then?

Not to be disheartened by the familiar conditions we continued inland when a random school memory crossed my mind. There I was sitting in class flicking through an old geography textbook, when I came across a set of intriguing images depicting the massive earthquake that nearly obliterated the city many years ago. I couldn't have been more then twelve at the time but I remember thinking what sort of crazy person would want to live in such a place. Who in their right mind would live in a city that literally paved over the cracks of the earth? More fool them. I would later learn that *that* earthquake was *the big one* of 1906 that nearly wiped out three quarters of the city, and as for that huge crack? Well that was the infamous San Andreas Fault line and the only thing separating two of the largest opposing tectonic plates on earth. For the record, San Francisco quickly recovered, growing into what many consider to be one of the most charismatic cities in all of America.

A quick drive around the city and it soon became apparent why so many people choose to run the gauntlet and live here. If there were league tables for the coolest cities to reside in then San Francisco would surely be challenging for the top – as unlike many other cities that seem to have an endless sprawl of urban wastelands, San Francisco does not. What it does have is a diversity of compelling neighbourhoods, each one unique, but all happy to serve its own community in whatever way it can. The Beat Generation of the fifties brought with it a gay-friendly, multicultural society with a sense of liberalism that few other places can match. Localism is everywhere – on the street, in every district, each one cradling its own idyllic community, with an appropriate mix of artisan style cafés, bistro restaurants and hippy boutiquey shoppe fronts. They really are all quite wonderful places, so near in distance, yet so far removed from the financial district in which they so closely encircle. Although without doubt the overriding feature of San Francisco is the multitude of spectacular hills on which it resides. In total they reckon the city is built upon forty-three hills. An intriguing thought as not only was someone actually tasked to go out and physically count them – *which in itself is a fairly pointless exercise* – but for the sheer question as to what exactly constitutes a hill in the first place? Does it have to be a certain height? Particular width, perhaps? What about that bump in the road, does that count? And what happened at the end of the day when the hill counter was no doubt probably on his knees losing the will to live.

'*Thirty-one... 32... 33... Right, sod this for a living, I'm bloody knackered. There's gotta be at least another ten of those mothers out there? I'm off to the saloon!'* It's not like anyone would ever be in a rush to check his work?

We checked into our hotel, a rather professional looking Marriott in the heart of town, and then ventured on foot to the Powell Street cable car on the corner of Market and 4th Street.

'Sod this for a wait. I'm walking up the next block to catch the tram,' Angie piped up, noting the line of tourists patiently waiting for a lift up the hill to Fisherman's Wharf.

'I've heard only tourists and idiots wait in this line,' she smiled, nodding in my direction. 'I'm a seasoned traveller, you know,' she boasted, clearly impressed with her local knowledge.

Not one to argue with a girl on a mission I followed behind and to my surprise a much shorter queue presented itself the next block up.

A short while later the cable car arrived and we wasted little time jumping upon its faded wooden steps. The tram ascended the hill and memories of the Corkscrew at Alton Towers came immediately flooding back, as the rickety old carriage jerked and juddered its ascent before coming to a complete halt on the brow of the hill. Looking down the hill, the driver announced we were now overlooking Lombard Street, the most crooked street in America. Quite why someone felt the need to build a street with hairpin bends fit for only a racing driver is anyone's guess? But that didn't appear to deter the line of eager cars queueing up to have a go.

The views from the top were stunning. In the far away distance the prominent island of Alcatraz patrolled the icy waters, while downhill the rows of Victorian townhouses oozed with a charm I hadn't experienced since our visit to the colonial Deep South. The driver released the handbrake and we hurtled downhill towards the bay. I grabbed a leather handle and leant out as far as my outstretched arms would allow.

'Wahaaaaaaaay!' I screamed. 'Look at me, baby, I'm flyyyyyying!'

'Wahoooooooooo!' Angie yelled, wind gushing through her hair. 'I love you, San Franciscoooooooo!' she proclaimed to the world.

Turning inwards I scanned through the carriage. Rarely had I seen so many smiling faces staring straight back at me. It's no wonder why everyone loves San Francisco, I thought to myself. In a place where anything goes, nothing else quite epitomises that kindred spirit than to be whizzed around the city on the back of an old tram.

The tram terminated at Fisherman's Wharf, San Francisco's unique fishing quarters and historic gateway to the east. Once a thriving harbour filled with Irish fisherman and Chinese immigrants, the Wharf is now a popular tourist Mecca famed for its boating tours, bouncing sea lions and about as much street entertainment as you could possibly stomach. After a quick detour into yet another Irish bar we continued down the hill to the main entertainment hub situated on Pier 39.

'Right darling, I fancy some chilling... Just sitting on the dock of the bay... Just wasting timmmmmme... Just waaaaasting timmmmme,' I began to sing, strutting my stuff down the street.

'Oh my gosh, so that's where that song comes from! I never knew that?' Angie excitedly smiled.

'Stick with me darling and I'll show you the world,' I declared confidently.

'Yeah yeah Jamie, whatever. You think you're so clev... Arrrrrhhhhh!' Angie screamed as a frightening man in dreads leaped out from behind a bush.

'Bloody idiot. You could have given me a heart attack,' she shouted, clenching her fists. I was about to pile in myself and give him a piece of my mind when I heard a child shout out.

'Look, Mommy, he got them good that time. That man with the bush is funny, isn't he?' I turned towards the boy to see a line of people pointing and laughing and like so many before we had now been officially rumbled by San Francisco's notorious 'Bushman'.

Crouching behind his now legendary handheld bush, the homeless street performer has made a career from scaring the living bejesus out of unsuspecting tourists. Selecting his targets carefully, the sneaky Bushman lies in wait before pouncing in their path like a demented jack in the box. All very childish really but the locals seem to thrive on it. A large crowd had now gathered waiting for the next victim. A middle-aged man with two daughters unwittingly approached the dreaded bush.

'Booooo!' the Bushman yelled directly into the man's ear.

They say the old ones are the best ones and watching the man nearly knock over his two startled daughters was humour I hadn't experienced since I left the playground.

'You squeal like a girl, sir,' a voice shouted, much to the amusement of the baying crowd.

'Wish I could jump that high,' another jested.

Angie, who had now recovered from her initial shock, tossed a dollar bill into the Bushman's bulging collection pot.

'Bet this guy makes a fortune,' she said.

'He must do if he's good enough to extract money out of you, my darling.'

'Well actually he should be thanking you really since it was your 10 bucks you left behind in the Jeep, my friend!'

'Really? You thieving little scoundrel. I thought it strange you volunteering to pay for the beers earlier,' I said, shaking my head.

That evening I googled the Bushman, intrigued as to what if any information I would find. Amazingly Wikipedia had a whole page dedicated to him, YouTube countless videos and believe it or not the cunning prankster's even got his own Facebook page. Over the years the Bushman has become so popular he's starred in numerous documentaries and has even got his own miniature Lego model terrorising the streets of Legoland. Oh what a legend, and if his claims are to be believed then he's also doing rather well thank you very much to the staggering tune of $60,000 bucks a year to be precise.

All very impressive really and just goes to show that given the right opportunities even the less privileged people can live out their American Dream as well!

Feeling somewhat inspired by the Bushman's antics we decided to plough on with our own adventure, and besides, I was keen to reacquaint myself with the warm Californian sunshine we had become so readily accustomed to. San Francisco may have been fun, but it was colder than our annual family pilgrimage to the chalets of Pontin's Pakefield.

The next day we drove north and almost immediately the fog cleared as we entered the sun-drenched hills of the Napa Valley. Winding down the window I turned on the radio and contemplated what wine I would sample first. You see up until now my knowledge of the wine industry had always been somewhat vague. A red generally tasted like vinegar, was supposed to be for connoisseurs, yet somehow managed to deliver the hangover from hell, while a white tasted okay, got you giddy at first, but was way too embarrassing to buy at any respectable drinking establishment. And as for determining a wine's quality, well that was a mystery wrapped in an enigma and hidden in a riddle. As far as I was concerned a good wine could be carefully selected from the wooden racks of Waitrose, whereas a bad one could be seen rattling around the empty racks of Aldi. Clearly like many others I still had much to learn about the fabulous world of wine.

The Wine Valley

It was late afternoon when we checked into a very pleasant Springhill Suites on the outskirts of Napa. Feeling hungry, we decided to pop into town to grab some lunch while sampling a few cheeky glasses of wine in the process. On the drive up to town Angie had done her research and identified a suitable vegetarian restaurant which we simply had to try.

'I don't care what you say, James, we're going and that's final!' she said, holding her ground. 'Look, it's got 5 stars on Trip Advisor so it's gotta be good, right?' she continued.

To be honest, vegetarian establishments ain't exactly my thing *give me a real cowboy roadhouse any day,* but every now and then there comes a time when a bloke's gotta ignore the blatant alarm bells ringing in his head and do as his missus demands.

'Ok darling, whatever you say I'm sure it will be lovely,' I said trying my best to sound enthused. 'What's the name of the place you're looking for, darling?'

'It's called Unbumtu I think?' Angie replied scanning the store fascias for a match.

'What sort of bloody name is that? Um... Bum... too? What the hell is that supposed to mean? Hardly an encouraging name for a restaurant, is it darling?'

'I've got no idea Jamie, and frankly I don't care. The important thing is that we're doing something I want to do for a change... Oh look, it's over there,' she said, scurrying to the front door.

A balding man with thick rimmed spectacles immediately welcomed us into the groovy looking restaurant.

'Ya, hello madam, sir, welcome to Umbumto. Do you have a reservation with us tonight?' the snotty man enquired softly.

'Err no we don't,' I said, sensing an opportunity. 'Oh well never mind, we'll have to come back another day,' I concluded heading for the door.

'Not so fast, buster,' Angie said, tugging my arm. 'I rang up earlier and was told we didn't have to book if we ate at the bar,' she told the man.

'Oh... right... ok... yah... normally this establishment only allows reservations made a month in advance, madam,' he replied looking to his supervisor for advice.

A seductive blonde-haired vixen sauntered over.

'That will not be a problem, madam. You're more than welcome to join us in the bar area. Craig will happily look after you,' she said, pointing to another immaculately well-groomed man serving shots from behind the bar.

Craig immediately set about pouring some wine as he formally introduced us to 'Umbumtu'.

'Ya... this place is absolutely amazing. Utterly divine,' he said, handing Angie a free taster. 'Ya... It was the first vegetarian restaurant to open in the valley. I would introduce you to Sandra the owner if I could. What an amazing and absolutely inspirational women she has been to us all. But regrettably I can't as she's teaching yoga in Thailand these days,' he said, passing over the menus.

'Oh wow, that's amazing,' Angie smiled gazing into the handsome barman's eyes. However the flirtatious biting of the lip soon dropped to the floor the moment she began to unravel the menu's velvety bind.

I watched with intrigue as Angie's eyes flickered nervously over the pages and after much deliberation she whispered into my ear.

'Babe, you can have one item from the menu only. It's so expensive in here. Actually, I'm not really sure if we should eat here at all?' she said, running her finger down the pricing column.

'Oh, that's great babe, drag me in here, get me comfortably seated and just as I'm about to tuck into my free shot of wine you tell me to make our excuses and leave? No way, babe, this was your call, darling. You've been banging on about this all bloody day. We're going nowhere, my friend.'

'Fine, James. One item only. No arguing!' Angie reiterated. Regaining control of the situation.

I scanned down the menu:-

Garden lettuce with shredded carrot $22

Garden lettuce with green beans $22

Garden lettuce with red onion $22

Garden lettuce with tomato $22

And the Unbumtu special of the day...

Roasted lettuce on seasonal petals freshly plucked from the garden $32

You've got to be kidding me!

I deliberated for a moment, before finding a bean stew saviour on the back of the menu. Feeling pleased I had swerved the lettuce I placed our orders at the bar.

'Ya, will there be anything else, sir?' the barman asked.

'No, I think that's it!' I replied.

'Sir, we do recommend that our guests have at least three of our entrees?' he insisted.

'That's fine. I'm not really that hungry,' I said, smiling through gritted teeth.

A while later the waiter delivered our food and to say I was disappointed was the understatement of the year. My 22 buck bean stew turned out to be nothing more than a few miserly mouthfuls of froth you could have easily poured into my free shot glass. There was one bonus, I guess. It did come with a complementary slice of lettuce leaf served on a black ceramic tile.

'Excuse me sir, is this plucked from the garden as well?' I said, gazing down at my single slice.

'Oh yes, sir,' the waiter replied. 'This is one of our finest pieces, sir. Sandra planted it herself!'

'Oh, wow, that is amazing,' I replied with just a hint of irony.

The restaurant then bestowed an eerie silence, as for the next two minutes the only sound to be heard was the pitter patter of my spoon scraping along the bottom of my bowl. Then like a caged baboon unable to contain my wild scavenger instincts, I grabbed the leaf and frantically began mopping up the last few droplets of bean I could salvage.

'Oh, that's disgusting, babe,' Angie shouted as I shovelled the last remnants of leaf into my mouth.

'And you can keep quiet, girl. What do you expect when you place a friggin' quota on my order? Now pass me your leaf will you, I'm bloody Hank Marvin!'

I think it's fair to say that if this had been our first dinner date I doubt there would have been a second, but unfortunately hunger can have no pretend. Shortly after we made our excuses and retreated to the comfort of our hotel to plan the next day's activities. Grabbing a couple of flyers from reception, I fired up the laptop for a quick history lesson on the surrounding area.

Known as the gateway to the Californian wine country, the Napa Valley is itself actually rather small. Spanning a valley of no more than thirty miles in length, the wine produced from the region accounts for only 4% of US wine. However, what it lacks in size it more than makes up for in dollars. For what was once a backward cowboy watering hole is now considered to be the premier wine region in America, accounting for over 20% of its entire wine revenue. Now that's some serious cash and probably goes a long way to explaining the type of snooty nose folk we encountered that afternoon.

The next morning we drove along the Silverado Trail, an old stagecoach trail so called due to the large amounts of silver deposits discovered in the mid 19th century. For the next hundred years or so nothing happened, until one day in the summer of 1976, one of its small wineries won a blind drinking contest in the heart of Paris – an event that would shock the world of wine, much to the horror of the French judges who to this day remain convinced they had been secretly duped. *'Excuzzzy this cannot be? Someone must have switched zer glasses?'* Anyway, after much head scratching, the Californian wine was reluctantly crowned king, and the Napa Valley officially unveiled to the world of wine. Today the Silverado Trail is home to over forty wineries – from the world-famous Rutherford's to the smaller vineyards that dare to live the dream. Running parallel to the main highway, the trail is affectionately referred to as 'The road less travelled' and is considered the most scenic way to explore the area. So with time on our side we meandered our way up the sun-drenched valley with the speedometer rarely exceeding 30. There really are few things in life that quite rattle the senses then cruising through a majestic wine region in the height of summer – and with the windows down and air rushing through, the smell of summer was all around. A warmth of contentment flushed through me as I gazed around at my surroundings. It was as if we were driving into the heart of a Tuscan oil painting, drifting and weaving through the wandering lanes that zig zagged their way up the lush green valley. Every so often we would stop off to pluck a ripening grape from a random roadside vine.

'Perhaps we should relocate out here? Start afresh?' I said sucking on another grape.

'Wouldn't it be amazing,' Angie smiled, hair swaying in the gentle breeze.

We continued north to Calistoga, a charming little town located high in the upper valley. My parents had visited the place a few years before and recommended we visit a particular vineyard for the sole reason it had an aerial tramway ascending over 300 feet to the castle's mountaintop entrance. Never one to take my father's advice lightly, we found ourselves ascending high over the valley in what has to be one of the most impressive entrances to a vineyard anywhere in the western world. The formalities ended once inside as a self-audible tour guided us through the complicated world of wine. We ambled around the exhibits taking as much in as we could, but as fascinating as it was you couldn't help conclude that it really was an industry where the marketing man is truly king. Someone clearly gave these guys a blank canvass to work on, as the lengths they go to distinguish one near identical product from the next is mind boggling. If listening to top quality bullshit is your thing then you're definitely in the right place. Starting with the vine, they focus heavily on where it's grown, how it is cut, how it is treated. They talk about the soil, its fertility. Then there's the temperature, humidity and altitude of the valley to consider. Then we must understand what type of grape it is, when it was picked, how it was picked, where it was stored. If that's not enough to baffle, then the taste sensations derived certainly will. A typical Pinot Noir is said to be spicy while oozing a soft and fruity blackcurranty essence. Sorry, but is it me? Am I the only one who's confused here? Shouldn't it supposed to taste of grape? But then that would be really dull wouldn't it? And is there really that much variance to a Pinot Noir grown in one region to the next? I don't see other fruit producers claiming such merits. Surely one Granny Smith grown in an English orchard tastes remarkably similar to one plucked from a Del Monte tree? And why should I challenge at all? What do I know, I hear you say. Well what I'm going to tell you now may surprise you or may even shock you perhaps. You see many years ago on my first backpacking excursion to Australia – my friend and I were lucky enough to secure some fruit picking work – nothing much, just picking some apples in a blazing hot Queensland orchard. The season was coming to an end and the farmer had hired as many casual workers as he could to gather the last few remaining ripe apples. What we didn't know at the time of our two minute interview, was that many of the apples had fallen into decay and were already infested with a swarm of wasps. *'Blimey! Wouldn't want to be the poor sod who's gotta clear that sorry mess up.'* We laughed while naturally opting to cherry pick the good ones from the bottom of the tree. Unfortunately, when we retuned the tractor trailer with a half empty load, the farmer wasn't best pleased and insisted we go back and gather all the rotten ones as well. *'They're be awright for juicing, lads. Don't you worry about that no one will ever know!'* he jested, tossing a handful of brown ones onto the heap.

So there you go. Nothing goes to waste in farmland. All those rotting apples you see falling by the wayside each and every September? Well I guarantee they'll be heading your way to a supermarket near you. Utterly disgusted but severely strapped for cash we had little choice but to do as the farmer wished, and so for the next few days we were left with the unenviable task of scooping up the half eaten remains into our buzzing baskets. However, being the plucky little fighters that we were, we were naturally able to make light of the situation and laugh at our misfortune. Every time we would come across a particularly gross one, I would shout over the tree in my best foreign accent. *'Look, Mr Del Monte, I found another manky one. It's a good quality, yeah?'*

While my best buddy Martin, would pick up his pretend phone, request to speak to Mr Del Monte and shout across the field.

'The man from Del Monte, he say a yeah. It's a perfect!'

A fascinating insight into the world of agriculture, but disturbingly very true. The moral to the story being don't believe everything you read on the label. You see those oaky smokey flavors and spicy blackcurrants fusions of crunch, may well in reality be something very different indeed.

We finished the tour and drove the short distance to the town of Calistoga. My previous night's research had suggested that the area had its very own 'Yellowstone' type Geyser located somewhere off the main road – so not wanting to miss out we popped into the local tourist office to get some directions.

'Hello, sir, and how can I help you today?' an elderly lady enquired from behind her desk.

'Hi there, I'm looking for the Old Faithful geyser. Do you know where I can find it, madam?' I replied.

'I sure do, honey,' the old lady smiled. 'You gotta go right outta town and down the old A65. You can't miss it... but you don't want to go there, sweetie,' she said, shaking her head.

'I don't?' I said, slightly startled. 'This is supposed to be the tourist office, isn't it? Aren't you supposed to tell me how wonderful this mysterious place is and I'd be a fool to miss it? You know like it's the best thing I've never done?' I replied, scratching my head.

'You ever been to Yellowstone, honey?' the old lady interrupted.

'Well, yes, I have actually, now you come to mention it. Couple of weeks ago. Amazing place.'

'Well, honey, they have proper geysers there. In their natural environment. Not like this one. Damn greedy owner came in and built a God damn fence round this one. Even went as far to plant a whole bunch of trees to obscure the view from the road. Then he goes and makes you pay a lousy 10 bucks for the privilege. As I said, honey, you don't want to go there. Go sample some wine, get a little merry and have some fun. We gotta lotta fine wineries here in Napa.'

The old lady had caught me off guard. It had been a while since I had encountered such brashness.

'You not from round here?' she continued. 'Where you from, if you don't mind me asking, honey?'

'England, ma'am, near Windsor, not too far from the Queen.'

'Well, young man, that is sure one fine almighty country. And what do you folks do for a living over there in Engerlaaand?'

'Technically nothing, I guess?' I said fearing further interrogation. 'We quit our jobs to go travelling.'

'What? You telling me you quit everything you had without having some sort of backup plan,' she said, pausing for a moment. *Oh here we go again, another telling off...*

'Well you know what, honey. I think that's mighty brave of you, sir. I respect that. Life can go by so quickly that we often miss what's right in front of our very own eyes. It's like a steam train, you see. It starts kinda slowly, speeds right up around your teens, then goes completely outta control by the time you hit your twenties. Then within a flash you're in your forties and wondering where the hell it all went wrong. And hell, you won't even remember your thirties as you were far too busy sucking up and doing everybody else's dirty work for a living. *"Yes boss, no boss, anything else I can do for you boss?"*

'Absolutely,' I said intrigued by her wisdom.

'Life sure is a funny thing. When we're young we're all too wrapped up in our own problems to really appreciate what we have. It's only when we get older we realise we got our priorities wrong from the very start.'

I turned to Angie and like me she was captivated by her words of wisdom. Then the old lady said something I will never forget.

'Honey, come closer,' she said, whispering me in. 'Let me tell you something I learnt a long time ago. You should be able to take your retirement now then work right up until your eighty. Maybe then we'll appreciate how precious this life really is. Go see the world when you're young, fit and able, and maybe then we can all give something back. To me it's obvious. I'm just surprised nobody thought of it first,' the wise old lady said with a mischievous glint in her eye. 'Now, anything else I can do for you, sir?'

I was gobsmacked. What began as a polite conversation turned into an inspirational moment which will stay with me forevermore. The irony was not lost on me that this old lady was happily out there mingling with strangers, not rattling around some poky little home on her own. She really was a very wise old lady indeed.

Later that day we passed the Old Faithful geyser and it was exactly how the old lady described it. A large roadside sign directed cars to a nearby parking lot. A clump of newly grown trees acting as a shield obscuring any possible sighting from the road. What surprised me most was the queue of cars eager to pay their 10 bucks for what was effectively an overpriced peep show. This didn't sit too well with me. I don't mind paying to see nature and would happily pay over 20 bucks for an entrance ticket into one of America's vast national parks. Unfortunately, the 'Geyser of California' had long since succumb to greed and was now a sad indictment of man's blatant attempts to profiteer. Such a wonderful natural occurrence shouldn't be kept hidden away in a box.

The next day we packed up our rucksacks and headed north. California was proving to be a fascinating place. In a matter of days we had crossed the mountains, rode over plains, and touched the waters of the Pacific Ocean. However, the best was definitely yet to come. In a few hours' time we would step foot into Redwood country and literally enter into another world altogether. A world so enchantingly big, that not even man could hide away into a box.

The Redwoods

There are some things in life that we all earmark to do from
an early age. In recent times this has become known as your
bucket list – your very own list of things you want to
experience before it is too late. Some want to walk the Great
Wall of China, while others climb the Empire State. One
thing's for certain, one's bucket list is as varied as the next.
Looking deeper, something may well have occurred in our
lives to have influenced our list, a random event or specific
incident directing us towards a path. Mine was when my
grandfather presented me with an old Polaroid of my
grandma, steering her car through the belly of an old drive-
thru tree on one of their fabulous American journeys. How
amazing, I thought, that you could actually drive your car
through the middle of one of those gloriously wide trees. I
may have only been six at the time, but it would be my first
entry onto that never-ending list of things I wanted to do.

It was late afternoon when we entered the Avenue of
Giants, a 31 mile stretch of forested highway snaking its way
through the heart of Redwood country. Running parallel to
the freeway, the scenic road cuts a swathe through some of

the largest remaining primeval redwoods in North America. We had literally entered another world, a majestic world so ancient it is said to house the oldest living beings on earth. Impressive stuff, but it's bewildering to think that these almighty beings were once so nearly destroyed.

At the onset of the Californian Gold Rush it was estimated there were over 2 million acres of Redwood forest in North America. Yet within fifty years, nearly all had been virtually wiped out; fallen victim to the wide scale logging and rapid construction of the railroad. Westward expansion had certainly come at a price. Today only 5% of the ancient forest remains. A paltry figure I'm sure you'll agree, but in reality it could have been far worse had it not been for the formation of the *Save the Redwood's* conservation group, a powerful group of activists who lobbied intensively for their survival – although it would take another 50 or so years for the state and national government to eventually buy back the vast swathes of land which had fallen victim into private hands.

Keen to check out our giant surroundings, we ditched the Jeep and followed an enticing little trail deep into the forest. The main road may have only been a few feet away, but it was as if we'd entered another time and place altogether, our immediate surroundings being so quiet and peaceful. And so for the next half hour we were completely alone, venturing ever further away from the safety of civilisation. Somewhat precariously we continued walking, eager to discover where the lonesome trail would end. A muffling of voices echoed somewhere in the distance, a clapping of leaves overhead. It was the eeriest of feelings. Was it me? Was I going mad? Or could I somehow hear strange whispering noises coming from all around? Were the trees actually communicating to themselves, alerting one another to our presence? Maybe, maybe not? But if a single tree can outlive every other organism then we shouldn't be so dismissive of their powers.

With an average life expectancy of over 800 years, the giant Redwoods are without doubt the most incredible living beings on earth. Able to produce a natural self-protecting resin, the wily old trees are said to even combat the effects of fire. Fed on a rich diet of natural water drifting in from the Pacific, the coastal Redwoods are also the largest living life forms on the planet. Reaching heights of up to 400 feet and weighing anything up to 1.5 million pounds, the giant Redwood is one monstrosity of a tree and you certainly wouldn't want to hear the word *Timmmmbeeeeeerrrrr* when standing under one of these old fellows. Somewhat miraculously, we are able to determine which one is the tallest. From the untrained eye it would surely be like finding a needle in the densest of haystacks. Therefore, even more surprising to learn that even in the age of technology, experts still rely on the good old-fashioned tape drop method to officially decide the tallest. This primitive process requires one guy *usually the boss* to stand at the bottom of the tree, while the other guy *usually the Rookie* is bundled into a harness and given the unenviable task of climbing high into the canopy, before dropping the tape back to earth for the official measuring to begin. Unfortunately, by the time our hero emerges from the tree, his devious little boss has already fixed a commemorative plague to the stump of the tree, and named it 'The Rupert Tree' in honour of his great achievement. *Yep we've all been there, haven't we?*

With the light fading we wandered off the main trail, quickly finding another path drifting deeper into the woods, the faint sound of children's voices becoming ever more distant. Then, like a bolt from the blue, my senses came to the fore dragging me out of the peculiar trance in which I had now drifted. Where the hell were we? What if we got lost? And what if we weren't the only ones out here? Wasn't BIGFOOT supposed to roam these murky parts? It's fair to say it wasn't the first time this trip I'd found myself a little scared.

Said to be half man, half ape, tales of the hairy creature dates back as far as the Indians. Although it wasn't until 1958 when the legacy really caught the world's attention, when a local construction owner discovered a set of unusually large footprints encircling his site. Worried that no one would believe him, the canny worker immediately set about creating a set of plaster casts – presenting his findings to the media, who duly labelled his huge casts as Bigfoot. It was America's very answer to Loch Ness and extraordinary to think such a beast still existed. I'll certainly never forget the first time I saw those grainy images of that strange ape-like creature darting through the woods, pausing momentarily only to acknowledge the jerking camera. That infamous 1967 film was captured by a man called Paterson who by sheer chance was also searching for Bigfoot evidence at the time. What an amazing coincidence that turned out to be. Looking back, it's crazy to think how gullible we all were. Surely it must have been obvious it was just a man twatting around the woods in a monkey suit? My suspicions were confirmed years later when a famed Hollywood director later declared it all an elaborate hoax, claiming one of his crew had commandeered a costume from the upcoming movie *Planet of the Apes*, staring the one and only Charlton Heston. I can't believe we all fell for it. Perhaps it was Charlton himself taking a stroll through the woods that day? Come to think of it the two do look remarkably similar, don't they? Who's to know? But despite the doubters the Bigfoot industry is well and truly alive in Northern California and you can't go anywhere without passing a Bigfoot Drive-Thru, a Bigfoot steakhouse, a Bigfoot motel, or some other commercial venture trading on his name. But then I guess in these parts it would cost too much *not* to believe, wouldn't it?

We returned to the car, pulling over a few minutes later outside the park's main visitor centre – a cute, quaint little log cabin engulfed by a hundred trees. In truth there wasn't really too much to see – a few flyers, couple of maps, and of course the customary Bigfoot souvenirs. One of the Rangers recommended we take a hike around the Rockefeller Forest, which is said to house the oldest living trees in the park. We drove the short distance and once again found ourselves embarking on another mysterious trail leading through the densest of woodland. We followed the path, climbing over several fallen trees along the way. Where dead trees lay, new growth was now beginning; the young flourishing of the old in a natural cycle of life and death. Venturing ever deeper we followed on the coattails of an elderly couple, shortly finding what we were looking for. The huge tree opposite the stream was exactly how it appeared in the old black and white photograph back in the visitor centre. Only this time there were no funny looking men with goofy grins but just an ancient forest whispering in the wind. I paused for a moment looking high into the canopy. No amount of photography can replicate the true sense of scale that these majestic beings exude. To be in their presence is a truly humbling experience, one so deep you begin to question your own significance. And like a tiny ant looking up into the heavens I was in awe.

That evening we arrived in the town of Fortuna, checking into a Best Western motel a few minutes' walk from the centre. Somewhat surprisingly it was only the second time we had checked into a motel on our trip. Up until now *and thanks to Angie's Dad* we had been rather spoilt, choosing to stay in modern mid budget holiday suites rather than the more traditional types of motel. In truth you couldn't really go anywhere without coming across a newly developed Courtyard, Residence Inn, or Fairfield Inn complex. So, for a couple of extra bucks a night it was the natural choice. Unfortunately, the town of Fortuna didn't offer such privileges, leaving us little option but to check into the only available motel with a vacancy sign overhead. Once nicknamed *No tell hotels* due to their long association with adultery, one of the major benefits was that you could park your car right outside your door, thus avoiding any potentially awkward conversations with the overzealous sales receptionist. '*And would you like any half price chocolate with that, sir?*'

'*What the hell are you suggesting!*'

Anyway, upon reflection that's probably where the benefits of a drive-thru motel ends, as I can tell you now it's altogether a completely different experience the moment you enter your shabby little room. If the pitter patter of footsteps outside your door doesn't start to irritate, then the heavy clunking of slamming trunks most certainly will. It's only then you realise the only thing protecting you from that creepy looking man who's been watching you all afternoon is one of those crummy old key chains uselessly dangling down from the side of your door. Well thanks a lot, mate, that makes me feel so much safer now.

'Nice job, James, this is just lovely. You really know how to woo a girl, don't you?' Angie said rather sarcastically.

Outside the room there was a hive of activity. The annual rodeo was in town and by the sound of things it appeared every redneck in the county had rocked up to the party. A line of empty four by fours lay dormant, while a rowdy bunch in cowboy attire attended to their steaks on the outdoor BBQ pit. Picking up a flyer from reception I was keen to see what all the fuss was about. Angie on the other hand needed a little more convincing.

'Babe, do we really have to go to the rodeo? I don't really want to see all those poor animals get mistreated. It's so cruel, you know,' she said a little concerned.

'Bloody hell, babe, you're a fine one to talk, what with you living in Barcelona on your gap year. Not exactly a bull friendly city, is it!'

'Yes, well I'll have you know I never saw a single bullfight while I was there, thank you very much.'

'Well you must have been a very lonely girl then darling, as I bet every other mother was out in the street baying for blood!' I smiled.

'Whatever!' Angie replied, shaking her head.

'So it's settled. We'll pop over have a look and if you don't like it we'll come straight back,' I said glancing at the flyer for directions.

Like most outsiders, my knowledge of an American rodeo was limited to somewhat disturbing images of sexually charged men riding sexually deprived broncos, while repeatedly spanking them as hard as they could on the backs of their very sore bottoms – a trifle worrying I'm sure you'll agree? However a quick Google search soon revealed that the sport actually originated in Canada and was designed to test the skill, speed, and dexterity of a cowboy. To win a rodeo event is considered to be the ultimate cowboy accolade. Events are varied, challenging, and dare I suggest a little intriguing. With names such as Mutton Busting, Tie Down Roping, Team Roping and perhaps best of all... Bareback Riding. I can only imagine the queuing cowgirls must have been quaking in their knee-high boots?

The main rodeo event itself is the culmination of an intensive week of activities, ranging from street parties, carnival processions, numerous BBQs and about as much live country music as one could possibly stomach. And if that's not enough then there are always the classic street games of stick horse, egg toss and dummy roping to keep the kids amused throughout the day. Although regrettably by the time we arrived the last event had long been contested and much to my dismay even the beer boys were packing down for the night.

'Oh dear, looks like it's just finished. Oh well, can't say I didn't make the effort can you, darling,' Angie said with a smile.

Disappointed, we trundled back in the direction of the hotel, although by the sound of Angela's cheerful whistling I suspect I was the only one who was downhearted.

That evening we planned our final moves. With our outbound flight to Boston fast approaching, something was going to have to give. Up until now our westward planning had been intense but more or less straight forward – as in truth all we really had to do was follow the trail west. Heading back on the other hand was an entirely different matter, as without a specific trail to follow difficult decisions now had to be made.

I didn't recall encountering such problems navigating around Australia all those years ago on my first backpacking adventure? Flying into Melbourne, we booked ourselves a one-way Greyhound pass and followed the road north all the way up along the east coast. The only decision we had to make was who was first in line to the pay phone to blag their old man for another boat load of cash. Fond memories, but in some ways I also recall it being a far more primitive process of travel. There were no mobile phones, the Internet was in its infancy and the most reliable way to communicate was by airmail *or slow mail* as we used to call it. Astonishingly it took us nearly two weeks before we could be bothered to make our first long distance telephone call and when we did finally connect, you had to deal with an annoying 3 second time delay between one side speaking and the other side hearing. Try doing that when you've had a few sherbets. Communication has certainly come a long way in the last twenty years.

Switching on my Mac, I opened up Google Maps and began zooming back and forth between various cities. From our location in the north there appeared to be two obvious paths to Vegas. The first was to head inland, driving through Yosemite National Park, before entering the desert of Death Valley, allegedly the hottest place in America – or alternatively drive south along the Great Ocean Road where we'd eventually end up in LA. Once again we were at another crossroads. Either way the lure of Vegas was becoming ever more apparent. Although the bright lights would also signify the beginning of the end of this long and crazy westward adventure, after which we'd be heading to Phoenix to catch our returning flight east. Not at all influenced by the filming of George Clooney's *Ocean's Eleven*, we shamelessly booked ourselves a luxurious room in the Bellagio hotel. All that for a mere 200 odd bucks a night. Not bad really especially when you consider most basic Premier Inns back in England have stealthily crept up to around 80 or 90 quid a night. *29 quid a night, yeah right!* The homeward plan was beginning to play out. We were now what Americans commonly refer to as 'all set'; one last push around California before our final blowout in Vegas. Four days and counting, the clock was now ticking. The only question being which way would we go now?

The Ocean Road

The next morning we headed south along the tree-lined highway towards the coastal town of Monterey. It had been a close call, but after careful consideration Angie had made her feelings perfectly clear what our chosen path should be. 'Darling, it's my holiday too,' she began in a now very familiar tone. 'I'm sure Yosemite is very nice, but come on baby, how many mountains do we have to go and see this holiday? Don't you think we milked it a little? And as for Death Valley, well quite frankly I want to get home ALIVE. No, we're doing something different, something I want to do for a change, we're going to Hollywood and that's final, my darling!' she insisted.

About an hour later, yet still very much in Redwood country, we passed the most famous tree of them all, the Chandelier drive-thru tree, which incidentally was the very same tree in which my grandfather had shown to me all those years ago. Now this famous old tree was just like any other, until one day in the early 1930s some trigger-happy chainsaw operator thought it a bright idea to hack out a whacking great hole right through the centre of its trunk. I can only assume the Save the Redwood League of conservationists must have been away on vacation that week as how this one slipped through the net is beyond belief. Quite how any living thing can survive such a gaping wound to its structural make up is a true testament to nature. On the flip side though few can argue that the image of an all American Chevy driving through the belly of a Giant Redwood is one of the finest pieces of marketing you'll ever likely to see – and so like many before, we found ourselves joining the back of the queue, lured in by an unexplainable urge to drive through the heart of one of nature's greatest giants. Convincing ourselves it was going to be another one of those *once in a lifetime opportunities* I handed over my 10 bucks, slipped the car into first and rolled the car into the mouth of the tree.

'Smile, baby,' Angie shouted pointing her camera in my face.

'Yes, darling, but can you make sure you get my head in this time please. My forehead's beginning to get a complex,' I smiled scrunching my head into the base of my neck.

'Oh, sssshhh you,' she replied, taking the shot.

'Ahh wicked, baby, this one's definitely going on Facebook later,' she confirmed, admiring her photography skills. But the reality being it was a hollow moment *if you pardon the pun* as what may constitute a great photo doesn't always translate in a great experience. To say it was an anticlimax was an understatement, especially when compared to our surreal experience walking in the woods the day before. It was all over in a flash of a button and I was left wondering what was the point of it all? How ironic then, we both left feeling empty as we drove away from the giant hole in the tree.

We continued southwards for the remainder of the afternoon, the wooded surroundings so peaceful it was hard to believe we were cruising through America's most populous state. Picking up the interstate north of San Francisco, we bypassed the urban sprawls of Oakland and Fremont before eventually rejoining the 101 south of San Jose.

It was late afternoon when we finally reached the Pacific's edge, rolling into the historic town of Monterey. On first impressions it was hard to believe this quaint little seaside town was once the thriving heartbeat of the old west. First settled by the Indians, then colonised by both the Spanish and Mexicans, Monterey was the original capital of California until the gold rush eventually sparked a mass exodus to the hills. Over the years the town may have lost much of its political clout but this has probably been somewhat of a blessing in allowing it to retain much of its natural beauty. Situated alongside the neighbouring towns of Carmel and Pacific Grove – and with the mighty Big Sur to the south – the Monterey Peninsula is said to be 'The greatest meeting of land and sea in the world'. A bold claim, but with its warm Mediterranean climate, rugged coastline, pine covered forests, and glorious sunsets, it can come as no surprise that the area has been a haven for artists and writers alike – most notably that of John Steinbeck, *another of my literacy idols* who set many of his books in and around the coastal area. Unfortunately the grim weather of San Francisco had followed us down the coast, providing us with about as much inspiration as a wet weekend in Wales – quickly learning that it doesn't really matter where you go, if the weather's grim then more likely you will be too. Upon reflection I'm sure most parts of Britain would be very pleasant too if it wasn't so bleeding miserable all the time. In recent years our summer aspirations have dipped to such lows that we now count ourselves lucky just to experience a few days of consecutive sunshine. And when the good weather finally does arrive we must be the only country in the world whose national media feels it a necessity to splash provocative headlines all over the covers of every red top newspaper the following morning:-

'Brighton bathes while it rains in Spain'

'Blackpool sizzles as Greece suffers more downpour misery'

'Temperatures hit 90. Eat that, Turkey!'

All rather pathetic, really. Anyway, depressed and reminded of exactly why we left England in the first place, we decided to move on at first light.

The next morning we continued our journey southwards, following the coastal highway around the rugged cliffs of the Big Sur. Rising from the depths of the Pacific, this mountainous wilderness was once so inaccessible the early settlers commonly referred it to as 'The big country to the South'. It wasn't until the mid-thirties when authorities finally gave the nod to construct a highway linking San Francisco to the north and Los Angeles to the south. Today the 90 mile stretch of highway that weaves its way around the Pacific edge is considered to be one of the most scenic drives in North America. With its majestic vistas, quirky bridges, and dramatic waves crashing a thousand feet below, it's easy to understand why 3 million visitors annually choose to cruise along the stunning highway. Unfortunately though the dire weather of the last few days had developed a plucky streak and was insistent on following our every turn. The poor visibility, sharp bends and Angie's persistent reminders to keep my eyes firmly on the road ensured a cautious progression – which was not necessarily a bad thing considering the road is deemed to be one of the most dangerous in all of California. Roadside collisions are common occurrences and driving in the backside of meandering cars so frequent that officials have had to introduce new laws insisting vehicles must pull over if five or more cars are tailgating behind. Driving southbound is particularly dangerous, as your car is effectively driving on the wrong side of the hairpin bends, and with no side rails to protect you any miscalculation could see you plunging over the edge.

We continued southwards and a few hours later the clouds parted to reveal a magnificent palace gleaming high in the hills above. The story of Hearst Castle is an intriguing one, and perhaps more than any other tale, epitomises the westward fever of the time.- Average Joe *who we shall call Senior Hearst* heads west to seek his fortune. After early struggles, invests some cash in an old abandoned mineshaft. A short while later the jammy git strikes lucky only to discover he's sitting on the largest cache of silver ore in American history. Nice, but not content in owning the largest private mining corporation, the new senator acquires an ailing newspaper company, which he hands over to his grateful son, William. And so with the help of his father's fortune, Junior is able to become one of the most powerful and controversial media moguls the western world had ever seen. However all was not well, as accusations of news fabrication begin to spiral. Junior's waning popularity takes another battering when it is alleged that his newspaper stories nearly cause a full-on Cuban war. Keen to redress his tainted image, he commissioned the top female architect of the day *nice touch* to design and build him a lavish palace where he can relax, unwind, and flaunt his ludicrous wealth to Hollywood's finest. It's fair to say I was beginning to dislike this chap already – but with time on our side we turned off the highway, hopped aboard a tour bus and chugged our way to the top of the hill, where an elderly man greeted our arrival.

'Hi yer folks and welcome to Hearst Castle. My name's Dwaine and I'll be your guide for the next couple of hours. Please step this way folks as we gotta lotta wonderful things to see,' he said enticing us towards the building. 'Right folks, you're now standing at the main entrance to the castle...'

'Absolutely stunning isn't it, Angie... Angie...?' I said, turning to see she was no longer at my side, although she hadn't gone far. In fact she was standing directly opposite Dwaine squinting her eyes and tilting her head like an obedient little puppy. I watched with intrigue as she pulled out her phone and began to frantically tap away with her right thumb. She repeated this bizarre ritual several times – looking up, listening, looking down and tapping, looking up, listening, looking down and tapping. *Oh my god she's actually taking notes! She's... she's... she's a complete NERD!* Shocked by this unexpected yet joyous discovery I crept up behind her.

'What are you doing, Einstein?' I said looking over her shoulder.

'I'm taking notes,' she said, still tapping away.

'What you doing that for? It's not like you're getting tested at the end, you know?'

'Ssshhhhhhh you, I'm learning. Maybe you should take some notes too, Desmond!'

'What you talking about dear?'

'Desmond Tutu. You only got a 2:2, remember? Maybe if you had taken more notes you may have got a proper degree, like me!' she shrugged, eyes firmly fixed on her phone.

'Yeah thanks darling, thanks for reminding me. I'll have you know I'm very proud of my drinking degree.'

'Yes, well you were always easily pleased weren't you, darling.'

'I certainly was, sweetheart,' I said stroking her back. 'I certainly was!'

'Now leave me be, I'm trying to concentrate!' she replied, digging her elbows rather annoyingly into my chest.

Oblivious to his new best friend, Dwaine guided us to the outside pool area where a magnificent Roman style columned fascia drew gasps from the group.

'Welcome to the Neptune pool and gardens everyone. This is perhaps the most popular part of the castle where Hearst's guests would come and relax for the day. The great Howard Lloyd and Charlie Chaplin were notable regulars on these two particular sun loungers,' Dwaine smiled, gesturing towards a couple of recliners that lay dormant in the afternoon sun. 'It is believed Hearst sought inspiration from his early childhood where he accompanied his mother around much of Europe. The young Hearst was so impressed he insisted the original Roman columns that you see before you be imported directly from the continent,' he continued.

'That's a bit unnecessary, isn't it,' Angie whispered into my ear. 'Imagine the hassle trying to get those things through customs?'

Dwaine upped the pace leading us through one of the several summer houses that overlooked the pool. 'This is where the English Prime Minister Winston Churchill would often come to relax,' he said, pointing to a plush leather desk overlooking a garden full of swaying Cypress trees.

After a quick nose, we exited the summer house and entered the main castle passing through the Great Hallway, a billiard room, an extravagant assembly room, before ending up in the main dining room where we came to a halt in front of a large mahogany table in the centre of the room.

'Welcome to the Refectory, ladies and gentleman. You are now in the main room of the house. As a guest of the castle you were free to do whatever you wanted on the sole condition that you joined Mr Hearst here in the refectory for evening dinner and drinks.'

'Seems a fair deal to me. I wonder if they had champagne,' Angie said with a twinkle in her eye.

'Now if you were new to the castle Mr Hearst would insist you sat directly next to him in the centre of the table. After dinner you would then be expected to perform at the table in accordance to your particular talent. So if you were Cary Grant you might have acted out a new scene...'

'What about Harold Lloyd then?' a member of the group said, stroking the edge of the table. 'Would he have had to balance across on his tippy toes?'

'Yes, very good, sir,' Dwaine nodded although not really appearing to appreciate the joke. 'Guests were free to stay as long as they liked but with every new day they would be placed further along towards the end table until... well, you kind of got the hint,' he laughed.

'Silly man,' Angie snarled.

'Why what did I do this time?' I replied somewhat startled.

'Not you, bozo. Him, good old Hearsty boy. Fancy making his guests perform like dancing monkeys. What sort of man puts Winston Churchill at the end of their dining table? He should have paid his guests a little more respect, don't you think?'

'Absolutely baby, nobody puts our Churchill in a corner, nobody!'

'Yes, Jamie, I'm glad we can agree... and err... since when did you become a fan of *Dirty Dancing* anyway?' Angie shrugged.

The tour ended and we were escorted back down the hill to the main reception. We entered the main foyer and Angie's eyes immediate lit up, which could only mean one thing... cheap rubbish! Although to my sheer amazement she didn't spend a single cent.

'You know what, my friend? I don't need to buy anything here today. Shall we hit the road?' she said, not really impressed with it all.

I glanced around one last time but couldn't help but notice the lines of tourists queuing up for the tour specials, of which there was plenty of choice. The most popular seemed to be the night time tours of the castle, the queue for the special bedroom tour was also quite impressive, and bloody hell there was even a few in a queue for the costumed tour of the castle. Now that's a bit keen really, as why anyone would feel the need to dress up in fancy costume really defies all reasonable logic. Although what struck me the most were the eager beavers signing up to receive the monthly Hearst Castle newsletter. Now come on, that's taking it a bit too far don't you think? It's hardly bloody Disney World, is it? But in a poignant way the excessive marketing and sheer willingness to consume it really did sum up what we had encountered in recent weeks – be it the Old Faithful of California, the fine wines of Napa, the giant hole in the tree, or the magical mystery tour of Hearst Castle. Each one had a vastly different offering – but the principle remained the same: create the fantasy and milk it for every last dollar and dime. The American Dream is still very much alive.

That evening we stopped off in the beautiful wine region of the Santa Ynez Valley, in what would prove to be our final night on the West Coast. Located a mere 100 miles from LA, the small valley is neatly tucked away between the San Rafael mountains to the north and the Santa Ynez mountains to the south – effectively cocooning it from the searing hot deserts to the east and sprawling metropolis to the south. On first impressions it is as if the area has been plucked straight from an ancient European countryside, it's gorgeously green Tuscan like hills providing the idyllic setting for its characteristic villagers to quietly go about their business. One of which we passed through was the delightful hamlet of Solvang. Touted as the Danish capital of America, the enchanting town is an exact recreation of what you'd expect to find in 19th century Denmark. Chocolate box houses, Danish bakeries, and olde worlde antique shops lined the streets, while silly old men dressed in lederhosen entertained the picnicking crowds lazing on the immaculately kept lawns. We stopped off briefly, munching on a couple of Danish pastries and soaked up the last remnants of the afternoon sun. A final calm before the storm that would inevitably follow. I sat on the grass and pondered. Tomorrow we would head for LA and all that entailed. It may only have been a short drive around the coastal mountains, but what would await us would no doubt be a vastly different world to the tranquil one in which we were sitting.

The truth being if I had known then what I know now then I may well have decided to give it a miss altogether. We live and learn I guess, we live and learn.

Los Angeles

As I mentioned a few chapters back there are various reasons why we travel. At the outset of our journey, one of my many challenges was to find the perfect American town where perhaps one day we could eventually settle down. Well you can't blame a man for dreaming, can you? I might not have become accustomed to rocking back and forth on a sun decked verandah but that's not to say my future children shouldn't be denied such a privilege. So far there were several contenders for the crown of the best town, most notably that of Denver and Colorado Springs in the state of Colorado. Not only were these places warm and friendly, but they were affluent, sunny, situated at a healthily high altitude and right on the fringes of what has to be one of the most spectacular sights in America – the Eastern Rockies – and I doubt you'd ever get bored having those big babies on your doorstep. That was the central region taken care of but what about the east? Many would no doubt choose New York and I can understand why, but to me the Big Apple is just way too friggin' hectic, give me the more refined city of Boston any day. Then there are the New England towns of Hanover and

Stowe to consider. Both situated in the northern Appalachians, both stunningly beautiful, and both offering a lifestyle one can only dream about. I could visit New England every season for the rest of my life and never tire of its white clapboard churches, picturesque villages and dense forested woodland. Only downside being I'm not too sure how much sun you'd get on the north east coast. Therefore another warm weather challenger was needed *hey it's my game I can have as many entrants as I like!* And the moment we passed through the sunny seaside town of Santa Barbara early the next day I knew we had another serious contender on our hands.

The truth being I'd always suspected Santa Barbara may be a little bit special. You see as a youngster it wasn't just the repeated playbacks of Barry Manilow and his endless hours of seventies cheese that my mother thrust upon me – she would also subject me to countless hours of daytime television mediocrity. The list of these low budget, second rate gap fillers were endless, but a few in particular will forever haunt me – *Sons and Daughters*, *The Sullivans*, *Knots Landing*, *A Country Practice*, and *Santa Barbara* are just a few of the horrors that immediately spring to mind. As you can see my mother was a very busy lady indeed. Now I don't really recall much of Santa Barbara *apart from the usual – beautiful women bitching about their no-good rooting tooting cheating men* but loosely remember it being set in lavish hilltop apartments overlooking the glistening ocean. However, it would be a travesty to associate Santa Barbara solely on some dodgy two-bit of a soap opera that was rightfully axed years ago.

Drenched in colonial history, the city dates back to the 18th century and was one of the special twenty-one sites chosen by the early Spanish settlers to build their Missionary outposts. These large inhabited compounds were ambitious attempts by the Spanish to convert the local Indians to their Catholic way of life. And come to think of it the promise of free dwellings in a posh Spanish villa must have been highly appealing even for the most fearsome of warriors. *'So, do you promise to serve the Catholic faith to the best of your ability, my son?'*

'Not sure, Chief. Don't think Crazy Horse be too happy with another traitor? He is a little crazy after all innit. Tell you what boss, give Geronimo room with sea view and Geronimo be very happy!'

The Spanish preachers may have long gone but their cultural influences clearly remain. Adobe buildings sprawl high into the hills, while its leafy downtown has a distinctly laid back and enchanting Mediterranean feel. We originally hadn't intended to stay for long but found it increasingly difficult to leave this delightful seaside town. A romantic walk on the harbour was soon followed by a leisurely stroll along the beach. Angie even found time to complete her own westward mission by dipping her toes in both sides of the ocean – the Atlantic Ocean in Atlantic City and now the warm waters of the Pacific Ocean. After that we stopped off for lunch in one of the many plush downtown tapas bars. Sprawling out into the street, we ordered a round of cocktails and watched the beautiful crowds saunter on by. A strapping man with a chiseled jawline strutted past, a striking young blonde dressed in the tiniest of skirts soon followed. Angie turned to me and smiled, I smiled back. One drink led to another as lunch slowly drifted into the afternoon. It really was the perfect way to spend a day. A while later we begrudgingly pulled ourselves away and headed to the car, but even then we couldn't quite say goodbye, allowing ourselves one last final drive into the Santa Barbara hills to deliberate on where we would live if our lottery numbers ever came in.

It was quarter to three when we eventually departed Santa Barbara and headed in the direction of LA. What the hell were we thinking? As who in their right mind would choose to time their arrival to coincide directly with the LA rush hour. This was surely naivety on a massive scale. Quite frankly I have never embarked on such a drive before and will never ever put myself through such an ordeal again. We only had ourselves to blame, it's not like Michael Douglas hadn't already warned us in that appallingly bad movie *Fallen Down*. You know the one? The one where the grumpy old man gets dumped by his wife, gets stuck in a traffic jam, then throws a complete paddy and goes off on a mass killing spree. A bit unnecessary I'd always thought; a wafer-thin plot Angie had commented. Little did we know how testing the next few hours would be.

I should have known we were heading for trouble the moment we deviated off the main highway and decided to take the scenic route towards the beach town of Ventura. Upon reflection only a fool could plump for such an option, as surely any sane person would have realised that an hour of faffing around over here would almost certainly mean another hour and half of rush hour hell over there. We weren't exactly prepared for a diversion either. My iPhone's GPS was up to its usual tricks, randomly bouncing across the screen, while my back up print outs only covered the main route from the highway. Personally, I was blaming Angie for all the chaos, as I specifically remember her interrupting the salesman at the car hire counter and confidently declaring, *'Sat Nav? No, I'm sure we can survive without it, thank you very much,'* before whispering into my ear... *'If they think we're paying another sixty-five bucks for a friggin' Sat Nav that should come as standard then they can go and take a running jump, my friend!'*

But it never ceases to amaze me how any given situation can blur with time.

'I hope you know what you're doing, Jamie?' she piped up.

'That Sat Nav you declined would have come in pretty handy now, don't you think? I really hope you know what you're doing?'

'Pardon me? I seem to remember it was you who refused that sat nav, my friend. What was it you quoted to the man...?' I challenged back.

'Whatever, James! You just better make sure you know where you're going, buster. This is all your fault, you know!'

'Yes darling, it always is,' I said shaking my head.

Unfortunately I hadn't a clue where we were going and my cunning plan of following the road signs was proving not particularly cunning at all – the road we were following suddenly coming to an abrupt halt at a junction of derelict playing fields *what the...?* Leaving us with little option but to retrace our route all the way back to the main highway we had departed thirty minutes earlier. It was fair to say I wasn't a popular chappie that afternoon.

It was approximately four o'clock on a steaming hot Thursday afternoon when we finally hit the back of the LA rush hour somewhere along highway 101. It took another three hours of stop start, bumper to bumper traffic before we finally reached the city's limits, still someway short of our intended destination.

'This is ridiculous,' Angie huffed. 'It's all your fault for taking us on that ridiculous detour. I dunno, Jamie, what were you thinking?'

'Yes, in hindsight it probably wasn't the best idea, darling,' I muttered. 'But do you really think we would have magically missed all this? It must have been building up for BLOODY hours?' I shouted, striking the horn in frustration. Honk Honk Honk!

'And smacking the car is not going to help you now, is it?'

'No, maybe not but it makes me feel a whole lot better.' Honk Honk Honkkkkkkkkk 'FUCK OFFFF!' I screamed out my window to no one in particular.

To those in the know the sound of hooters and driver turrets is a common occurrence in these parts. According to the Texas Transportation Institute, the official body which tracks congestion statistics, LA is officially the worst city in America for traffic congestion. Traffic can get so bad that they reckon every man, woman and child spends an average 72 hours a year stuck in gridlock. Now that's a lot of time to spend watching your evening slowly dissipate away, so it's no wonder why one may occasionally feel the urge to vent one's fury. *Michael Douglas, I take it all back. Maybe it wasn't such a crap movie after all*. There are various theories as to why it's so bad. Some point to the fact that LA has the highest concentration of people per square mile. At last count it was creeping up to 6,000, that's nearly 50% more than New York. Others suggest that locals simply love their cars too much, driving on average 23 hours a week and nearly double that of any other major city. While the majority of people simply bemoan an inadequate transportation system, claiming the city's metro just doesn't go where it needs to go. One thing's for certain, it's not for a lack of road space. LA has a plethora of road networks and with an average of twelve road miles packed into every square mile, the city has more road space than it could possibly need.

However, on further analysis this could actually be part of the problem. A quick perusal of the city's road network reveals a bewildering set of highways, byways, intersections, and spaghetti like junctions intercrossing the city. To the casual observer the road layout bears more resemblance to a set of Russian nesting dolls than it does a coherent road system. The complex network of roads is effectively a set of grids within a set of grids within a grid. *Stay with me here.* The largest grid is the main freeway system that dissects the city *think big squared graph paper where the edges are the freeways. The* secondary grid system is the main artillery roads or surface streets that feed each freeway system *now think of a load of smaller squares sitting within a bigger square.* Whilst the third set of grids are the residential streets that sit within each surface grid. And if you think that's confusing enough you wanna try driving it – which kind of explains all the chaos in the first place as no one clearly has the foggiest idea as to where the hell they're supposed to be going?

They say you never get a second chance to make a first impression and regrettably our chaotic experience had somewhat skewed my opinion before our visit had really began. Los Angeles may well be home to Hollywood, Santa Monica, Pamela, and the movies – and yes I'm sure it would have been nice to have checked out the hills, pay homage to the stars, and even taken in a few adventure parks – but sadly it wasn't going to happen. Not this time anyway, as somewhere in the gridlock we had taken the decision to move on, forget about LA and continue with our journey onwards. You see, that's the beauty about travelling, there are no rules, no real regulations or timeframes to stick to – you can stay as long as you want or as little as you like, it's entirely up to you.

Our time in California was nearly complete and I certainly didn't want to remember it like this – a sprawling metropolis of congestion and chaos. As despite what you think you've seen in the movies, California really is a truly wondrous place – full of diverse landscapes, stunning scenery, while packed with a sense of optimism that can only really come in a land full of plenty. I for one wasn't going to let one smoggy afternoon of bumper to bumper traffic fray my perceptions any further. So when Angie somewhat inevitably popped the question '*Oh sod this, shall we sack this off?*' she got no argument from me. I simply glanced down at my spaghetti map of junctions, passed it across the dashboard and said.

'Take me home, baby. Take me home.'

It's a good job we weren't in any rush.

Palm Springs

And so we headed east to begin our journey home, and for the first time in a long time the setting sun was now very much behind us. Crossing LA that evening had been slow and tedious. The traffic may have eased somewhat but the road was still dotted with a line of cars stretching out as far as the eye could see. One accident now and there would be tailbacks for miles. Drifting into a daze I was reminded of a journey long ago, where a few of us from Uni *and apparently 2 other million folk* set out one night along the M4 corridor to catch a rare glimpse of the last ever solar eclipse of the 20th century. Never before had I seen a motorway so densely packed, it was a miracle the road never crumbled under the sheer weight of cars, yet somehow the traffic still flowed. It really was an extraordinary sensation driving along the road to Devon that night. It was as if we were riding upon an unstoppable tide, along an imaginary river of cars. And as for the solar eclipse? Well that was one of the most remarkable things I had ever seen. From the rapid decrease in temperature, to the eerie silence that bestowed as a thick blanket of dark shrouded day into night. But most of all I will never forget those birds, those crazy disorientated birds so confused they didn't know which way to fly...

Sometime later we left civilisation and entered the clutches of the Californian desert. As to when exactly, I couldn't tell you. A combination of poor road signage, sleepy eyes and even poorer lighting gave little away as to what lay beyond the next turning. Eventually we picked up the trail for Palm Springs and shortly before midnight arrived in what would be our final destination before the big blow out in Vegas.

The next morning we were up surprisingly early considering we'd spent much of the previous day locked in heavy traffic – yet my growing suspicions we'd be doing very little were immediately confirmed the moment I spoke to the hotel's dippy young receptionist.

'Good morning and how are we today?' I said causing the girl to snap from her gaze.

'Errr yeah, errrr... very well, I guess? Errr sorry I was likeeee miles away.'

'Don't worry, I'm not your boss,' I smiled. 'I won't tell.'

The young receptionist stared back blankly. A large yawn crept across her face.

Well there's no need for that, my sweet pickle. It was only a bit of bloody banter.

'So what can I do for you, sir?' she said, glancing down to fiddle with her nails.

'Yes, well I was wondering if there was something you can recommend we do today? We're only in town for a couple of days and haven't really had much time to do any research.'

The young girl looked up from whatever she was doing, drew a big sigh and puffed.

'Well it is kinda hot around here, you know,' she said, pointing in the direction of the leaflet counter. 'I suppose you can play golf? Lotta folk around here like to play bitta golf I guess.'

'Anything else? Not really much of a golfer I'm afraid,' I said, hoping for a little more.

'Well I guess you're like kinda screwed then, ain't yer,' she said with a petulant shrug of the shoulders. 'Not much else to do around here.'

'Nothing?' I challenged back somewhat surprised by her nonchalance.

'Uh uh,' she replied, shaking her head.

'Surely there must be something?'

'Well I guess there's the aerial tram in town.'

'Oh really? Great, that sounds perfect,' I smiled, feeling we were finally making progress.

'But you don't wanna go up there,' she said, shaking her head.

'I don't? But it sounds a fantastic idea. Why on earth not?'

'Because it's closed, sir.'

'Closed?'

'Absolutely, sir.'

'Oh well that's handy, isn't it. Any particular reason as to why it's closed?' I asked.

'Errrr yeah... because it's like way too hot up there!' she said with a derogatory shake of the head. 'Like I told you, no one goes into the mountains this time of year. Only people with a screw lose wanna go in the mountains when it's this hot!' she giggled, rolling her eyes and spinning her little finger around her ear.

'Really? Well thanks for the tip I'll bear it in mind,' I replied concluding it probably best to end the conversation right there.

Seeking answers I retreated to our balcony, flipped open my laptop and Googled Palm Springs. After a quick view of some overhead aerials it became abundantly clear what Palm Springs was – a purpose-built resort town located on the outer fringes of the desert. The actual town itself is barely 100 miles east of LA, but the four separate mountain ranges that encircle the valley, may as well put it on an entirely different planet altogether. However, it was the advent of the car that changed everything and it was this coupled with the perceived climatic health benefits that encouraged widespread migration in the early 20th century. The resorts and stars soon latched on and by the late 1920s Palm Springs had become *the* holiday destination for many of Hollywood's finest. And that's about it really, that's all the history I could muster up for this steaming hot desert town.

And I must also confess we did absolutely nothing in the next couple of days and I'm at pains to say the dizzy receptionist was right all along. You see in Palm Springs it really is too hot to do anything remotely constructive and in a place where temperatures regularly exceed a hundred, even the simplest tasks can become highly demanding. Out in the desert there can be no room for mistakes and any slip ups are immediately punished. Take for example starting up your car. What should normally be a simple case of starting the ignition and pulling away, is complicated by the fact that overnight your steering wheel has somehow morphed itself into the devil's ring of burning fire, scalding everything that crosses its path, including the palms of your hands – hence the name Palm Springs. And you thought they named this town after an oasis? Ok I completely made that up but you nearly believed me, didn't you? Note to self – never ever park the car out in the open. There's a reason why every other car parks under a tree!

Things don't get any easier by the pool, especially if you've accidentally left your flip flops out melting in the afternoon sun. A school boy error if there ever was one, as your path to the pool is now completely blocked by a searing hot layer of molten concrete, leaving you little choice but to dance around like a complete numpty as you prance your way forwards to the perimeter of the pool.

Note to self – flip flops must be placed under sun lounger at all times!

'You want to be careful, James,' Angie giggled. 'Keep that up and you might have just secured yourself a role in the next Riverdance tribute act'

'Yeah yeah very funny, girl, and thanks for reminding me about the flip flops. Nice to know you've got my back... Not!'

Most important note of all – Angie can no longer be trusted!

That evening we dined at the local Applebee's restaurant. I had my usual chicken wings and baby back ribs, while Angie, conscious that we were both piling on the pounds, decided she would set the example and opt for a rather dull house salad instead. Supping on my Bud Light I took a moment to absorb our immediate surroundings. In less than two weeks' time we'd be back on a plane and all this would be gone. A tinge of sadness came upon me. I was going to miss this place that was for sure. I'm not afraid to admit it but I had completely fallen in love with it all. The irony is that we all have our preconceptions of America and not all of them are good. A combination of ill-advised foreign policy and general movie stereotyping has led many to lay judgement before they have even set foot in the place. It's amazing how many times you hear people talk in negatives only to later confess they've never actually visited the place. Sometimes you just have to look a little further, dig a little deeper to truly understand the meaning of a place. Take for example a regular American bar. To some it may be nothing more than a crude drinking establishment with rowdy folk drinking very light beer. But to me it is a reflection of everything that is good about the American way of life. From the bright lights, big screens and generous servings of succulent food – to the twinkle in the eye of the smiling waitress wishing you all have such a wonderful day. But above all I would miss that overwhelming sense of can-do positivity that is very much prevalent in these parts. In a country where hard work and effort is rewarded rather than frowned upon it's no wonder why so many people achieve so much. It's amazing to think the things you can accomplish in life when you put your mind to it.

I supped on my beer and let out a big sigh. It's fair to say I had never felt more American than I did that day, on that early summer's evening in the baking hot town of Palm Springs.

Las Vegas Part 1

They say there are some things in life you are born to do, and other things you are trained to do. Yes, I'm talking about the nature nurture theory here. Now you're probably wondering where I'm going with this and what the hell it's got to do with Vegas. A very good question, as by making this statement I'm clearly alluding to the fact that I was either a born gambler *which is completely nonsensical as have you ever seen a baby toddle into a bookies?* Or over the years I have skillfully educated myself into the art of deception to become one of the greatest card sharks the world has ever seen – which incidentally were it to be true I'd no doubt have been beaten to a pulp and banned from every Vegas casino a long time ago! Regrettably *for my wallet* I am none of the above, but like many of my peers I do enjoy the occasional flutter, most notably on my weekly football accumulators that promises so much yet ultimately delivers so very little. Although what really gets me going is a good game of cards and I can think of nothing better than pitting my wits against fellow card players wherever the place may be.

My passion for cards began a long time ago and for this I can solely lay the blame of responsibility squarely upon my father's broad shoulders – for it was him and his fellow card buddies that got me well and truly hooked the moment they invited me into their secret card society way back in the summer of 1991. Now to many, my father was generally regarded as a rather cautious, pragmatic banker who spent the majority of his time tucked away in some poky little room, dishing out small business advice to every Tom, Dick and Harry on the east side of the estate. To say he was bored and needing a bit of excitement was an understatement. So one day he and his fellow banking buddies created this underground card school, where they would reconvene on the final Friday of every month to gamble away their hard earned cash. In total there were four of them – my dad, his best mate Dave, Phil the wheeler dealer, and Brian the hairy one. Each month the venues would change, but the majority of games were either played at David's small bachelor flat in Burnham or around our family home in Langley, on the proviso that me and my big sister were kept firmly out of the way. Over time my father would ease on this ruling, allowing us a few moments to greet the gang and if we were really lucky, bad boy Phil would beckon us over for a quick swig of his frothy brown beer and sneaky sniff on his packet of Silk Cut Lights! *Ahhh those were the days!*

The games they played would inevitably vary. Phil liked Bragg, my father preferred poker, while Brian didn't really care at all as long as he was well stocked up on the monkey nuts. The majority of the time they would play this crazy game called Phat, a kind of mad cross between Bridge and Trumps, where the aim of the game was to team up with your partner and win as many tricks as possible. Any trick won with an Ace would score your team 4 points, a King 3 points, Queen 2 points and Jack 1 point. The only other two scoring cards were the nines and fives and these were the big ones to go after. A nine would score you 9 points, a five would score you 5 points, unless of course it was the designated trump suit which would then count for double. The winning team was the first to peg over 180 points. Each player would take it in turns in calling the trumps and therefore taking on the responsibility in leading the team out from the front. However, woe betide anyone that lost the nines and fives on their call, for this was regarded as a home defeat and there'd be some serious questions raised about the caller's carding ability. Occasionally the guys would let me in on the odd dummy hand to teach me the basics. The main skills being to determine the strength of your partner's hand, whilst learning of your opponent's weaknesses. They all agreed that without doubt it was the finest card game they ever played. Then one day out of the blue Phil suddenly left the country and never came back. To this day we still have no idea why he suddenly disappeared and for years they all speculated. David always thought it was the taxman, Brian was convinced it was the mafia, while my father just missed his old buddy. Either way there was now a huge vacant void in the gang that desperately needed filling. Over the next few months there were many contenders. Nigel, Bob, and John all gave it their best shot, but none were considered a patch on Phil. Then one day David, who was regarded as the most talented player of them all, invited me to join in for proper, and, impressed with my skills, he declared to the gang, *'Guys, we can stop looking now. I think we've found our man!'*

Yes, it's fair to say I was probably nurtured from a young age to love the game of cards so it was only natural that one day I'd want to test my skills in the biggest arena of them all. In hindsight I often wonder why it took me so long to actually reach Vegas, but now I was here I was going to explore its entirety in every last detail. They say Vegas is not a place, but a state of mind; an adult's Disneyland so to speak. So what better place to get a feel for the real Vegas *not on the Strip where we would inevitably end up* but out on the outskirts of town in the JW Marriott, home to the legendary Rampart Casino and holy grail to every old fart and dreamer in town. There were other reasons why we chose to temporarily stay off the main strip – basically we were knackered and the thought of lounging around a sun-drenched pool, knocking back the cocktails all day was naturally a very appealing one – and in terms of relaxation the JW did not disappoint. Set in over 10 acres of lush tropical gardens and with stunning westerly views, the hotel was quite frankly the finest place I'd ever stayed in. And so for the next few days we did exactly as intended, but as hard as my body tried I refused to let it unwind. I had waited far too long to let anymore time simply idle on by.

'Do you fancy a wee gamble, my dear?' I said with a hint of a flutter and to my great surprise Angie replied with a smile.

'I thought you'd never bloody ask!'

We were finally ready to gamble. But let's not make any bones about it, the Rampart Casino that was attached to the hotel bore more resemblance to my grandfather's bingo hall than it did a swanked up Vegas casino. A classic Facebook moment this most certainly was not. In fact, it's fair to say that in the space of a few short hours, I had to swerve past more speeding Zimmer frames than I did in the entire week working as a builder's tea boy back in the local old folks' home on my first ever work experience. Some work experience that turned out to be, as the only thing it taught me was that I never ever wanted to work again.

Anyway, not to be put off by our mature surroundings, we immediately embraced the Rampart for what is was: the real Las Vegas, the off the beaten path Las Vegas, where only locals and those in the know would come to seek their fortune. With an average age well above sixty, the Rampart Casino was clearly the place where folk from far and wide would come for one final flutter, one last hurrah before being hurriedly packed off to the nearest retirement centre. Some would come just for a holiday while others would clearly stay for longer. One thing's for sure though you couldn't help but admire their sense of adventure. Many will no doubt say it's a sad way to end your days, but I for one wholeheartedly disagree and besides what's the alternative? Being cooped up in a crusty old folks' home where the only highlight is counting the number of times the builder's sloped off for tea? I know what I'd prefer, that's for sure.

We circled the floor and what immediately struck me was the velocity of the gaming machines. Maybe it was the mesmerising flashing of lights or the constant ringing of bells that initially drew me in. Or perhaps it was just the sheer weight of numbers that had me reaching for my pocket. Either way there must have been over a thousand shiny machines spinning away, all grouped in their little clusters. The vast majority of which were occupied by one old timer or another frittering away what little remained of their meagre inheritance. A wry smile crept over my face. With an official payback of just 94% on every dollar spent, it must be every middle-aged child's worst nightmare to discover that your parents have just packed up and buggered off to Vegas.

We headed for the Roulette tables and were soon devising our own fool proof strategies. I went for the cover as much of the board approach, placing my chips on every line, corner and number. Whereas Angie would randomly place her five chips *the minimum bet* on selective numbers, before carefully tucking the remaining chips into the depths of her handbag, in a pathetic attempt to convince herself it really was going to be her last bet after all. Needless to say, it wasn't and we soon found ourselves caught in conversation with an elderly lady who had clearly been drinking all afternoon.

'Ah wow, are you guys really from Engerlaaaaaad?' the lady shouted across the table.

'Indeed we are,' I replied politely, doing my best to deflect yet another *Yes I'm from England* pointless conversation.

'Oh, I just love little old Engerlaaaaand. Did you know my ex- husbaaaaand was English?' the old lady slurred.

'No, can't say I did,' I replied glancing back at the table.

'Oh yeah he most certainly was, bless his cotton socks,' the old lady smiled.

'So why did you guys spilt up then?' Angie piped up from out of the blue.

'You can't say that, isn't it bloody obvious!' I whispered subtly pointing to the lady's long line of finished drinks.

'Ah well honey, he didn't like to smoke, he didn't like drink, and he certainly wasn't much of a gaaammmbleeerr. Hell, it was never going to work!' She shrugged. 'But hey that don't matter now as I got myself a new maaaan you see. Yeah, I know sweetie, he ain't that much to look at but he sure knows how to treat a woman and that's all that matters to me, honey,' she said taking a huge slurp of her cocktail.

'We'll I can see he's a very lucky man,' Angie smiled with just a hint of sarcasm.

'Why, thank you, dear. Ain't she just the sweetest thing?' the lady replied, slobbering over the table.

We carried on playing, but my strategy of covering two thirds of the board was slowly dwindling my chips. Deciding to hedge my bets, I changed tact concentrating all my chips on the first third of the board, spreading them around the number 5 for no particular reason. It must have been a gut feeling or something as moments later the number 5 dropped in delivering with it a cool 84 bucks!

'Get in the hole!' I roared clinching my fists then spinning Angie high into the air.

'Go Englaaaaaaad,' the old lady screamed, blowing plumes of smoke across the table.

'About tiaaaaaaaaaaaame,' Angie giggled in her best American accent.

And yes perhaps in hindsight the celebrations were a tad excessive but the exhilaration of that first win will stay long in my memory.

Dinner came around resulting in an immediate exodus from the tables, with everyone heading towards the dining area to claim their free complementary buffet. One by one the old folks shuffled forward, swiping their player's cards at the head of the queue.

'How many points do we need to qualify?' Angie asked the greying couple in front.

'Oh, it's all changed now,' the old lady answered. 'In the old days 200 points would buy you a breakfast and 300

286

points would gettcha dinner. Nowadays you need 500 points to get yourself a free meal.'

'Lotsa changes, lotsa changes,' the old man chipped in shaking his head.

'When we first moved here from New York, back in '69, a win used to feel like a win,' the old lady continued. 'Nowadays they just print you out this little ticket,' she said pulling a crumpled piece of paper from her purse. 'This don't feel like real money, not anymore, now it feels more like Monopoly money. They do this on purpose so you end up putting it all straight back in. I swear they're all in it now, all of them. Me? I put my ticket in my purse, like this you see, and then put another $20 in. That way you know where you are so you can track your winnings. You gotta have a strategy, honey, you gotta have a strategy.'

It was fascinating speaking to the old couple and as much as they hated to admit it they were both completely and utterly hooked.

'Now it's all run by these computers,' she continued. 'Back in the old days, back in '69, you used to get 250 flushes a week on those slots. Now nothing, not a God damn dime!' she said shaking her head.

'But you still come back for more? You must still enjoy it?' I questioned.

'I'll tell you a little story, sonny,' the old man interrupted, pointing his finger into my face. 'When we first started playing, back in '69, we came to Vegas with the New York gambling club. The first time I played craps, I bet 40 dollars and this young Asian lady, rolled straight through twenty-nine times. I walked away with 27 thousand dollars that day, son. And you know what, my friend? I've been looking for that lady ever since,' he smiled with a wry shake of the head.

I gave Angie a shrug and a smile. Whether the story was true or not I guess we'll never know. All I can say was that the old man was pretty damn convincing.

We finished dinner and headed back to the tables, although all I could think about was that young Asian lady rolling through twenty-nine times. Did she really roll straight through twenty-nine times? Shit, I didn't know what the hell that even meant but it sure sounded good to me. If the old man could get lucky then maybe we could too. Maybe all those years of training in my old man's card school would finally begin to pay off. I was certainly in the right town that was for sure, now all I had to do was go and find out if I could still do it. And there was only ever one place that was gonna be!

Las Vegas Part 2

My fascination for Vegas began in the summer of 1982, where I recall sitting in front of my grandfather's television set watching the opening credits to *Viva Las Vegas*, in a vain attempt to console myself from England's devastating elimination from the Spain '82 World Cup. What an introduction to football that turned out to be. England had desperately needed a win that night and with the score 0-0, Kevin Keegan, the alleged saviour, came off the bench to find himself totally unmarked, inside the box and with the ball spinning towards his legendary girlie perm. This was it, this was his moment, his destiny so to speak, for all he had to do was stick out his massive head, make any sort of connection and we were on our way to the next round. Regrettably our curly-haired friend completely fluffed his lines, put the ball wide and the rest is as they say history. England were sent home packing despite not losing a single game in the whole tournament.

'But I don't get it, Grandad? How can we be out if we didn't lose a single game? Doesn't make any sense?' I said scratching my head.

Try explaining that one to an inquisitive seven-year-old.

'Well you see, son... it's all about the goal difference? Oh, never mind!'

At the time my grandparents had just returned from their own westward adventure, a three week Californian holiday, ending up in Vegas.

Oh, how I loved visiting my grandparents at such times, for as well as filling us with tales of their travels, they would inevitably shower us with gifts the moment we entered their house. On this particular trip I had been given a very rare PAL video cassette of *Viva Las Vegas*, in what many consider to be one of Elvis Presley's greatest ever movies. And so, in a blatant attempt to divert me from my persistent questioning, my grandfather suggested I go be a good little boy and quietly watch the movie. As with all distant memories the images of that day are somewhat hazy, but I vaguely recall being swept through this mad, illuminated, flashing city with Elvis singing along to some catchy Hawaiian tune in the background. It was only later I would learn the street in which the camera was panning over wasn't the world famous Strip in which we've all become accustomed to, but Fremont Street in the old town, which up until recently was considered to be *the real* Las Vegas – the one where Elvis, Frank, and the rest of the gang had clearly fallen in love with all those years ago.

Like most westward towns, Las Vegas had blossomed with the advent of the railroad. Its central location between Denver, Salt Lake City, and Los Angeles initially put the town on the map, although it was its access to water that really elevated it into the premier stopover destination. Indeed, the name Las Vegas translates into 'The Meadows', implying the immediate area was surrounded with vegetation, not just barren wasteland in which we all associate with it today. However, what really separated this town from the rest was the legalisation of gambling in 1931. This newly found freedom, coupled with the mass migration of men working on the nearby Hoover Dam project was just the spark the town needed. As a result the downtown area flourished, with

Fremont Street quickly becoming its glittering heart and soul. Over the next few years numerous western style casino hotels sprang up – Binion's Horseshoe, The Golden Nugget and my particular favourite, The Pioneer Club with its legendary 40 foot smoking cowboy – helped propel the town into the neon mecca it is today. Mafia money soon flowed in, and with it the rapid growth in the number of luxury themed hotels. Perhaps the most famous hotel at the time was the Flamingo Hotel. As well as bringing in the stars and the shows, it was also the first big casino to be located outside the city limits on the major highway, which would soon become known as the Strip. Investment continued throughout the sixties and with the completion of Caesars Palace in 1966, the first all purpose mega resort hotel had been born.

Four decades later and arguably the Strip's most accomplished development, the Bellagio, was presented to the world, starring in the 2001 remake of the Rat Pack classic *Ocean's Eleven*. Inspired by the Italian mountain village of Bellagio, the hotel was the world's most expensive development when completed in 1998. Costing a staggering 1.6 billion dollars, the casino broke conventional design by creating a gaming environment based on seduction rather than distraction. With an emphasis on low lighting, glass chandeliers and extravagant furnishings, many considered it to be a privilege just to be within. While some even believed the interior to be so immersive it was irrelevant whether they won or lost. However, it was its stunning fountain display that featured so prominently in *Ocean's Eleven* that shot the hotel into immortality. That 30 second film clip of a smooth George Clooney and suave Brad Pitt overlooking the dancing fountains probably did more for local tourism than any cheesy commercial could ever have done.

Well it certainly worked for me anyway, as no sooner had we arrived we found ourselves following the crowds into the hotel lobby where an impressive glass ceiling of coloured flowers welcomed our arrival.

'Wow, that's amazing!' Angie smiled, before being rudely barged by a horde of snappy happy Japanese photographers.

'Bloody tourists. Some people have no manners,' she huffed.

'Bloody cheapskates, they should get themselves a friggin' room,' I said with a disappointed shake of the head.

The queues for the front desk were unsurprisingly busy. Not that I was complaining, on the contrary, I saw it as an opportune moment to take in our lavish surroundings. To my right, a splendid conservatory housed a vivid display of seasonal flora, on the walls hung fine art, while through the windows you could just about make out the tall cypress trees surrounding what looked like a Roman themed pool.

'This is the life, my darling? One day this could all be ours when I eventually write my book!' I said as we approached the front desk.

'Yeah, whatever, darling. Then I guess you won't mind giving me a hefty advance then, will you. Anyway, your treat, remember? You promised,' she smiled.

'Oh really, Angela? Well it would be, wouldn't it? I don't remember making such a promise? I'm sure your devious little mind conjures these things up.'

'No way Jose, it was your big idea to stay here. I would happily have stayed at the Bally's. I'm easy to please me, although unlike you, my friend, you were always a bit of a Peter Pan weren't you, Jamie?'

'Babe, that's the nicest thing you've ever said to me. Think I'll take that as a compliment, thank you very much.'

'Well you shouldn't, dear,' she replied, grabbing my American Express and placing it firmly into the hands of the very handsome receptionist.

'Allo my name is Helmut and welcome to Bellagio,' the smiling man said in his best Eastern European accent. 'How can I help you?'

'Room with a view please,' I replied, showing a print out of my hotel reservation.

Helmut took the paper and began to tap away.

'I'm sorry, sir. The reservation you made is for a standard room. Unfortunately, the standard room does not come with a view of the fountains, sir,' he said shaking his head.

'Really? Well I'm not happy about that as the agent on the phone promised us a free upgrade you see?' Angie promptly responded.

'No, I'm sorry, madam, this cannot be so. It appears this was an Internet booking? I do not believe our website employs agents, madam?' Helmut replied, shaking his head.

'Ohhhh nice try, babe, nearly got it through. Any chance of an upgrade then?' I said unfolding a crisp twenty-dollar bill onto the counter.

Helmut paused glancing down at the shimmering twenty.

'I understand, sir. You come all is this way, you spend all this money, and you don't want a view of a car park now, do you?' he suggested, tapping away on his keyboard.

'I couldn't have put it any better myself,' I smiled, sensing we were closing in on a deal.

'Ahh yes we have a room on the 25th floor overlooking the fountains. I trust that would be suitable, sir?'

'That would be lovely, my good friend,' I said slipping another twenty across the table. Angie immediately tugged me aside.

'Steady on, James, you had him at twenty. Call yourself a salesman?'

'Give me some flaming credit, will you. I got you the room, didn't I? How about a pat on the back for being so brave?'

'Yes, very impressive, Jamie. Anyway, where did you learn to pull a stunt like that?'

'It's all about spotting the window of opportunity, my dear. That's what a real salesman does you see, strikes while the iron is hot. Perhaps I'll teach you someday? You know, show you the ropes and all that,' I said, merrily skipping into the very same casino where Brad, Andy, Julia, and George once so famously strode.

And what a casino it was too. They say you never forgot the first time you grace the Bellagio's illustrious floor, and with each paying guest having to walk through the very centre to reach the elevators on the far side of the casino, it's an experience you're never likely to forget. Angie later told me she felt like a million dollars that day rolling her luggage through the heart of that casino and I agreed, comparing the experience to a scene from *Catch Me If You Can* where the young Leo waltzes through the airport surrounded by the most beautiful of air hostesses. Only this time it wasn't a bunch of sexy air stewardesses causing a stir – just me, my girl, and our trusted North Face backpacks. And so for the briefest of moments the floor of the most famous casino in the world was completely ours. Heads held high we swaggered our way through the casino like we were the most important people in town. A young man playing Roulette clocked our luggage, immediately giving out a wry smile. *Yes, my friend, your eyes are not deceiving you, it is true, we will be staying tonight. Amazing, isn't it.* We continued onwards, turning left at the blackjack tables, catching the eyes of the croupiers as we passed. One by one they all looked up nodding their heads in silent approval. I puffed out my chest just a little bit more to acknowledge their interest. *Yes, my friends, it is true, we are indeed staying here tonight. It is very expensive, you know!* We were more than just players now, we were the big time and every single person in the room knew it too. I turned to Angie seeing the excitement in her eyes.

'Still want to stay at the Bally's my friend?'

'Oh, shut up,' she replied, pouting her lips to anyone that cared.

We eventually reached the lifts where an elderly man and woman attempted to operate the card slot. Only this time they weren't staying at the Bellagio, so unfortunately for them their brief tour of the Bellagio would soon be coming to an end, right there by the lifts, oh such a shame. I retrieved my card and waived it high into the air.

'I'll get this one, darling. What floor we staying on?' I said, flapping it wildly in front of the old couple.

'Erm? I think it's the one that overlooks the fountains, darling?' Angie replied, getting into the spirit.

I'm sure you'll forgive us for our petulance. It's not every day you get to stay at the Bellagio, you know.

We spent the rest of the day casino hopping along the Strip. The weather may have been sweltering but the pace was relentless. With so much to do and so little time, you find yourself frantically whizzing from one hotel to another, yet barely scratching the surface.

Starting at the Bellagio, we crossed the road into Paris, walking through 18th century Parisian streets then into the Bally's for a quick game of roulette. *That was Angie's call. She does love a cheeky gamble that one.*

We continued up the Strip, venturing into Venice for a grande latte and quick ride on the gondolas. Next to that was the Wynn, where we marvelled at the dramatic waterfall, and then crossed the road to watch the pirates at the entrance of Treasure Island. Turning back on ourselves, we checked out the huge Mirage volcano before spending what felt like an eternity walking through the streets of Rome in the colossus that is Caesars Palace.

It was frantic stuff but wholly addictive and fuelled by an unexplainable desire to experience *just one more world* we gallantly soldiered on – passing the Bellagio fountains, sampling life in the Big Apple, dodging the kids in Fantasyland, before finally ending up in the Mandalay Bay on the far end of the Strip for a well-deserved cocktail and some much-needed light reflection.

A mad, hustling, bustling of a city it most certainly was, but one with a sense of anticipation, not trepidation that you may normally encounter when being so rushed. But above all there was this vibe, a perennial buzz of excited optimism flowing throughout the city, one of which I had not encountered before or anytime since. Yet without doubt there is most definitely a darker side to Vegas. Look beyond the glamour and you can see it everywhere, hidden within the phone boxes and lurking on every street. It ain't called Sin City for nothing and within moments of setting foot on the Strip you are soon confronted by the infamous card slappers clicking their cards to the chorus of a thousand crickets – and before you know it some little cheeky bugger has handed you a calling card of some exotic lady charging you sixty-five bucks for an evening of anal. A bargain at twice the price the man assured me, but not the best thing to be caught with while walking down the street with your loved ones.

'What you got there then, babe?'

'*Errr nothing, darling? Wow, is that the Bellagio. Doesn't it look amazing!*'

The next day entailed more of the same – more food, more beers, more hotels and lots more Roulette in between. It was all thoroughly exciting stuff, yet there was so much we didn't get to do. Time flies in Vegas. It's common knowledge that the casinos try to confuse you by bearing no natural light or real time clocks, although that's only the half of it. The other half is completely unexplainable. You walk in one moment, depart the next only to discover that three hours of your life has mysteriously disappeared, vanished like it never even existed. *Where the hell did that go?* you wonder to yourself. *I only had a quick game? And where's all my bloody money gone*? Time distorts in Vegas. Like a weird, messed up time warp it sucks you in, casts its spell, only to spit you out when you've completely blown away all your chips. The irony being I had come here to test my Poker skills, yet I couldn't pull myself from the Roulette tables, so addictive they had become.

'James, you sure you don't want a quick game of Poker? Your dad will be very disappointed with you,' Angie commented.

'No, I'm fine, darling,' I responded. 'Doesn't feel quite right playing without him. Maybe I'll drag the old boy out here next time?'

'Any excuse to come back, hey, babe,' Angie said with a knowing smile.

We finished our tour of Vegas where it all began, in the old town in the centre of Fremont Street. So much has changed in recent years I doubt the old Rat Pack would recognise it now. The multi-million-pound light extravaganza that is now 'The Fremont Street Experience' is quite a piece of work. Covering over four blocks, downtown's newest attraction is a dazzling light display projected onto a canopy high above your head. Housing over 12 million LED lamps, it's really quite a show. Although rather ironically the highlight is the moment they pull the plug, leaving you in total darkness. Local officials will no doubt tell you the project has been a success and few can argue as the downtown area is now flooded with tourists once again. But impressive as it is, I left somewhat disappointed. Maybe I was being selfish, but part of me wanted to experience the old downtown, like it used to be, the one where Elvis and the boys used to go to all those years ago.

Rather fittingly then I guess it kind of sums up what Vegas is all about. With new casinos popping up all the time, it's an ever-changing, ever-evolving, 24-hour city lusting for more dollars. Stop feeding it and it can be very unforgiving, knocking down the old to be replaced by the new. This is a city that never stops, not for anyone and not even for Elvis. There's no time for sentiment in Vegas, it's only the here and now that really matters. Love it or hate it – it is what it is – a microcosm of life itself, a mad encapsulated experiment reflecting the greater world in which we now live in – and maybe just maybe that's why we all love it so very much?

Leaving Las Vegas

We said goodbye to Vegas feeling somewhat deflated, barely saying a word to one another for the remainder of the morning. We had lived through the highs and now it was time to experience the lows. *Please, Angela, please, just one more game pleaaaaassseeeeeee.* It was depressing stuff alright, as not only were the fun and games well and truly over, but leaving Las Vegas would also signify the end of our long and wonderful American adventure. In a few days' time we'd be catching our plane out of Phoenix, being one step closer to home and all the uncertainty that entailed. I wasn't ready to go home yet, not by a long stretch.

A couple of hours later we passed the most famous dam of them all, the Hoover Dam, and agreeing it might improve our moods we pulled over for a quick visit to peek over its precarious edge.

'No, I'm sorry Angie, it's just not happening for me anymore. I can't take it... I'm... I'm... I'm going over,' I said staring down into the concreted abyss some 700 feet below.

'Well, before you jump can you sign everything over to me, please, babe?' Angie replied, handing me over a tissue.

'And if I'm really lucky there may even be a few dollars left in your empty pot to pay for my ticket home!' she giggled.

'Yeah thanks dear, knew you'd talk me out of it,' I replied stepping back from the edge. The dam itself is hugely impressive and when completed in 1935 it was the largest federal project ever undertaken. Measuring over 1,200-foot-wide and 700 feet high, the concreted arch gravity dam was the largest man-made structure ever made. As a result, the mighty Colorado River was successfully tamed, while providing irrigation and much-needed flood relief to the local area. To top that, they reckon the power generated from its massive hydroelectric generators is enough to light up the entire west. Now that's some piece of work alright and it's no wonder engineers are still literally wetting their pants over it to this day.

Deep in thought we headed back to the car and continued along the I-40 towards Kingman, some 100 miles south east of Vegas. It was one of the quietest journeys I had ever encountered with barely another car passing us by. Then out of the blue something very strange happened. Something so instantaneous and had we taken the wrong decision the consequences could have been devastating. We had just past the town of Kingman when I spotted her – a well-dressed middle-aged woman waving her arms at us from the side of the road.

'Babe, is that a woman waving at us?' I said, sensing something wasn't quite right.

'I think it is, Jamie, shall we pull over and pick her up?'

I slowed down as we approached the lady to assess the situation. I was suspicious from the moment I looked into her eyes. Here was this calm middle-aged woman casually flagging us down in the middle of nowhere. And where was her car? Surely she must have had one? Could it have been hidden behind that enormous boulder that she was rather conveniently standing in front off?

'Come on James, let's pick her up, we can't leave her out here,' Angie requested.

I slowed some more. Something wasn't right. She was too calm. If it were me, stuck out here on my own, in the middle of all this wasteland I would be close to panic, not casually waving to passers-by.

'No. I don't like it. Someone else can pick her up,' I said shaking my head.

'You sure about this, James?'

'Positive. A trucker will pick her up. Probably welcome the conversation.'

'Your call, James. But on your head, be it,' Angie replied, notching up the pressure somewhat.

I veered back to the centre of the road, tapped the accelerator and watched the lady gradually disappear from my rear-view mirror. It was a big call leaving her out there, in all that scrubland. Had I made the right choice? Had I just left a stranded woman alone in the desert? What if a trucker didn't come along? She could be out there all night? With no access to water? She could...? No that wasn't worth thinking about, but for the next few hours I could think of nothing else, going over it again and again in my head. If she really was in trouble then why didn't she show it? Why didn't she beg us to stop? Was she ruffled? No. Was she tearful? Most certainly not. There was just something about her I didn't like, something I saw in her eyes, something I didn't trust. She was too cool, too calculated, like she was hiding something perhaps. She wasn't scared, she wasn't desperate, but in a peculiar way she was kind of nervous. I'd seen that look a thousand times before on the Poker table and I knew she was bluffing the moment I first laid eyes on her. If I was wrong I'd have to live with it, deal with the consequences later but there are just some times in life you have to go with your gut, even if it appears the totally wrong thing to do. The moment I looked her in the eye I knew something was wrong. I could feel it aching away deep inside me, like a natural inbuilt alarm system warning me away from danger. All those years of playing cards in my father's card school were finally going to pay off, only not in the way I had previously imagined. My gut had never let me down before and it wasn't about to fail me now.

We arrived in Flagstaff a few hours later to discover it was all over the news.

'Police are warning residents not to approach them. The fugitives are armed and considered highly dangerous' a panicked broadcaster told a gripped nation. We watched with intrigue as the story evolved right in front of our eyes. There had been a prison break on the outskirts of Kingman. A middle-aged woman had thrown a pair of bolt cutters over the fence in an elaborate attempt to free her boyfriend and two other convicted murderers. Reports continued to flood in.

'It's believed the gang hijacked a truck at gunpoint on the outskirts of Kingman, forcing the driver to take them to Flagstaff. Police are advising residents to stay indoors. We repeat, residents must stay indoors as they are considered armed and extremely dangerous!'

I shuddered, remembering the strange lady, playing it back in my head. She fit the description, the timing was right, the location spot on and as for that huge boulder behind her? What the bloody hell was that concealing?

Over the subsequent weeks the breakout caught worldwide attention in what was to become known as the Arizona prison break. The whole region was on edge – mass murderers were officially on the loose. The story dominated the news, with the whole nation tuning in for updates. The truckers that were high jacked outside Kingman were lucky, escaping with their lives, but two other tourists were tragically murdered in the days that followed. The convicts, labelled the new Bonnie and Clyde, refused to turn themselves in, setting up camp in Yellowstone National Park. Cornered and with nowhere to run they were eventually detained but only after a fierce gunfight in the woods.

To this day we will never really know how close we came to the unthinkable. Several times I've googled the events of that day and studied her mugshot in considerable detail. It's amazing to think one moment we were innocently driving along listening to Taylor Swift's 'Love Story' then the next there was the real possibility we could have been robbed, hijacked, or possibly even worse? That thought alone will forever send a chill down me, but it just goes to show that you can never take your safety for granted. I guess we'll never really know what happened on that lonely afternoon on the I-40 but I for one truly believe we had a very lucky escape indeed.

The next day we headed north into canyon country. News of the prison break dominated local networks – with alleged sightings in southern Arizona, New Mexico and as far away as Texas and Oklahoma. Thankfully none of them in our direction.

'Right, I hope you don't mind, darling, but if we do happen to come across a stranded woman I'll be quite frankly SPEEDING up this time. You ok with that, dear?'

'Yes, grumpy, we live and learn, don't we?' Angie replied whilst rather appropriately summing it all up.

Putting our Vegas hangover and near abduction aside, there was another reason for my grumpiness – the weather. The thing is I'd waited years for this day, ever since a random school outing to Thorpe Park when I experienced my first ever helicopter ride over the magnificent Grand Canyon on the newly installed cinema 360 ride. Watching our tiny silhouette flying above the dusty terrain was one of the most exciting things my tender years had ever experienced. It may only have been a simulation but it was as if we were there flying through the canyon itself, not watching from the comfort of a packed auditorium. Oh, how we gasped as we descended into the almighty depths and wooed as we skimmed along the river's surface. Then without warning the camera jerked up, propelling us high into the bright blue sky, before slamming on the breaks nearly knocking us off our feet. We laughed, we screamed, some even tapped their hearts, they were so excited, but most of all we clapped and cheered. What an amazing ride we all agreed and maybe one day we would experience it for real. And so here we were years later, only yards away from the most famous hole in the ground, yet all we could see was an endless layer of heavy fog. I was gutted. How could this be? It wasn't supposed to rain here. We were in the heart of Arizona; a dusty desert by all accounts. Three hundred days of sunshine they keep telling us.

We parked the car at the South Rim visitors' centre and carefully followed the path to the edge. Nothing. It was out there somewhere, but it might as well have been a bloody pothole for all I could see. I walked to the edge peering out into a white shroud of unbroken cloud.

'Careful, babe,' Angie said from behind. 'Don't get all depressed on me again.'

'I'm not depressed, darling. Could be worse, at least we didn't pay for one of those all exclusive, non-refundable, 200 buck helicopter rides. Never feels quite as bad when somebody else has it worse off than you, does it?' I chuckled aloud.

'Yes, well you can thank me for that, dear,' Angie winked.

'Indeed I can. Your deep pockets saved us a small fortune, I reckon. Never thought I'd say it but thank you very much for being so prudent. Anyway, I've had enough of this, shall we sack it off then? It's never gonna to clear up.'

'No way Jamie, we've come all this way. Who's to know, it may get better. Look, let's go check out the visitors' centre, get a bite to eat and see where we are after that. You've gotta have faith, my darling.'

We spent the rest of the morning trudging around the visitors' centre being constantly reminded of what we would have seen if we'd actually bothered to have checked the forecast. It all looked so wonderfully amazing, which made the whole experience even more frustrating considering it was literally just a hop, skip and jump away – although probably not the wisest activity to be undertaking in these parts.

That's it, darling, it's not going to clear. I think we should head back.'

'Come on, babe, don't give up. Why don't we take one last drive before we go? Never know we might get lucky,' Angie said.

Impressed, and dare I say it a little shocked by her steely determination, I agreed and much to my surprise no sooner had we hit the road than the fog began to part.

'You see, I told you it would be alright,' Angie said gleefully.

Eager for our first proper look, we rushed to the rim's edge to see the canyon revealing itself in all its glory. With its multitude of layers and contrasting colours it was as if we were peering into time itself. Each layer not only representing a distinctive time period, but its vast contrasting landscapes are said to replicate over 70% of all living life zones. I stood back, taking it all in. In Vegas we had seen the future; now, peering into the depths of the Grand Canyon, we were most certainly seeing the past.

Snaking through 277 deserted miles and with depths of up to 6,000 feet – a crow would have to fly another 10 miles just to get to the other side on the North Rim. Now that's one hell of a crack and hard to imagine the culprit was that innocuous glinting little river trickling way down below. We proceeded with caution along the rim's edge. It was spine-tingling stuff but not actually that dangerous. The reality being you'd have to be very unlucky to tumble inside, as despite being more than a mile deep, the topography of the rock contours outwards rather then immediately downwards, therefore restricting the amount one can fall. That said accidents do happen as the edge is notoriously slippery. Officially fifty-four people have fallen to their deaths since the park opened in 1878. The most recent being in May 2012 where a young man got too close, slipped and plunged over 600 feet to his death. I stood back just a little, then without any warning the fog reappeared as quickly as it dispersed, ending the afternoon matinee before it had really begun. Shame.

The next morning we departed Flagstaff and headed south towards Phoenix. Winding our way up through a succession of elevated forests, the two-hour journey was perhaps one of the most spectacular drives I had ever encountered. The lush green cacti landscape was a welcoming change from the all too familiar sagebrush and boulder.

The following day we caught a plane out of Phoenix, touching down in Dallas to refuel. Several thoughts crossed my mind. How appropriate our westward adventure should come to an end where arguably the Wild West may have truly begun. For it was from these nearby cattle ranches that many a returning confederate soldier would start again, steering their herds of Longhorn to the newly formed railroad towns of the ever expanding west. Without the Texas Longhorn there'd have been no cowboys, without the cowboys there'd have been little need for the railroad towns, and without the railroads? Well, the Wild West would have been a very different place indeed.

I looked out of my window into the bright blue Texan sky. Not too far from here JFK was shot down in Dealey Plaza on that infamous November afternoon. Apparently, the old book depositary building, where the fatal shots rang out, has since been converted into a museum allowing you to gaze out the very same window where a hot and sweaty Lee Harvey Oswald notoriously once stood. Somewhere else on the outskirts of town lay Southfork Ranch. Wednesday nights were never the same again when *Dallas* came off air. Oh, how I missed JRs legendary scheming and classic one liners *'Sue Ellen, you're a drunk, a tramp and an unfit mother!'*

I sat alone as the plane refuelled and began to plan our next adventure. Starting in Dallas we could follow the Chisholm Trail retracing the pathway west. We could set off again from Independence but this time following the Oregon Trail to the coast. Maybe we could venture deeper into cowboy country, exploring the states of Wyoming, Montana and South Dakota. Heading south there was a whole lot more to see as well – we had barely touched Utah and Colorado and how could we miss out on Tombstone, one of the most famous cowboy towns of them all? We could do it all again, but completely differently. There were so many more journeys to take, so much more history to learn.

An hour or so later we were back in the sky and heading for Boston. Our westward adventure may have officially come to an end but there was still one more thing Angie just absolutely had to do.

Back East

Montreal

We touched down at Logan airport, checking into the nearest available hotel. It had been a long three months since we were last in town but I remembered it as if it were yesterday. I liked Boston, I liked it a lot, it was where our journey began and so will forever hold special memories for me. It was also our first introduction to the American way of life, so it was only fitting that we should return to relive some of those early experiences. The irony being we had travelled the continent in search of adventure but there wasn't another place I would have rather been on that late summer's afternoon.

Unfortunately though, Angie had other ideas and contrary to my best efforts there was absolutely no way I was talking her out of this one.

'You sure about this, babe?' I questioned one last time. 'To be honest, Canada's the last place I wanna go right now.'

'Sorry, darling, you promised, remember, and now it's time to deliver on that promise, my friend,' she said with a smile.

Rather reluctantly then I was left with little choice but to agree to her demands. Montreal was only a four-hour drive away and there were only so many Canadian cities I could realistically dodge. And so with a week to go Angela had finally gotten her own way and would get to live out her Canadian dream.

The next day we collected our car rental and headed to the border. The drive itself was fairly uneventful, barring Angela's childlike insistence in singing aloud to the tune of that rather annoying car insurance advert *'Go Compare, Go Compare, Go Compareeeeeeeeee'*, only this time cleverly replacing the catchphrase 'Go Compare' with 'Montreal' instead. I'm not sure what's worse? Listening to Angie gloating all morning or being repeatedly reminded of that irritating chubby bloke who starred in that terrible commercial?

It started the moment we got in the car.

'Montreaaaaaaaaaaaalll!' she randomly blurted out.

'Yep, well done, dear, that is indeed where we're heading on this bright and sunny morning.'

'Montreaaaaaaal!'

'Yes, dear, I heard you the first time.'

'Montreal... Montreal... Montreaaaaaaaaaalll!'

'Yeah alright girl, you can stop milking it now, it's getting a little tiring, you know.'

'Montreaaaaal...'

And so she went on for the remainder of the journey – watching me from the comfort of the passenger seat while occasionally bursting out her tune. Thing was, it was so annoyingly catchy, by the time we got to the border I was bloody well singing it too. All I can say it's a good job nobody was watching us as we must have looked like a right pair of idiots.

However our jovial mood soon changed at the border, and I knew I was in trouble the moment Poiret, the French speaking customs officer, singled me out for some extra special attention.

'Bonjour, sir. Can you confirm your name pleazzzzze,' he enquired with a steely glaze.

'Errr yeah? James... James Taylor?' *The same as it says on my passport? And what's with all this French nonsense anyway?*

'Oui... and can you confirm your middle name pleazzzze, sir?'

'Err... Christopher?' *Where the bleeding hell is he going with this?*

'And 'ave you ever been to Canada before pleazzzzzze?' the scary man persisted.

'No, never... errr well actually technically yes? We stopped over in Nova Scotia waiting for our connecting flight.'

'Oh really?' he replied staring squarely into my eyes.

'Yes, but we never left the ho... ho... ho... hospital though,' Angie suddenly chirped up, spluttering all over my shoulder.

'What the bloody hell was that about? Are you trying to get us both friggin' arrested?' I said scratching my head, not quite believing what I was hearing. 'I don't know what you used to get up to, my friend, but this *hospital* shit has gotta stop right now, you hear me?'

For some unknown reason men in uniform always seemed to have this effect on her. Nowadays even the sound of a passing siren is enough to make her burst off into a sprint?

'Excuzzzzzee madam, you say you were in the hospital?' the officer replied, looking suspiciously into my eyes, reaching for what I can only assume must have been his gun? Worse was to follow. Struggling under the soft interrogation, Angie's brain continued to crumble. In a moment of sheer desperation she thrusted her arm high into the air like an eager school kid waiting to be questioned.

'No, no, no. I'm sorry I didn't mean that. I meant the hotel, shit, I mean the airport. Definitely not the hospital!'

I was absolutely furious!

'Leave it out babe, or you'll get us both arrested on grounds of spluttering a complete pile of nonsense. And what's with this hospital shit anyway?'

'Sorry, Jamie, he's making me nervous.'

'He's making *you* nervous! Look, button it up and let me try and sort this out before we both get carted off to the nearest asylum centre!'

There was a pause as the customs officer assessed the situation. Clearly not impressed by our dithering I was subjected to further questioning.

'Can you confirm your date of birth pleazzzze, Mr. Taylor, stating when you last entered Canada?'

What the...? This was not looking good. What could I have possibly done? I answered both questions to the best of my knowledge, but the second was slightly tricky considering we had briefly stopped over in Canada before landing in Boston.

'Well technically we were here in May... but only for a few hours... as Angie here had to apparently go to the bloody hospital!'

'Your passport pleazzzze,' the officer requested.

I handed it over, noting the queuing cars behind. Never before had I looked so shifty.

'There you go, my friend,' I said, doing my best to befriend my inquisitor.

'Pleazzzzzze, sir, I am not your friend,' he replied, a bit too seriously if you ask me.

The officer slammed down the window and began dialling his phone. Several minutes passed and still no news. Through the window I could see the officer chatting away, occasionally shaking his head in obvious disgust.

'What's going on, James?' Angie said. 'This doesn't look good, what have you done?'

'Bloody nothing, dear, I've been with you for the last three months, remember?'

By now a bottleneck of cars were forming behind, no doubt all speculating on what crimes I had previously committed. Then finally the inspector opened his window.

'You are not lucky?'

My heart sank.

'Sorry, inspector, is there a problem?'

'Some bad guy has the same name as you and exactly the same date of birth!'

'Wow, really? Is he English as well,' I said.

'No, he is an American.'

'Is he on the wanted list? Like FBI top ten? Like a murderer or something?'

'He is just a very bad man!' the inspector replied not giving anymore away.

'Well I can assure you that I am a very nice man,' I smiled, sensing the panic was over.

Much to my relief the inspector smiled back and waved us through. Although walking through airport security will never be the same again that's for sure – and to be fair I'd often wondered why they'd always given me that suspicious look before marching me off for a good old frisking in the airport corner. Well at least I'll be better prepared next time I guess.

We arrived in Montreal shortly before dusk, checking into another Residence Inn in the heart of the old town. Keen to check out our new surroundings we headed out to town, although it didn't take us long to realise that perhaps Montreal wasn't for us after all. On the surface Montreal appeared to have it all – a quaint little old town, cobbled streets, chic restaurants, and a bustling town square jigging to the sounds of a dozen street buskers. It really was quite an atmosphere.

However, despite all its initial charms there were several reasons which caused me to question the purpose of our visitation. First and foremost, it just wasn't America. In distance it may be near but culturally it was an entirely different proposition altogether. It soon became evident that Montreal must be one of the only cities outside France that desperately craves to be French. Now, I have absolutely nothing against the French, on the contrary, I absolutely love the place, with their fine wines, elegant cuisine, bistro bars, and quaint little coffee shops. However, this was supposed to be an American adventure, and in truth, I guess I wasn't quite ready to return back to the Old World and all that entailed just yet. Although I was left in no doubt that this far flung Parison outpost, must have been one of the most confusing places I had ever been too. What other western nation is so persistent in having two national languages? What other place so adamant for French to be the number one language on every sign, street and corner. Let's make this clear, Canada is officially an English-speaking country and with the exceptions of Montreal and Quebec, the rest of the country has absolutely no desire for all this nonsense. It may only be a few hours north of the border, but the reality being Montreal was a vastly more serious experience to the one we had just encountered. To say things were a little awkward was an understatement to say the least. I can only assume the locals didn't particularly warm to our London accents, as some of the hospitality we immediately encountered was a trifle rude to say the least. Such a contrast to the effervescent Americans only a few hours further south.

Anyway, always the eternal optimist I was willing to give Montreal a go. Granted it certainly wasn't America but now we were here it would be foolish not to go and check out the numerous bars and restaurants that the old town undoubtedly had to offer. After much walking we finally ended up in a cool looking bar a short walk from the hotel. Feeling peckish I decided to go for my usual three way combo of wings, ribs and a pint of Bud to flush it all down, while Angie on the other hand had taken a firm look at the menu and not for the first time this trip declared that she wasn't really hungry after all.

'Go on girl, you bloody well better choose something. You can't just sit there and watch me eat again.'

'No way James, have you seen these prices. Your ribs alone cost more than 30 bucks. And do you really need a full rack again?'

'Yes, I do need a full one and now we're here you might as well embrace it, darling. We're not going anywhere else.'

'Fine, have it your way,' Angie replied, sensing defeat. 'But really, a full rack?'

'Don't have a pop at me? It was your call to come. You remember? Montreal and all that jazz.'

The food soon arrived and as succulent as it was, the final bill confirmed what we had already expected; everything was just so incredibly expensive. One minute you're south of the border paying 20 dollars for a tank of petrol, the next you're in Canada getting robbed over 70 bucks for a spoonful of steak and a slurp of a beer. Now where's the value in that, hey? It may only have been one meal but I was beginning to understand why so many Canadians regularly choose to queue up at the border each and every Friday for their weekly grocery shop.

I guess it was only inevitable that a short while later Angie would swallow her pride and suggest an immediate retreat to the scenic woodlands of Vermont. Naturally I was absolutely delighted with this and on the returning journey south I simply couldn't resist blurting out with the occasional...

'Montreaaaaal, Montreaaaal, Montreaaaaaaaaaaaalll!' for old time's sake, so to speak.

The Final Chapter

The last few days of our trip were very sad – not a sad sad but a happy sad – and so where better place to spend it than the Residence Inn in Hanover, our home away from home as we liked to call it, for this fabulous little spot in the far corner of America was the closest we'd ever come to a home in the last couple of months. Nestled high above the main road overlooking the valley below, the hotel would serve as our sanctuary for the final few days. It really was the perfect setting as we lazily sat outside, supping on our beers, while watching the afternoon sun set slowly behind the wooded mountains for another day's rest.

I turned to Angie and smiled. I might not have always acknowledged it but she had become my rock over the last few months. I really don't know how I could have done it all without her. They say trips like this are supposed to test your relationships, but where others may easily have fallen we had come through with flying colours. Angie looked at me and smiled back. It was perhaps the closest we had ever been. There are simply times in life when you look around and realise you are in that perfect moment. This was our moment.

On our last afternoon we decided to treat ourselves to a chowder lunch at the Hanover Inn. We pulled up at a roadside table overlooking the immaculate college green. Hanover really is the perfect town. A splendid little place situated right in the heart of the Appalachian Mountains, yet seeped in college history. For the next hour we sat in silent contentment watching the young and beautiful going about their business – all in the prime of their lives, all happy and smiley, all very much enjoying the late summer's sun under the protective gaze of the Dartmouth clock tower. We could easily have been in a movie set, so perfect was this small American town.

On our way home we stopped off at the Quechee Gorge, Vermont's very own answer to the Grand Canyon *be it slightly less grander* yet still a fabulous little canyon in its own right. Parking close to the bridge, I noticed a sign proclaiming we were exactly 175 feet above the gorge. Deciding the half mile trek may indeed be the best way to walk off our creamy chowder, we agreed to take the trail to the river below. What a wonderful decision that turned out to be. On reaching the riverbed we were greeted by scores of happy people, all stripping off their clothes and jumping into the warm canyon waters. Angie wasted little time joining in, removing her top to reveal a rather seductive looking bikini.

'How lucky was that!' she giggled before shouting 'Come on baby, take my picture, I'm jumping in too!'

I took her picture and within a blink of an eye she was off floating downstream.

'Come and join me, baby,' she shouted. 'It's wicked. The water's really warm.'

'I'd love to but I haven't got my swimming trunks on, darling. I'll get soaked,' I said pointing to my pants.

'Don't worry about that they'll dry off,' she smiled, beckoning me in.

Not to miss out, I stripped down and plunged in, letting the warm canyon waters carry me downstream. Others from the sidelines quickly followed, joining the growing band of adventurers bobbling up and down in the crystal warm waters. It was a surreal moment floating down that river, the canyon waters so enticingly fresh you'd be forgiven for having a quick slurp if you really had a thirst. It really was another perfect end to another perfect day.

We returned to the hotel to watch one final sunset sink below the valley. Our American adventure had finally come to an end. For the past three months we had lived the American Dream – we had followed in its history, learnt its cultures, listened to its wisdoms and marvelled at its beauty. We had crossed the entire continent by rail, from north to south and east to west. Riding along ancient frontier trails, we had crossed the Rockies, skimmed the deserts, and woke up to some of the most amazing sunrises you could ever have the fortune to see. We had driven through fifteen contrasting states, visiting every region – the East Coast, the Deep South, the Mid West and of course the Wild West and all that entailed. On our travels we passed through over thirty cities, and in most cases lugging our entire worldly possessions on the base of our backs.

And so after ninety days and nearly forty hotel rooms later it was finally time to say goodbye to our great American adventure. Driving through the rolling hills of Vermont, Angie turned to me and said.

'James, I don't get it? I thought we were supposed to find ourselves on this journey. I thought we were supposed to go away and come back all refreshed and get a job like everyone else? The only thing I want to do now is travel some more. Oh, Jamie, I'm so confused?'

'I know how you feel, babe,' I said nodding in agreement. 'I'm not sure what I want to do either. All I want to do is go home and write. Share this wonderful experience with everyone else.'

'Well then, Jamie, I think you've just answered your own question, haven't you!' she replied in her wisdom.

We may have only been on the journey for three months, but deep down I guess I'd always known something – that the day would finally come when I'd leave the world I knew behind and head off to a faraway land. Before I started this journey a friend once said to me *'I hope you find what you're looking for?'* I'm not sure we ever know what we're looking for; I'm not even sure why we even feel the need to look at all? Maybe we are all born to travel, not just to simply stay in one place. All I knew now was that I wasn't ready to go back and rejoin the rat race just yet. You see after many years of searching, maybe I was now finally onto something. It may not have been what I was looking for, but my destiny was certainly not to go back to the way it was before. I had finally moved on, broken the shackles of expectancy and for the first time in my life I was free, ironically in the land of the free.

Our experience of America had taught me many things. You can do anything in life if you put your heart and soul into it. Life is full of challenges with people telling you that you can't do rather than you can do. But now I know otherwise, now I believe you can achieve anything in life as long as you have the desire to do so.

It may have been the end of our trip, but our journey hadn't finished yet, not yet, not by a long way, for there was one more thing I needed to do – I needed to go back and tell the tale.

Thanks

Where to start, hey? I seriously believe that without the advances in modern technology I would never have been able to complete this book. It may have taken nearly ten long years of frequenting coffee shops, and squeezing the odd paragraph out between lunch breaks, but having the world at your fingertips certainly enabled me to get this one over the line. For this alone I would like to thank Google and Wikipedia for allowing me to research my book for free. Speaking of technology, I would like to thank Apple for inventing the iPad. I can honestly say I was one of the first to purchase this shiny new device, and will never forget the looks I got on the Amtrak as I pulled out this unheralded space age device from my backpack during the summer of 2010. Without the iPad there'd definitely be no book, as for the first time ever, firing up a computer actually felt like a leisure pursuit rather than a work chore.

In addition, I would like to thank every museum we visited on our travels for beautifully telling the story of the great westward migration. One museum in particular, the National Frontier Trails Museum in Independence, deserves special praise, as it was this museum that actually gave me the inspiration for the title *Westward Fever*.

I would like to thank my dad, for being the first to critique the book. New Generation, for giving me my big break, and Christina Campbell, for her help with editing. I would also like to thank Angie's Dad and my Grandad, who both inspired us to follow in our dreams. Sadly neither are no longer with us, but without them this journey most certainly would never have happened. Most importantly I would like to thank my companion and soulmate Angie, who after all these years still has to listen to me bang on about our great American adventure. Sadly, only recently Angie was diagnosed with Mycosis Fungoides, a rare type of Non-Hodgkins lymphoma. Luckily for Angie, she is blessed with the most amazing courage, and with the support of her family and world class doctors we are determined to beat this thing.

When writing *Westward Fever* it was always my aim to inspire the reader like the westward migration inspired the mind all those years ago. Who knows what happens now, but if just one person picks up this book and decides to tell their boss to *go stick it!* Then I can honestly say I have accomplished my mission.

Happy travels, my friend! xx

Lightning Source UK Ltd.
Milton Keynes UK
UKHW042058040121
376432UK00001B/221

9 781800 319608